Discovering Process

Stephen C. Lewis
M. Cecile Forte
Suffolk Community College

MACMILLAN PUBLISHING COMPANY
New York

COLLIER MACMILLAN PUBLISHERS
London

Macmillan Publishing Company
866 Third Avenue, New York, New York 10022

Collier Macmillan Canada, Inc.

Library of Congress Cataloging in Publication Data

Lewis, Stephen C.
    Discovering process.

    1. English language—Rhetoric.   2. College readers.
I. Forte, M. Cecile.   II. Title.
PE1408.L414   1985   808'.0427   83-9385
ISBN 0-02-370500-0

Printing: 1 2 3 4 5 6 7 8   Year: 5 6 7 8 9 0 1 2 3

ISBN   0-02-370500-0

Discovering Process

Meaning and Form in Reading and Writing

Acknowledgments

From "To the Reader" in MEMORIES OF A CATHOLIC GIRLHOOD, © 1957 by Mary McCarthy. Reprinted by permission of Harcourt Brace Jovanovich, Inc.

From "The Saving of the President" by John Pekkanen (August 1981). Reprinted with permission from The Washingtonian magazine.

From "People Aren't Born Prejudiced" by Ian Stevenson. Copyright © 1960 Parents Magazine Enterprises. Reprinted from PARENTS by permission.

From "The Libido For the Ugly" by H. L. Mencken. Copyright 1927 by Alfred A. Knopf, Inc. and renewed 1955 by H. L. Mencken. Reprinted from A MENCKEN CHRESTOMATHY, by H. L. Mencken, by permission of the publisher.

From "Salvation" in THE BIG SEA by Langston Hughes. Copyright 1940 by Langston Hughes. Renewed © 1968 by Arna Bontemps and George Houston Bass. Reprinted by permission of Hill and Wang (now a division of Farrar, Straus, & Giroux, Inc.).

From "A Medical Marvel in Your Kitchen" by Jack B. Kemmerer. Reprinted from Family Weekly, copyright 1982, 1515 Broadway, New York, New York 10036.

From "When I Was a Child" by Lillian Smith. Selection is reprinted from KILLERS OF THE DREAM, by Lillian Smith, Revised Edition, by permission of W. W. Norton & Company, Inc. Copyright 1949, © 1961 by Lillian Smith.

From "In the Eye of the Beholder" by Phillip Moffitt. Reprinted with permission from Esquire (June, 1981). Copyright © 1981 by Esquire Associates.

From "Body Parts" by Priscilla Flood. Reprinted with permission from Esquire Magazine (June, 1981). Copyright Priscilla Flood, first published in Esquire Magazine, New York.

From "Casting Commercials: It was easier to find Scarlett O'Hara." Reprinted with permission from Joan Walker.

From MacNeil/Lehrer Report, Show #7051. Reprinted with permission from The MacNeil-Lehrer Report, WNET/THIRTEEN, 356 West 58th Street, New York, New York 10019.

From "Confessions of A Token Black" by Roger Wilkins, from A MAN'S LIFE. Copyright © 1982 by Roger Wilkins. Reprinted by permission of Pocket Books, a Simon & Schuster division of Gulf & Western Corporation.

From FROM SLAVERY TO FREEDOM: A HISTORY OF NEGRO AMERICANS, Third Edition, by John Hope Franklin. Copyright 1947, © 1956, 1967 by Alfred A. Knopf, Inc. Reprinted by permission of the publisher.

From *Foundations of Psychology,* by W. Edgar Vinacke © 1968, American Book Company, NY, pp. 186–187.

From "Protestors Silent on Smoking," by Jack Mabley. Copyrighted, 1979, Chicago Tribune. Used with permission.

From the book THE MAGIC OF THINKING BIG by David J. Schwartz © 1959 by Prentice-Hall, Inc. Published by Prentice-Hall, Inc., Englewood Cliffs, NJ 07632.

From *Passages* by Gail Sheehy. Copyright, ©, 1976 by Gail Sheehy. Reprined by permission of the publisher, E. P. Dutton, Inc.

From "Sociocultural Barriers to the Reading Habit: The Case of Iran" by Glenn D. Reckert, May 1982, *Journal of Reading.* Reprinted with permission of Glenn D. Reckert and the International Reading Association.

From "Educating About Compassion" by John Agresto. This article first appeared in the Summer 1982 issue of the AMERICAN EDUCATOR (Vol. 6, No. 2), the quarterly Journal of the American Federation of Teachers.

From The Hofstra University Bulletin, edited by Virginia Grimes and Helen Topf. Used with permission.

From LET US NOW PRAISE FAMOUS MEN by James Agee and Walker Evans. Copyright 1939, 1940 by James Agee. Copyright 1941 by James Agee and Walker Evans. Copyright © renewed 1969 by Mia Fritsch Agee. Reprinted by permission of Houghton Mifflin Company.

From "Backdrop of Poverty" in SPANISH HARLEM by Patricia Cayo Sexton. Specified excerpt (pp. 1–2) from Chapter 1. Copyright © 1965 by Patricia Cayo Sexton. Reprinted by permission of Harper & Row Publishers, Inc.

From "The Wonderful Lousy Poem" by Bud Schulberg. Reprinted with permission of FAMILY WEEKLY, copyright 1964, 641 Lexington Avenue, New York, New York 10022.

From MEN AND NATIONS: A WORLD HISTORY, Third Edition, by Anatole G. Mazour and John M. Peoples, © 1975 by Harcourt Brace Jovanovich, Inc. Reprinted by permission of the publisher.

Excerpt from the Introduction to MODERN AMERICAN SCENES FOR STUDENTS, edited by Wynn Handman; copyright © 1978 by Bantam Books, Inc., New York.

From "Picking out a perfect crab-apple tree," by D. X. Fenten. Reprinted with permission from D. X. Fenten. Sunday Newsday, August 28, 1982, pt. 11, p. 40.

Condensed from "The new leader of the Pac is funky Donkey Kong," PEOPLE Weekly, May 31, © 1982, Time Inc.

From *Introductory Laboratory Exercises For Human Anatomy And Physiology* by Donald S. Kisiel. Published by Avery Publishing Group, Inc. Reprinted by permission of the publisher and the author.

From "Dear Ann" by Ann Landers. Permission from Ann Landers, Field Newspaper Syndicate and Newsday.

From "Royal wedding, Royal birth, what's next?" Reprinted with permission of Ernest A. Kehr. *Newsday* (Aug. 29, 1982).

From Foerster/Grabo/Nye/Carlisle/Falk: *American Poetry and Prose,* Fifth Edition, Part I, pp. 770–773. Copyright © 1970 by Houghton Mifflin Company. Used by permission.

From "L.A. Rock: From Mellow to Bellow," by Wayne Robbins. *Sunday Newsday,* August 29, 1982, Part II, p. 25.

From "The Two Americas," in THE ARROGANCE OF POWER, by J. William Fulbright © 1967, p. 245, Random House, Inc., New York.

From "A Versatile Actor's 'Nine' Lives" by Jerry Parker. *Sunday Newsday*, August 29, 1982, Part II, p. 4.

From "The New Ideal of Beauty." Time Magazine, August 30, 1982, pp. 72–73. Reprinted by permission from Time. Copyright 1982 Time Inc. All rights reserved.

From "Letter from Birmingham Jail, April 16, 1963" in WHY WE CAN'T WAIT by Martin Luther King, Jr, specified excerpt (pp. 83–84). Copyright © 1963 by Martin Luther King, Jr. Reprinted by permission of Harper & Row, Publishers, Inc.

From SILENT SPRING by Rachel Carson. Copyright © 1962 by Rachel Carson. Reprinted by permission of Houghton Mifflin Company.

From "Odd Balls" by Wright Morris, in The Atlantic, June, 1978. Reprinted by permission of Russell & Volkening as agents for Wright Morris. Copyright © 1978 by Wright Morris.

From "Southpaw Stigma" by Perry W. Buffington, in Delta SKY Magazine (Dec. 1982). Reprined through the courtesy of Halsey Publishing Co.

From "Salamanders: Clandestine Creatures of the Night" by Whit Gibbons, in Delta SKY Magazine, 1982.

From VIOLENCE: AMERICA IN THE SIXTIES by Arthur Schlesinger, Jr. Copyright © 1968 by Arthur Schlesinger, Jr. Reprinted by arrangement with The New American Library, Inc., New York, New York.

From "Who Said Wild Women Don't Sing the Blues?" by Margo Jefferson, *MS.*, April 1979.

From "Intellect and Intelligence," in ANTI-INTELLECTUALISM IN AMERICAN LIFE by Richard Hofstadter, Random House, Inc., New York, New York. Used by permission.

From "To Err Is Human," in THE MEDUSA AND THE SNAIL by Lewis Thomas. Copyright © 1976 by Lewis Thomas. Originally published in the New England Journal of Medicine. Reprinted by permission of Viking Penguin Inc.

From "Why We Make Excuses" in MERE CHRISTIANITY by C. S. Lewis. Copyright 1943, 1945, 1952 by Macmillan Publishing Co., Inc. Copyrights renewed. Reprinted with permission of Macmillan Publishing Company.

From "Why the Justice System Fails" by Roger Rosenblatt. Copyright 1981 Time Inc. All right reserved. Reprinted by permission of TIME.

From Daniel Boorstin's "The Prison of the Present." Reprinted by permission of Random House, Inc., New York, New York.

From "A Yo-Yo Going Down" in STOP-TIME by Frank Conroy. Copyright © 1965, 1966, 1967 by Frank Conroy. Reprinted by permission of Viking Penguin Inc.

From "A Delicate Operation" in WRAPAROUND by Roy C. Selby. Copyright © 1975 by Harper's Magazine. All rights reserved. Reprinted from the Decembr 1975 issue by special permission.

From "How to Mark a Book" by Mortimer Adler. *Saturday Reivew of Literature,* July 6, 1940. Coyright © 1940 by Mortimer J. Adler; Copyright © renewed 1967 by Mortimer J. Adler. Reprinted by permission of the author.

From "How to Change Your Point of View" by Caroline Seebohm. Courtesy HOUSE & GARDEN. Copyright © 1974 by The Condé Nast Publications, Inc., New York, New York.

From POWER: HOW TO GET IT, HOW TO USE IT, by Michael Korda. Copyright © 1975 by Michael Korda and Paul Gitlin, Trustee for the Benefit of Christopher Korda. Reprinted by permission of Random House, Inc.

From SECOND WIND: THE MEMOIRS OF AN OPINIONATED MAN, by Bill Russell and Taylor Branch. Copyright © 1979 by William F. Russell. Reprinted by permission of Random House, Inc.

From "Packaged Sentiment" by Richard Rhodes. Reprinted by permission of JCA Literary Agency, Inc. Copyright © 1971 by Richard Rhodes. Originally appeared in *Harper's Magazine*.

From DOWN AND OUT IN PARIS AND LONDON, copyright 1933 by George Orwell, Copyright © 1961 by Sonia Pitt-Rivers. Reprinted by permission of Harcourt Brace Jovanovich, Inc.

From WHAT TO LISTEN FOR IN MUSIC by Aaron Copeland. Reprinted with permission of McGraw-Hill Book Company, New York, New York.

From "In Bed" in THE WHITE ALBUM by Joan Didion. Copyright © 1979 by Joan Didion. Reprinted by permission of Simon & Schuster a division of Gulf & Western Corporation.

From "To Noble Companions" by Gail Godwin. Copyright © 1973 by Harper's Magazine. All rights reserved. Reprinted from the August 1973 issue by special permission.

From SOCIOLOGY (second edition) by Paul B. Horton and Chester L. Hunt. Copyright © 1968. Reprinted with permission from McGraw-Hill Book Company, New York, New York.

From "Expressive Language" by Amiri Baraka. Originally published in HOME: SOCIAL ESSAYS by LeRoi Jones. Copyright © 1963, 1966 by LeRoi Jones. By permission of William Morrow & Company.

Preface

Our goal in this text is to enable students to produce good writing and to improve their comprehension of materials they read. This goal requires little explanation: control of written language, either as a writer or reader, provides a level of control of reality, for language shapes our perceptions of the world.

Research in writing and reading has indicated that both activities are best understood as processes which require critical thinking. Consistent with this understanding, this text encourages students to *think* their way through the composing and comprehension processes. To this end, we emphasize discovery in both reading and writing by stressing the development of a questioning attitude. This approach permits students to realize that they should become active readers of their own material and to revise their work from that perspective; that is, they should anticipate the questions and responses their writing will produce when read by somebody else.

Revision, in fact, naturally ties together the idea of process in writing and reading. As we read, we revise and refine our understanding of an author's message, and as we write we revise our material so as to improve reader comprehension. Each chapter in this book addresses revision as refinement and clarification of thinking, and the final chapter offers a fully developed model of revision in writing, from first to final draft. This last chapter demonstrates how a writer's awarenss of purpose and audience involves a progression from the question, "What do I want to say?" to "How can I best express my thoughts to my reader?"

We have organized our presentation according to three purpose categories which define a relationship among the writer, the reader (or audience), and the subject matter. Although all written discourse involves these three elements, different emphases can be identified. For example, expressive writing projects a sense of the writer; informative writing focuses on the subject matter; and persuasive writing attempts to change the attitudes or beliefs of the audience.

These purpose categories, although different from the traditional grouping—narrative, descriptive, expository, and persuasive—work better to promote the critical thinking which reading and writing require because they more nearly coincide with the meaning a writer intends and a reader comprehends. These purpose categories are particularly useful in a combined reading/writing approach because they underscore the relationship between the writer as transmitter, and the reader as receiver, of facts, ideas, and feelings.

A sense of audience, as well as purpose, is important to student writers and readers. Accordingly, we stress the idea that every piece of writing is directed at an intended audience. Directing writing at a defined audience sharpens the writer's approach to his or her topic. Moreover, it is useful for a student reader to recognize whether or not he or she is a member of the intended audience for a particular piece of writing.

After our treatment of purpose and audience, we devote Part Four of the text to traditional patterns of development: examples, comparison/contrast, cause/effect, classification, and definition. These patterns, of course, are available to the writer no matter what his or her purpose or intended audience might be, and since they so often shape the material a reader reads, recognition of them greatly improves comprehension.

In this section, we have stressed revision in each of the writing chapters by asking the student to approach his or her writing as a reader. Each of these writing chapters includes questions, first introduced in the reading chapters, which enable the student writer to check his or her work for purpose, audience, and organization. Revision, then, is not presented as editing or proofreading, but rather as the final stage of the composing process, one in which the effectiveness of the writing is measured as a whole experience for potential readers.

We include a wide variety of reading materials, mostly essays and excerpts from longer prose works. The writing sections present model essays which are developed from beginning to end in each of the chapters. Although not organized like a traditional reader, the text offers a comparable variety of reading materials.

We would like to acknowledge the work of James Kinneavy in developing the purpose categories to which we are indebted for a rhetorical model which relates reader, writer, audience, and subject matter. Our manuscript profited significantly from the suggestions offered by Joan Dagle of Rhode Island College, Joyce Middleton of the University of Maryland, Mark Edelstein of Palomar College, and Nancy Walker of Southwest Missouri State University. We would also like to thank our colleagues in various organizations including the International Reading Association, NCTE, CCCC, the Nassau Reading Council, the Northeast Regional Conference of English in the Two Year College, and the New York State Reading Association where we presented workshops and received criticisms which helped us refine our thinking. We would also like to acknowledge the SUNY Council on Writing which has helped stimulate and develop new work in composition theory and practice.

Our efforts were greatly facilitated by our editor at Macmillan, D. Anthony English, who provided invaluable guidance and support. Among our colleagues we would especially like to thank Charles Martin of Queensborough Community College and Louise Robbins and Lowell Kleiman of Suffolk Community College for their encouragement and willingness to listen.

The preparation of the manuscript itself was possible only through the efforts of Katherine Morrisette and Sharon Weeks whose patience and good humor prevailed as deadlines approached.

S.C.L.
M.C.F.

Contents

part FOUR
Strategies and Form

Selected Readings

part ONE

Before Reading and Writing

chapter 1
The Purpose of Reading and Writing

All communications contains three elements: a speaker or writer, a message or subject matter, and an audience. Communication begins when someone decides to make a statement or ask a question, and it ends when the audience understands the message.

Communication has to be about something. A person walking down the street muttering unconnected words is not communicating. If the words do not form a message, there is no understandable subject matter. If, however, this person were combining words into recognizable patterns, we could say that communication had begun, and an audience who understood the words would complete the communication.

For a writer, the *intent* to communicate to an audience is crucial. Even someone stranded on a desert island who scrawls a message on a piece of bark, puts it into a bottle, and throws it into the ocean is attempting to communicate. Although the bottle might never be found, the intent to find an audience differentiates this attempted communication from the unthinking mutterings of the individual walking down the street. The mutterer does not intend that anyone hear or understand his or her words, but the person on the desert island does hope that the bottled message will be received, understood and acted upon by someone.

An intended audience, then, sets the stage for communication, and the communication is realized when the message is received. The intended audience can be as limited as oneself or as general as the world. A diary's intended audience is only the writer himself or herself. The largest intended audience would be every member of the world's population whom a diplomat addressed in a speech at the United Nations.

These three elements—speaker, subject matter, and audience—form the communication triangle. Different types of communication stress one of these elements more than the others, and therefore, one way to classify communication is to decide which of the three elements is emphasized most. This kind of classification determines the *purpose* of a particular communication.

Purpose

If a writer intends to produce a best-selling novel, the writer's purpose probably is to make money. But although this may very well be true and although it may tell us something about both the character of the writer and the society in which he or she lives and works, it is not a very useful observation. Rather, it would be more instructive to determine which of the three communication elements is the most important. In the following discussion of purpose in writing, we shall use the term *writer* to mean the individual who initiates the communication process and the term *audience* to mean the reader of the writer's message.

We can identify purpose by determining whether the writing emphasizes the writer, the subject matter, or the audience. Although all communication includes each of these three elements, in nearly all cases one is more important than the others. For example, you may keep a diary to record your ideas, feelings, and observations. Because you are the center of interest, the diary's emphasis would be first on you as the writer and second on the other elements. In other kinds of communication, the emphasis is placed differently.

Sometimes, the subject matter of a written communication is the most important element. The writer's aim may be to present his or her subject as objectively as possible or to present it in such a way as to change the audience's view of the subject. Thus the writer's purpose can be defined according to his or her emphasis:

1. Expressive: emphasis on the writer.
2. Informative: emphasis on the objective presentation of the subject.
3. Persuasive: emphasis on the audience's perception.

In *expressive writing,* the writer's purpose is to communicate to the reader a sense of himself or herself. Expressive writing might be a description of a scene, or it might tell a story, but the writer's overriding concern will be to present the subject matter from his or her point of view. Thus the reader of an expressive piece will learn as much or more about the writer as about the subject matter. If the writer describes a rainy day or an incident at the motor vehicle office, the focus will be on the writer's own feelings about the weather or the bureaucracy.

Consider the purpose of the following:

> Hence, as a lapsed Catholic, I do not trouble myself about the possibility that God may exist after all. If He exists (which seems to me more than doubtful), I am in for a bad time in the next world, but I am not going to bargain to believe in God in order to save my soul. Pascal's wager—the bet he took with himself that God existed, even though this could not be proved by reasoning—strikes me as too prudential. What had Pascal to lose by behaving as if God existed? Absolutely nothing, for there was no counter-Principle to damn him

in case God didn't. For myself, I prefer not to play it so safe, and I shall never send for a priest or recite an Act of Contrition in my last moments. I do not mind if I lose my soul for all eternity. If the kind of God exists Who would damn me for not working out a deal with Him, then that is unfortunate. I should not care to spend eternity in the company of such a person.

This excerpt deals with a controversial subject, whether or not to believe in God, but the emphasis is not on the subject matter. What is most important in this piece is the writer's—Mary McCarthy's—attitude toward the subject matter. And although the reader might learn something—for example, about Pascal's wager—that is not the writer's intention. Moreover, McCarthy does not really attempt to convince the reader that her views are the only correct ones. Rather, she presents her feelings, her confession of being a "lapsed Catholic," in the hope that the reader will empathize with her and thereby better understand her attitude. This excerpt, therefore, is clearly governed by an expressive purpose.

Informative writing, on the other hand, does focus on the subject matter, and its purpose is to present it in such a way that the reader can learn new information. Textbooks are good examples of purely informative writing:

> The Employee Retirement Security Act of 1974 . . . protects the pension rights of workers if the employer goes out of business or if the worker quits or is dismissed after a certain period of employment. The term 'vesting' means that the worker's right to his or her accumulated pension benefits is guaranteed to the worker. The law does not require an employer to set up a pension plan. It does, however, set up regulations for company or union plans. A Pension Benefit Guarantee Corporation was created to pay workers whose pension plans fail due to employer bankruptcy or union corruption.

This selection from a business textbook tries to present an objective view of employees' pension rights. Consequently, there is very little sense of personality in the writing, as there is in McCarthy's piece; indeed, the personal views of the writers of this piece are not relevant. The principal aim of this writing is information.

Sometimes the purpose of a piece of writing is to persuade the reader to change his or her opinions. In *persuasive writing,* the goal is not to reveal the writer's feelings or to present information. Rather, the goal of persuasive writing is to change the reader's mind. One of the more obvious places to find persuasive writing is in advertisements:

> This year, the nation's colleges will graduate about one million students.
>
> Unfortunately, only a small percentage will be adequately equipped to deal with today's high-technology, information oriented society. While they might know a great deal about their chosen fields, too many will be scientific illiterates.
>
> The reason for this is that the traditional liberal arts education has become too liberal. Too fuzzy. Not disciplined enough. Insufficient.

The "unliberal" solution.

The solution is to make liberal arts less liberal. "Unliberal," so to speak.

We must return education to its origins, when students were given what they needed, not just what they wanted.

What's required is a revision of the solution first offered 2,400 years ago by Aristotle and enriched by Augustine, Aquinas and Newman. They created a "liberal arts" education that equipped their students to make more informed decisions and to become better citizens. . . .

The person who wrote this advertising copy intended to convince the readers, probably prospective college students and their parents, that they should consider a particular college, one that offers an "unliberal" education.

This piece uses both the emotional and the logical levels of persuasion. On the emotional level, it describes present college graduates as inadequately prepared to meet the real world and as "scientific illiterates." More subtly, it appeals to prejudice against *liberalism*, a term that describes a political philosophy that was popular in the 1960s. Because many people attribute the less than satisfactory state of American education to the social upheavals of the sixties, which in turn has become identified with the discredited political liberalism of that period, the reader is asked to return to more substantial values, here, to a curriculum based on the teachings of Aristotle, St. Thomas Aquinas, and John Henry Newman, all recognized as brilliant and influential thinkers. And the fact that Newman, who died a century ago, is the most modern, underscores this commitment to "older" values for a new world.

On the logical level, this advertisement argues that a "true" liberal arts education will prepare students for the world in which they will live after their graduation from college. This reasoning assumes that for today's conditions, scientific literacy is necessary, as is a return to a more disciplined approach. The ad concludes by stating that this "unliberal" curriculum emphasizes "three critical areas: (1) Computer knowledge. (2) Deductive reasoning. (3) Writing skills." It does not note, of course, that the last two items are the cornerstones of any program of higher education, liberal or not. Therefore, an "unliberal" curriculum really is one that stresses traditional educational values, that is, thinking and writing, along with computer skills. Persuasive writing, as seen in this advertising copy, emphasizes the audience, not the writer or the subject. The writer of this copy is largely invisible except in the tone of the piece which is forceful and reassuring, as if the writer had only the subject's best interests in mind. This tone does not reveal the writer but, rather, adds to the persuasiveness of the piece. And although the copy is about a college program, which is given a clever name, the passage does not really tell us much about the program, only that it is important. Persuasive writing can be more descriptive of the subject or reveal more of the writer's personality, but the audience will always come first.

Purpose and the Audience's Expectations

Different purposes in writing create different expectations in the audience. Expressive writing asks that the reader share an experience or emotion. Such writing, because it concentrates on the writer's personality and views, is interesting because it allows the reader to relate to and understand the writer as an individual. And because the writing is so personal, we can expect its style to be subjective or even poetic.

Because informative writing tries to be objective, the reader expects clarity of presentation instead of interesting style. The writer of informative material is important only in terms of his or her credentials; that is, the reader wants to know only that the writer is speaking authoritatively.

But persuasive writing should put the reader on guard. The writer is attempting to change the reader's views. The style of persuasive writing thus is important, mainly as a way of affecting the reader's feelings. Persuasive writing often is colorful or witty or ironic because the writer wants to drive home his or her points. Sometimes, persuasive writing is analytical and rational in approach because the writer wants to convince the reader by appealing to his or her intellect rather than emotions. When reading persuasive writing, we should be able to recognize when an appeal is being made to our reason and when to our emotions. Knowing about the writer is useful in determining why he or she wants to change our opinions on a subject.

Because different purposes in writing create different expectations in the audience, one measure of successful writing is how well the particular purpose is served. Being able to read well means being aware of this purpose and being able to evaluate the writer's success in achieving it.

Purpose	Emphasis	Audience's (Reader's) Expectation
Expressive	Writer	Empathy
Informative	Subject matter	Learning
Persuasive	Audience	Change of attitude or belief

Exercises

1. Identify the purpose of each of the following pieces:

a. The President Said:

By John Pekkanen

Just before 2:30 on the afternoon of March 30, the "white phone" in the emergency room of George Washington University Hospital—linked directly to the White House—rang. Wendy Koenig, an emergency-room nurse for two years, answered. The voice she heard was brusque and to the point: "The presidential motorcade is en route to your facility." That was all the voice said.

Kathy Paul, a 28-year-old emergency room nurse, walked toward the ER main entrance, which faces Pennsylvania Avenue. It had been less than three minutes since the first call on the white phone.

She watched in astonishment as a black limousine pulled into the ER driveway, stopped, and out of the rear door stepped the President of the United States. She noticed he was dressed in a pin-striped suit, but her eyes riveted on his face, which was ashen. He looked frightened.

He walked through the three sets of double doors and said, "I feel like I can't catch my breath." He groaned, his knees buckled, and he began to fall backward. At that point Kathy Paul no longer was astonished or awed. The President now was a patient.

She grabbed his arm and, with a paramedic and two Secret Servicemen, helped carry him the 40 to 50 feet to the trauma bay at the rear of the ER. They put him on a stretcher in 5A.

The President lay flat on the stretcher, bright lights in his eyes, his brows furrowed, his expression worried. There wasn't any obvious sign of injury, and hospital staffers had received no word in those first confusing minutes that the President might have been injured.

"I feel so bad," he said, laboring for air.

They began the trauma protocol.

Without apology, Kathy Paul leaned over the President and started ripping and cutting off his clothes. All of them. The President kept repeating that he felt bad, that he didn't understand why he was finding it so hard to breathe. She thought he must be having a heart attack. His paleness, his breathing and chest discomfort all fitted. She kept ripping. So did Wendy Koenig, who noticed an elegant RR monogram on his shirt just before she tore it off.

Now standing at the foot of the President's stretcher was the tall, quiet figure of Dr. Daniel Ruge, his personal physician. Ruge had been at the Hilton. After making certain none of the injured on the sidewalk was the President, he had jumped into an official car that followed the presidential limousine to GW. A well-known and respected neurosurgeon, he now put his hand on the President's foot to monitor his pulse, which was steady and strong. Ruge offered several reassuring words to the President.

Wendy Koenig put the blood-pressure cuff on the President's arm. She pumped it up and waited for the thumping sound of the pulse in her stethoscope.

Not a sound.

"I can't hear anything," she yelled. "I can't get a systolic pressure."

The President is arresting, she thought, right here in front of me. She had to fight back tears.

She pumped up the cuff one more time, and now she palpated an artery with her fingers. She felt the first throb, somewhere between 50 and 60 systolic, an ominously low pressure, suggesting shock. Normal would be 130. The President was at this moment more dangerously ill than the public would ever realize.

Less than two minutes had elapsed since Ronald Reagan had walked in.

In trauma resuscitation there is nothing more precious than time; speed is the inviolable first principle. It is during the "golden hour"—the first 60 minutes—that most trauma patients are either saved or lost. Most of those lost die from shock, caused when the body's blood volume becomes so depleted that there is not enough to go around. Even people in deep shock can be resuscitated. But if too much time is lost before shock is reversed, the major organs can't support the body, and the patient dies. He or she may not die that minute or even that day, but death is inevitable.

The President was ashen because his involuntary nervous system had taken over, redirecting his blood flow away from his skin and extremities and into his vital organs, which had a far more urgent need for it. There is little question that in those first few minutes he was very close to shock if not in shock itself—as one of his physicians later remarked, the President was "on the brink."

No one knew what was wrong, because there was no obvious sign of injury. Jerry Parr, the Secret Serviceman who had landed on the President in the limousine and then directed it to GW after he spotted blood on the President's mouth, an act which probably saved Ronald Reagan's life, thought he might have cracked one of the President's ribs. But in those first two or three minutes none of the nurses noticed any blood or other possible sign of injury. It was only when technicians saw blood on the President's hand and inside his mouth that they knew he wasn't arresting; he was hurt.

"I can't breathe," the President repeated. The nurses took turns holding his hand and reassured him. He lay with his arms at his sides, his expression worried, but he was conscious and calm.

Three IV lines were now pushing fluids and blood into him, boosting his blood volume.

Perhaps three minutes—at most—had elapsed since the President's arrival.

Dr. Wesley Price, a senior resident, and Dr. William O'Neill, an intern on the trauma team, were the first GW physicians to treat the President.

Both were stunned when they saw the President lying on the stretcher with lines going into his arms.

They made a rapid assessment. O'Neill, who had worked in the emergency room as an undergraduate, had seen a lot of trauma. "You develop an immediate gut feeling as to who is really sick and who isn't," he said later. When he saw the President he felt he was looking at someone potentially in jeopardy—on the brink.

The President's palpable blood pressure was up to 78 systolic—still abnormally low but an improvement. The fluids were doing their job. The President's pulse was 88 and steady, another encouraging sign.

"Mr. President, where do you hurt?" O'Neill asked.

"My chest hurts and I'm having trouble breathing."

"Do you know what happened?"

"Not really."

"Are you hurting anywhere else?"

"No, I don't think so."

No other symptoms were evident. The President was thinking clearly and able to move all four limbs. To ease his breathing, they propped his head up about 20 or 30 degrees.

Wesley Price, the son of a North Carolina preacher, put a stethoscope to the President's chest and listened for breath sounds. Listening to the right lung, he heard crackling noises. The breath sounds on the left side were markedly diminished. Air was not moving in and out freely. As Price continued to listen to the left side he noticed a small, jagged slit, like a buttonhole, but more vertical than horizontal, just below the President's armpit. There was a black spot around it and blood was trickling out.

More doctors were arriving.

Dr. Drew Scheele, a general-surgery intern who had been a helicopter pilot in Vietnam, where he had seen many gunshot wounds, including his own, looked at it with Price. They both realized they were looking at the entry wound of a bullet. Price turned to Jerry Parr, the Secret Serviceman who had thought he had broken the President's rib. "It looks like he's been shot," Price said.

Dr. Ruge gave Ronald Reagan this news. The President nodded. Ruge added reassuringly: "Everything is okay." Wendy Koenig asked the President whether he had had a tetanus shot recently. He couldn't remember. She gave him one.

They gently rolled the President from side to side, looking for an exit wound. There was none, so the bullet had to be in the chest or abdomen. Then Price and O'Neill thought they noticed distended neck veins, a disturbing sign because it could be caused by cardiac tamponade, the filling of the pericardial sac surrounding the heart. On the other hand, heart sounds were normal. It was too early for certainties.

The President's left chest was thumped with hands and fingers. Where it should have sounded hollow, there was a dull, flat resonance. His left pleural cavity was filling with blood.

Less than 12 minutes had passed since President Reagan's arrival at GW.

A chest tube was readied to remove the blood flooding his left lung. Dr. Joseph Giordano, a faculty surgeon and head of the trauma team, cut an opening through the skin and muscle wall. He stuck his finger into the opening to make certain he was into the pleura, put a clamp on the tube, and popped it into the hole. The President winced at the pain. The other end of the tube was connected to a suction device called a Pleur-evac.

Blood gushed out of the President's chest tube—1,300 cc's of it, perhaps a fourth of his total supply. No one was alarmed; chest tubes normally pull out a lot of blood when they are first inserted into a wounded chest.

Usually, when a chest tube is inserted and the lung re-expands, the uninjured vessels close off and the bleeding stops. In about 90 per cent of all cases involving this type of chest wound, surgery is not performed.

But in Ronald Reagan's case the bleeding didn't stop. That was the first thing that disturbed thoracic and cardiac surgeon, Ben Aaron. The second was the color of the blood. It was not the bright red of freshly oxygenated blood. It had a darker, ruby cast to it, suggesting venous blood. Aaron had opened thousands of chests in his day and he knew that venous blood coming out of the chest meant some part of the pulmonary artery—through which venous blood is pumped from the heart to the lungs—was injured.

Perhaps 18 minutes had passed since the President's arrival at the hospital.

The President's blood pressure was now nearly normal. His color was better, but he still couldn't breathe without difficulty. If the President kept losing blood, the doctors would not be able to keep giving him fluids indefinitely. When blood is replaced by fluids, the patient's hemoglobin diminishes; even though the blood pressure is normal, the tissues are deprived of oxygen, and the kidney, heart, and lungs lose function. If whole blood is administered for too long, the patient's blood loses its ability to clot. That possibility was approaching.

A portable X-ray machine was wheeled into the trauma bay, and within two minutes a chest film was taken and developed. Dr. David Rockoff, the head of chest radiology, was there to read it.

It showed that, with the blood draining out through the chest tube, the lung had re-expanded. Rockoff also noticed an irregularly shaped, hazy area where blood remained in the left chest cavity. Then he saw a small, slender metal fragment shaped almost like a comma in the shadow of the heart. It was the bullet. Ben Aaron also looked at the film. According to their viewing angle, the bullet could have hit the heart, the aorta, or the pulmonary artery. But the dark color of the blood coming from the President's chest still suggested that its source was the pulmonary artery, not the aorta, which produces bright-red blood.

Rockoff, a highly respected member of the GW faculty, needed to know the caliber of the bullet. If it was a .22, they were seeing all of it. If it was a larger caliber, another fragment might have hit a rib and been deflected into the abdominal cavity.

He turned to a Secret Serviceman who said he didn't know but would find out. What followed was one of the most inexplicable incidents in the President's shooting.

Rockoff listened as the Secret Serviceman turned to a superior and said, "They've got to know the caliber." The Secret Service agent went to a nearby phone and called the FBI. This is what was then overheard in the GW emergency room:

"What do you mean, you can't tell me?" the Secret Serviceman said. "The doctors here have to know."

He turned to his superior and shouted: "They won't tell me."

"You tell them they've got to tell you! It's the President."

His voice rising, the Secret Serviceman told the FBI: "We've got to know, and we've got to know now!"

There was a moment's silence before the Secret Serviceman turned to Rockoff and said: "It's a .38."

Rockoff, stunned by this information, relayed it to colleagues. "It's a .38," he said. "We need a belly film to look for the rest of the bullet."

This occurred approximately 20 to 25 minutes after the President was admitted to the ER. The error was never corrected by any of the authorities, nor was the reason for it ever given. Although much of the nation was soon to learn from television that a .22-caliber gun had been used, the physicians treating the President were not watching television. They worked now under the assumption that he had been shot with a .38 and they would continue to assume that until, approximately 60 to 90 minutes later, an intact .22-caliber bullet was removed from wounded Secret Service Agent, Tim McCarthy, confirming that a .22 caliber was the weapon.

An abdominal X-ray—the "belly film"—of the President was taken immediately. One would have been taken anyway, but if the doctors had had correct information about the caliber of the bullet, it would have been done later. If time had been a more critical factor, the misinformation about the bullet could have been costly.

The abdominal film was negative.

Nancy Reagan was ushered through the crowd in the ER and into the trauma bay. She held her husband's hand and leaned over to kiss his forehead. "Honey, I forgot to duck," he said.

His wife was controlled, but her face registered worry and fear. After a brief visit, she returned to the small interview room at the entrance to the ER to join Edwin Meese, James Baker, and Lyn Nofziger, members of the President's staff.

It was now obvious that surgery was the safest course. Was a large blood vessel in the wound ready to burst? Would the blood flow suddenly increase to 600 to 700 cc's every five minutes instead of the present rate of 300 cc's every 10 to 15 minutes? Those were the questions preying on Aaron's mind. He didn't want to be wheeling a 70-year-old patient who was in shock into the operating room for chest surgery.

Aaron now told the President that he wanted to go in and find the source of the bleeding and stop it. The President said go ahead. Aaron then spoke with Mrs. Reagan and explained options. She too said go ahead. They would operate.

The President had been in the hospital just over half an hour.

b. PEOPLE AREN'T BORN PREJUDICED

Ian Stevenson

What is prejudice? Its characteristics and origins have by now been carefully studied by psychologists and sociologists so that today we know a good deal about how it is transmitted from one person to another.

Prejudice is a false generalization about a group of people—or things—which is held onto despite all facts to the contrary. Some generalizations, of course, are true and useful—often needed to put people and things into categories. The statement that Negroes have darkly pigmented skin and nearly always curly hair, isn't a prejudice but a correct generalization about Negroes.

Ignorance isn't the same as prejudice, either. Many people believe that Negroes are basically less intelligent than white people because they've heard this and never have been told otherwise. These people would be prejudiced only if they persisted in this belief after they knew the facts! Well documented studies show that when Negroes are properly matched in comparable groups, they have the same intelligence.

Prejudiced thinking is rarely, probably never, confined to any one subject. Those prejudiced against one group of people are nearly always prejudiced against others. Prejudice, then, could be said to be a disorder of thinking: a prejudiced person makes faulty generalizations by applying to a whole group what he has learned from one or a few of its members. Sometimes, he doesn't even draw on his own experiences but bases his attitudes on what he has heard from others. Then he behaves toward a whole group as if there were no individual differences among its members. Few people would throw out a whole box of strawberries because they found one or two bad berries at the top—yet this is the way prejudiced people think and act.

The Different Paths of Prejudice

There are different kinds of prejudice, and two of these deserve separate consideration. First there is that loosely spoken, loosely held opinion that can be called conforming prejudice: people make prejudiced remarks about other races, nations, religions or groups because they want to conform to what they think are the conventions of their own group. Attacking or deriding members of another group who "don't belong" gives them a sense of solidarity with their own group. It's rather sad but also fortunate that most prejudice is probably this conforming kind. Fortunate, because this type of prejudice is easily given up when a new situation demands it.

A number of studies have shown that while people may protest about some social change, when the change actually takes place most will fall silently and willingly into line. It's the rare examples of change being resisted with violence that unfortunately receive most publicity. A psychologist interested in this phenomenon once made an amusing study of the differences between what people say they'll do and what they really do in a particular situation that evokes prejudice. Traveling across the country with a Chinese couple, he found that the three of them were received in 250 hotels and restaurants with great hospitality—and only once were refused service. When the trip was over, he wrote to each of the hotels and restaurants and asked if they would serve Chinese people. Ninety-two per cent of those who had actually served them said they would not do so!

The second kind of prejudice is less easily relinquished than the conforming type, for this second kind stems from a more deep-rooted sense of personal insecurity. A prejudiced person of this kind usually has a feeling of failure or guilt about his own accomplishments and, to avoid the pain of blaming himself, he turns the blame on others. Just as the Jews once symbolically piled all their guilt on a goat and drove it into the wilderness, so these prejudiced people make scape-goats out of Negroes, Southerners, Jews, Russians, or whoever else fits their need. Moreover, insecure people like these are anxious, too, and anxious people can't discriminate among the small but important differences between people who seem alike. So, on the one hand they often can't think clearly about other people; and on the other, they need to blame scapegoats in order to feel more comfortable. Both these mechanisms promote faulty generalizations; these people respond to others not as individuals but as Negroes, Russians, wom-en, doctors—as if these groups were all alike.

How Children Learn Prejudice

The first important point about how children learn prejudice is that they do. They aren't born that way, though some people think prej-udice is innate and like to quote the old saying, "You can't change human nature." But you can change it. We now know that very small children are free of prejudice. Studies of school children have shown that prejudice is slight or absent among children in the first and second grades. It increases thereafter, building to a peak usually among chil-dren in the fourth and fifth grades. After this, it may fall off again in adolescence. Other studies have shown that, on the average, young adults are much freer of prejudice than older ones.

In the early stages of picking up prejudice, children mix it with ignorance which, as I've said, should be distinguished from prejudice. A child, as he begins to study the world around him, tries to organize his experiences. Doing this, he begins to classify things and people and begins to form connections—or what psychologists call asso-ciations. He needs to do this because he saves time and effort by putting things and people into categories. But unless he classifies correctly, his categories will mislead rather than guide him. For ex-ample, if a child learns that "all fires are hot and dangerous," fires have been put firmly into the category of things to be watched care-fully—and thus he can save himself from harm. But if he learns a category like "Negroes are lazy" or "foreigners are fools," he's learned generalizations that mislead because they're unreliable. The thing is that, when we use categories, we need to remember the exceptions and differences, the individual variations that qualify the usefulness of all generalizations. Some fires, for example, are hotter and more dangerous than others. If people had avoided all fires as dangerous, we would never have had central heating.

More importantly, we can ill afford to treat people of any given group as generally alike—even when it's possible to make some ac-curate generalizations about them. So when a child first begins to group things together, it's advisable that he learn differences as well as similarities. For example, basic among the distinctions he draws is the division into "good" and "bad"—which he makes largely on the grounds of what his parents do and say about things and people. Thus, he may learn that dirt is "bad" because his mother washes him every time he gets dirty. By extension, seeing a Negro child, he might point to him and say, "Bad child," for the Negro child's face is brown, hence unwashed and dirty and so, "bad." We call this prelogical thinking, and all of us go through this phase before we learn to think more effectively.

But some people remain at this stage and never learn that things that seem alike, such as dirt and brown pigment, are really quite different. Whether a child graduates from this stage to correct thinking or to prejudicial thinking, depends to a great extent on his experiences with his parents and teachers.

Parents Play Role

Generally speaking, a child learns from his parents in two main ways. Each of these may contribute to his development either as a prejudiced personality or a tolerant one. First, a child learns a good deal by direct imitation of his parents. If parents reveal prejudiced attitudes, children will tend to imitate those attitudes. If a mother or father, for example, tells a child, "I don't want you playing with any colored children," they foster in their child's growing mind the connection between "colored" and "bad"—and thus promote the growth of prejudice. If instead of saying "colored children," a mother says "nigger" in a derogatory tone of voice, this makes another harmful connection in a child's mind. Even before he clearly knows to what the words Negro or "nigger" refer, he would know that these words mean something "bad" and hence indicate people for him to avoid. It may be that some colored children, like some white children, are unsuitable playmates. But the prohibition should be made on the grounds of the particular reasons for this unsuitability, not on the basis of skin pigment.

How parents actually behave towards members of other groups in the presence of their children influences children as much or more than what parents say about such people. Still, parents can and do communicate prejudices in subtle ways, by subtle remarks. For example, some parents take pride in belonging to a special group, lay stress on the child's membership in that group, and consequently lead him to believe that other people are inferior because they're outside this group. Sometimes parents are unaware that the pride they take in such membership in a special group can be an insidious form of prejudice against other groups. This isn't always so, because often pride in belonging can be related to the genuine accomplishments of a group. But just as often, pride stems simply from thinking of the group as special and superior because of its selectivity, not because of its accomplishments. However, this kind of direct transmission of prejudice from parents to children is the conforming type, and so can usually be modified by later experience if the child comes into contact with other unprejudiced people or if he has the opportunity to get to know members of the group toward which he has had prejudiced attitudes. For example, during the Second World War and the Korean War, many white soldiers of both North and South fought with Negro troops; knowing Negroes as people, they lost their old prejudices.

Unfortunately, however, parents tend to restrict their children's experiences with different kinds of people, for fear that the children might be harmfully influenced. This naturally prevents the children from unlearning prejudices. Unfortunately these children who most need broadening and correcting experiences are often deprived of them.

Parents promote prejudice in a second, more subtle and harmful way by their own treatment of their children. Studies of markedly prejudiced persons show that they usually come from families in which they were treated harshly, authoritatively and unfairly—in other words, they were themselves the objects of prejudice. This parental behavior promotes prejudice in the children—apart from their imitation of it—in two ways. First, if parents treat a child harshly and punish him unfairly, they are relating to the child in terms of power instead of love. Treated as if he were always bad, the child will respond to his parents as if they were always dangerous. Growing skilled in the quick detection of threats or possible injury, he becomes sensitive to danger not only from parents but from other people as well. He makes quick judgments in order not to be caught unaware. Quick judgments are a facet of prejudiced thinking. An insecure and easily frightened person makes sweeping judgments about whole groups, finding it safer to treat the whole group as if it might be harmful to him. He thinks, often unconsciously and always incorrectly, that then he can never be hurt.

Secondly, when parents relate to a child in terms of power, when they punish him, say, with equal severity for accidentally knocking over a dish or for biting his baby brother, he not only thinks of his parents as dangerous people but he thinks of himself as dangerous, too. He must be bad, otherwise why would he be punished so often? Given this low opinion of himself, he will often try to raise it by putting the blame on others—using the old unconscious scapegoat mechanism. Here again, psychological studies have shown that people who are able to blame themselves when they're responsible for things going wrong tend to be much less prejudiced than people who blame others when things go wrong. But a child can only learn to accept blame fairly if his parents attribute blame fairly to him. If he is blamed for everything, he may—in his own defense—grow up unable to accept the blame for anything. If he cannot blame himself he has to blame others—he has to see them as more deficient and blameworthy than they are—which means making prejudiced judgments about them.

School Plays a Role

School can help undo the damage. Actual personal experience with children of other groups can show a child directly, immediately and concretely that not all members of a group are blameworthy, stupid, dirty or dishonest. In addition, unprejudiced teachers can instruct children in the ways of clear thinking that underlie tolerance. There is definite evidence that education reduces prejudices. It's been found, for example, that college graduates are less prejudiced on the whole than people with less education. Direct instruction about different groups and cultures, another study shows, reduced prejudice in those who were taught.

Fortunately, we seem today to be making progress in the direction of less prejudiced belief and behavior. Today, parents treat children with greater respect for them as individuals—in short, with less prejudice. This will continue to exert a healthy influence on the next generation. In fact, one survey has shown that it already has! College students of our generation, it demonstrates, are less prejudiced than college students of the last generation.

But since prejudice against members of a minority group or the people of other countries is a luxury we can increasingly ill afford—no parent should relax his vigilance in guarding against sowing the seeds of intolerance.

c. THE LIBIDO FOR THE UGLY

H. L. Mencken

On a Winter day some years ago, coming out of Pittsburgh on one of the expresses of the Pennsylvania Railroad, I rolled eastward for an hour through the coal and steel towns of Westmoreland county. It was familiar ground; boy and man, I had been through it often before. But somehow I had never quite sensed its appalling desolation. Here was the very heart of industrial America, the center of its most lucrative and characteristic activity, the boast and pride of the richest and grandest nation ever seen on earth—and here was a scene so dreadfully hideous, so intolerably bleak and forlorn that it reduced the whole aspiration of man to a macabre and depressing joke. Here was wealth beyond computation, almost beyond imagination—and here were human habitations so abominable that they would have disgraced a race of alley cats.

I am not speaking of mere filth. One expects steel towns to be dirty. What I allude to is the unbroken and agonizing ugliness, the sheer revolting monstrousness, of every house in sight. From East Liberty to Greensburg, a distance of twenty-five miles, there was not one in sight from the train that did not insult and lacerate the eye. Some were so bad, and they were among the most pretentious—churches, stores, warehouses, and the like—that they were downright startling; one blinked before them as one blinks before a man with his face shot away. A few linger in memory, horrible even there: a crazy little church just west of Jeannette, set like a dormer-window on the side of a bare, leprous hill; the headquarters of the Veterans of Foreign Wars at another forlorn town, a steel stadium like a huge rat-trap somewhere further down the line. But most of all I recall the general effect—of hideousness without a break. There was not a single decent house within eye-range from the Pittsburgh suburbs to the Greensburg yards. There was not one that was not misshapen, and there was not one that was not shabby.

The country itself is not uncomely, despite the grime of the endless mills. It is, in form, a narrow river valley, with deep gullies running up into the hills. It is thickly settled, but not noticeably overcrowded. There is still plenty of room for building, even in the larger towns, and there are very few solid blocks. Nearly every house, big and little, has space on all four sides. Obviously, if there were architects of any professional sense or dignity in the region, they would have perfected a chalet to hug the hillsides—a chalet with a high-pitched roof, to throw off the heavy Winter snows, but still essentially a low and clinging building, wider than it was tall. But what have they done? They have taken as their model a brick set on end. This they have converted into a thing of dingy clapboards, with a narrow, low-pitched roof. And the whole they have set upon thin, preposterous brick piers. By the hundreds and thousands these abominable houses cover the bare hillsides, like gravestones in some gigantic and decaying cemetery. On their deep sides they are three, four and even five stories high; on their low sides they bury themselves swinishly in the mud. Not a fifth of them are perpendicular. They lean this way and that, hanging on to their bases precariously. And one and all they are streaked in grime, with dead and eczematous patches of paint peeping through the streaks.

Now and then there is a house of brick. But what brick! When it is new it is the color of a fried egg. When it has taken on the patina of the mills it is the color of an egg long past all hope or caring. Was it necessary to adopt that shocking color? No more than it was necessary to set all of the houses on end. Red brick, even in a steel town, ages with some dignity. Let it become downright black, and it is still sightly, especially if its trimmings are of white stone, with soot in the depths and the high spots washed by the rain. But in Westmoreland they prefer that uremic yellow, and so they have the most loathsome towns and villages ever seen by mortal eye.

I award this championship only after laborious research and incessant prayer. I have seen, I believe, all of the most unlovely towns of the world; they are all to be found in the United States. I have seen the mill towns of decomposing New England and the desert towns of Utah, Arizona and Texas. I am familiar with the back streets of Newark, Brooklyn and Chicago, and have made scientific explorations to Camden, N.J. and Newport News, Va. Safe in a Pullman, I have whirled through the gloomy, God-forsaken villages of Iowa and Kansas, and the malarious tide-water hamlets of Georgia. I have been to Bridgeport, Conn., and to Los Angeles. But nowhere on this earth, at home or abroad, have I seen anything to compare to the villages that huddle along the line of the Pennsylvania from the Pittsburgh yards to Greensburg. They are incomparable in color, and they are incomparable in design. It is as if some titanic and aberrant genius, uncompromisingly inimical to man, had devoted all the ingenuity of Hell to the making of them. They show grotesqueries of ugliness that, in retrospect, become almost diabolical. One cannot imagine mere human beings concocting such dreadful things, and one can scarcely imagine human beings bearing life in them.

Are they so frightful because the valley is full of foreigners—dull, insensate brutes, with no love of beauty in them? Then why didn't these foreigners set up similar abominations in the countries that they came from? You will, in fact, find nothing of the sort in Europe—save perhaps in the more putrid parts of England. There is scarcely an ugly village on the whole Continent. The peasants, however poor, somehow manage to make themselves graceful and charming habitations, even in Spain. But in the American village and small town the pull is always toward ugliness, and in that Westmoreland valley it has been yielded to with an eagerness bordering upon passion. It is incredible that mere ignorance should have achieved such masterpieces of horror.

On certain levels of the American race, indeed, there seems to be a positive libido for the ugly, as on other and less Christian levels there is an libido for the beautiful. It is impossible to put down the wallpaper that defaces the average American home of the lower middle class to mere inadvertence, or to the obscene humor of the manufacturers. Such ghastly designs, it must be obvious, give a genuine delight to a certain type of mind. They meet, in some unfathomable way, its obscure and unintelligible demands. They caress it as "The Palms" caresses it, or the art of the movie, or jazz. The taste for them is as enigmatical and yet as common as the taste for dogmatic theology and the poetry of Edgar A. Guest.

Thus I suspect (though confessedly without knowing) that the vast majority of the honest folk of Westmoreland county, and especially the 100% Americans among them, actually admire the houses they live in, and are proud of them. For the same money they could get vastly better ones, but they prefer what they have got. Certainly there was no pressure upon the Veterans of Foreign Wars to choose the dreadful edifice that bears their banner, for there are plenty of vacant buildings along the track-side, and some of them are appreciably better. They might, indeed, have built a better one of their own. But they chose that clapboarded horror with their eyes open, and having chosen it, they let it mellow into its present shocking depravity. They like it as it is: beside it, the Parthenon would no doubt offend them. In precisely the same way the authors of the rat-trap stadium that I have mentioned made a deliberate choice. After painfully designing and erecting it, they made it perfect in their own sight by putting a completely impossible pent-house, painted a staring yellow, on top of it. The effect is that of a fat woman with a black eye. It is that of a Presbyterian grinning. But they like it.

Here is something that the psychologists have so far neglected: the love of ugliness for its own sake, the lust to make the world intolerable. Its habitat is the United States. Out of the melting pot emerges a race which hates beauty as it hates truth. The etiology of this madness deserves a great deal more study than it has got. There must be causes behind it; it arises and flourishes in obedience to biological laws, and not as a mere act of God. What, precisely, are the terms of those laws? And why do they run stronger in America than elsewhere? Let some honest *Privat Dozent* in pathological sociology apply himself to the problem.

d. SALVATION

Langston Hughes

I was saved from sin when I was going on thirteen. But not really saved. It happened like this. There was a big revival at my Auntie Reed's church. Every night for weeks there had been much preaching, singing, praying, and shouting, and some very hardened sinners had been brought to Christ, and the membership of the church had grown by leaps and bounds. Then just before the revival ended, they held a special meeting for children, "to bring the young lambs to the fold." My aunt spoke of it for days ahead. That night I was escorted to the front row and placed on the mourners' bench with all the other young sinners, who had not yet been brought to Jesus.

My aunt told me that when you were saved you saw a light, and something happened to you inside! And Jesus came into your life! And God was with you from then on! She said you could see and hear and feel Jesus in your soul. I believed her. I had heard a great many old people say the same thing and it seemed to me they ought to know. So I sat there calmly in the hot, crowded church, waiting for Jesus to come to me.

The preacher preached a wonderful rhythmical sermon, all moans and shouts and lonely cries and dire pictures of hell, and then he sang a song about the ninety and nine safe in the fold, but one little lamb was left out in the cold. then he said: "Won't you come? Won't you come to Jesus? Young lambs, won't you come?" And he held out his arms to all us young sinners there on the mourners' bench. And the little girls cried. And some of them jumped up and went to Jesus right away. But most of us just sat there.

A great many old people came and knelt around us and prayed, old women with jet-black faces and braided hair, old men with work-gnarled hands. And the church sang a song about the lower lights are burning, some poor sinners to be saved. And the whole building rocked with prayer and song.

Still I keep waiting to *see* Jesus.

Finally all the young people had gone to the altar and were saved, but one boy and me. He was a rounder's son named Westley. Westley and I were surrounded by sisters and deacons praying. It was very hot in the church, and getting late now. Finally Westley said to me in a whisper: "God damn! I'm tired o' sitting here. Let's get up and be saved." So he got up and was saved.

Then I was left all alone on the mourners' bench. My aunt came and knelt at my knees and cried, while prayers and songs swirled all around me in the little church. The whole congregation prayed for me alone, in a mighty wail of moans and voices. And I kept waiting serenely for Jesus, waiting, waiting—but he didn't come. I wanted to see him, but nothing happened to me. Nothing! I wanted something to happen to me, but nothing happened.

I heard the songs and the minister saying: "Why don't you come? My dear child, why don't you come to Jesus? Jesus is waiting for you. He wants you. Why don't you come? Sister Reed, what is this child's name?"

"Langston," my aunt sobbed.

"Langston, why don't you come? Why don't you come and be saved? Oh, Lamb of God! Why don't you come?"

Now it was really getting late. I began to be ashamed of myself, holding everything up so long. I began to wonder what God thought about Westley, who certainly hadn't seen Jesus either, but who was now sitting proudly on the platform, swinging his knickerbockered legs and grinning down at me, surrounded by deacons and old women on their knees praying. God had not struck Westley dead for taking his name in vain or for lying in the temple. So I decided that maybe to save further trouble, I'd better lie, too, and say that Jesus had come, and get up and be saved.

So I got up.

Suddenly the whole room broke into a sea of shouting, as they saw me rise. Waves of rejoicing swept the place. Women leaped in the air. My aunt threw her arms around me. The minister took me by the hand and led me to the platform.

When things quieted down, in a hushed silence, punctuated by a few ecstatic "Amens," all the new young lambs were blessed in the name of God. Then joyous singing filled the room.

That night, for the last time in my life but one—for I was a big boy twelve years old—I cried. I cried, in bed alone, and couldn't stop. I buried my head under the quilts, but my aunt heard me. She woke up and told my uncle I was crying because the Holy Ghost had come into my life, and because I had seen Jesus. But I was really crying because I couldn't bear to tell her that I had lied, that I had deceived everybody in the church, and I hadn't seen Jesus, and that now I didn't believe there was a Jesus any more, since he didn't come to help me.

e. I AM TIRED OF FIGHTING (SURRENDER SPEECH)

I am tired of fighting. Our chiefs are killed. Looking Glass is dead. Toohulsote is dead. The old men are all dead. It is the young men who say no and yes. He who led the young men is dead. It is cold and we have no blankets. The little children are freezing to death. My people, some of them, have run away to the hills and have no blankets, no food. No one knows where they are—perhaps they are freezing to death. I want to have time to look for my children and see how many of them I can find. Maybe I shall find them among the dead. Hear me, my chiefs, I am tired. My heart is sad and sick. From where the sun stands I will fight no more forever.

2. As a reader, what would you expect to be the purpose of each of the following? For each, state whether you think the writer anticipated that you would empathize, learn, or change your attitude toward the subject matter.
   a. Instructions on a cake mix box.
   b. An article whose title begins "True confessions of a . . ."
   c. A newspaper editorial.
   d. A film review.
   e. A bulk-mail advertisement selling precious metals.
   f. A diet book.

3. Imagine that you are going to write about each of the situations listed below. State what you think your purpose would be, and explain your choice.
   a. A letter to a close friend describing your first impression of being in a new neighborhood.
   b. A letter to the editor of a local paper concerning a proposed nuclear plant.
   c. A report to an insurance company concerning an accident you witnessed.
   d. An ad you place in a newspaper to sell your car.
   e. A letter to your grandfather requesting financial help.
   f. A newspaper story about changes in the registration procedures at your college.

4. Choose one of the situations in Exercise 3 as the topic of a paper. State your purpose and the reaction you anticipate from your reader. Write a draft of the paper, and then try to read it objectively. See if the purpose is clear. As a reader, do you find yourself sharing the writer's feelings, learning about the subject matter, or changing your attitudes or beliefs? Rewrite the paper to improve the clarity of your purpose. Try to make your language and style suit your purpose.

chapter 2
Discovering Ideas When Reading

Philosophers have argued whether two people viewing the same object see the same thing. If two people bite into an apple, will they experience the same taste? Or, what terms are adequate to describe the taste of the fruit to another person? These questions concern both the nature of reality and our attempts to communicate what we think, feel, and experience. Written language is one way to communicate, but words are something like the apple mentioned above: they exist on the page, but they can mean different things to different people. Writing is a process in which the writer uses certain words to convey to the reader his or her ideas. Reading is a similar process in which the reader discovers the writer's intended meaning.

Both reading and writing try to make the reader see the same apple, to receive the same meaning from the words on the page. To aid these discovery processes, questioning stimulates thought and response and enables the reader and/or writer to read and write more efficiently.

Questioning to Discover Ideas

Although most of the questions that you answer in a classroom are asked by the teacher or by the author of the materials read outside the class, you should ask yourself questions as you read. Good readers do this almost without thought. As they read, they use what has been read, be it a phrase, a sentence, or a paragraph, to anticipate what will come next. Such anticipatory questioning increases their curiosity and provides a reason to continue reading.

These questions are answered (or discarded if they are inappropriate) as ideas are discovered and additional ones are created. Formulating questions and seeking answers as you read will enhance your comprehension of the material.

Anticipatory Questioning

Anticipatory questioning refers to those questions you should ask as you survey the material to be read. Surveying is seeking cues provided by the author that indicate the subject matter. Think of these cues as the border pieces of a jigsaw puzzle: they give you an outline of the content, just as the border pieces form the outline of the puzzle. Fitting together the border pieces before doing the rest of the puzzle will help you figure out where the other pieces belong. Likewise, putting together the cues before reading the body of the material will reveal useful preliminary information. These cues can be found in the following places:

Titles

Introductory statements

Beginning paragraphs

Organizational divisions

Illustrations

Authors' names

Biographical sketches

Summary statements

Ending paragraphs

These cues enable you to anticipate the material's subject, scope, and objective and to help you frame anticipatory questions.

The following are cues from several different sources. What can you find out by reading just the cues?

Title	**1. A MEDICAL MARVEL IN YOUR KITCHEN**
Introductory state-ment	*It deadens pain, retards bleeding and infection; it's safe and inexpensive—something you should learn to use in common household emergencies*
Author	**Jack B. Kemmerer**
Beginning para-graph	Suppose someone told you of an exciting new drug which kills pain almost instantly, helps control bleeding, is completely safe, prevents infection—and costs practically nothing.
Ending paragraph	One word of caution: doctors say that while ice massage relieves many types of pain—including the afterpain of a heart attack—it doesn't necessarily clear up the problem. Ice should never be used without proper diagnosis or knowing what's causing the trouble.
Source	*Family Weekly*

Title **2. WHEN I WAS A CHILD**

Author **Lillian Smith**

Introductory state-
ment

Biographical sketch

Lillian Smith (1897–1966) was born in Jasper, Florida, and educated at Piedmont College, the Peabody Conservatory of Music, and Columbia University. Her experiences in the South, especially her contact with the peculiar institution of racial segregation, became the principal subject of her writing for such magazines as *Saturday Review, New Republic,* and *The Nation.* Her books include *Strange Fruit* (1944), *Killers of the Dream* (1949), *Our Faces, Our Words* (1964), and *The Journey* (1965). "When I Was a Child," an excerpt from *Killers of the Dream,* is Smith's explanation of her family's values, and an account of the racial incident that caused her to question those values.

Beginning para-
graph

I was born and reared in a small Deep South town whose population was about equally Negro and white. There were nine of us who grew up freely in a rambling house of many rooms, surrounded by big lawn, back yard, gardens, fields, and barn. It was the kind of home that gathers memories like dust, a place filled with laughter and play and pain and hurt and ghosts and games. We were given such advantages of schooling, music, and art as were available in the South, and our world was not limited to the South, for travel to far places seemed a simple, natural thing to us, and usually there was one of the family in a remote part of the earth.

Ending paragraph

Something was wrong with a world that tells you that love is good and people are important and then forces you to deny love and to humiliate people. I knew, though I would not for years confess it aloud, that in trying to shut the Negro race away from us, we have shut ourselves away from so many good, creative, honest, deeply human things in life. I began to understand so slowly at first but more and more clearly as the years passed, that the warped, distorted frame we have put around every Negro child from birth is around every white child also. Each is on a different side of the frame but each is pinioned there. And I knew that what cruelly shapes and cripples the personality of one is as cruelly shaping and crippling the personality of the other. I began to see that though we may, as we acquire new knowledge, live through new experiences, examine old memories, gain the strength to tear the frame from us, yet we are stunted and warped and in our lifetime cannot grow straight again any more than can a tree, put in a steel-like twisting frame when young, grow tall and straight when the frame is torn away at maturity.

Title **3. IN THE EYE OF THE BEHOLDER**

Illustration

Source *Esquire*

Title **4. BODY PARTS**

Topic *Gentlemen, the question before us is what exactly* a woman of quality thinks of the male body. Now a woman of quality has been bold enough to oblige us. Part by part.

Reader's response *Brace yourselves*

Author **Priscilla Flood**

Introductory state-ment When she was five her father used to take her on his Saturday morning errands. She had learned the words to *"Oh, What a Beautiful Mornin',"* and they would sing it together as they bounced along in the old Ford. Every once in a while he would reach across the seat and give her knee a squeeze. His hands, gentle and strong, were large, with big veins and long fingers.

Source *Esquire*

Author's position The author of "Body Parts" is an executive editor of this magazine.

These cues tell you that the first selection concerns "a medical marvel in your kitchen" that "deadens pain, retards bleeding and infection," is "safe and inexpensive," that "you should learn to use it in common household emergencies," that it "costs practically nothing," and that the article about ice was written by Jack B. Kemmerer for *Family Weekly*. The second selection is a story, "When I Was a Child," by Lillian Smith, a well-educated Southern author (1897–1966), who wrote about racial segregation. This story explains her family's values and what caused her to question them. The first paragraph briefly describes the town and home she grew up in, and the last paragraph reveals her understanding of, and her reaction to, the world she lives in. The third selection offers only a title, source, and illustration, but they suggest that the article may concern female appraisals of males. Finally, the fourth states the subject in the title—"Body Parts"—specifically what "women of quality" think of the male body, warns the readers to "brace" themselves, and identifies the author and her position at *Esquire* magazine. The introductory statement hints that a girl's early experience with her father will somehow influence the discussion of the topic. These cues should then stimulate anticipatory questions for each selection.

For example, surveying the first selection may have prompted the following questions:

1. What is this "medical marvel"?
2. If it is ice, why is it described as a "new" drug?
3. Why is it referred to as a drug?
4. If it is "completely safe," why am I cautioned about its use?
5. Who is the author?
6. What is *Family Weekly?*

A survey of the second selection may have generated these questions:
1. Why does the author want to explain her family's values?
2. Why does she question them?
3. Why did she choose to write about it?
4. Does the fact that she was reared in "a small Deep South town," in what seems to be a well-to-do family, influence her reactions in the last paragraph?
5. Who was denied love and humiliated?
6. To what does the "warped, distorted frame we put around every Negro . . ." refer?
7. Why and how are whites "stunted and warped" as a result of what has been done to blacks?

The following questions may have been raised by a preview of the third selection:

1. Is the title related to the old saying, "Beauty is in the eye of the beholder"?
2. Does the magnifying glass suggest that a careful study of a man's beauty will be discussed?
3. If beauty is being studied by a woman, what kind of beauty is it?

Finally, surveying the fourth selection may have produced these questions:

1. To which body parts does the title refer?
2. What is meant by the phrase "woman of quality"?
3. Why is it "bold" for this woman to answer the question?
4. Why must I brace myself? (Why should gentlemen "brace" themselves?)
5. Why is it important to know the author's position at *Esquire*?
6. Does the fact that the article appeared in *Esquire* influence its content or the audience for which it is intended?
7. Why is the first paragraph about a five-year-old girl and her father?
8. Because the title of the article is "Body Parts," are the father's hands in some way significant to the article? How? Why?

Each question is based on the cues that each selection provides. Reading thus becomes the active search for answers to questions. Reader concentration is increased because it is focused.

Continuous Questioning

Continuous questioning refers to those questions you ask yourself as you read through a text. Continuous questioning includes (1) seeking answers to anticipatory questions and (2) formulating new questions based on ideas discovered in the material.

The first article, "A Medical Marvel in Your Kitchen," is presented in its entirety. Notice that some of the anticipatory questions are answered by the text and that continuous questions are created by certain ideas in the text.

A MEDICAL MARVEL IN YOUR KITCHEN

It deadens pain, retards bleeding and infection; it's safe and inexpensive—something you should learn to use in common household emergencies

Jack B. Kemmerer

Answer to anticipatory question

Suppose someone told you of an exciting new drug which kills pain almost instantly, helps control bleeding, is completely safe, prevents infection—and costs practically nothing.

You would demand to know the name of this exciting new wonder drug. Yet, without a doubt, you have plenty of it in your home at this moment. The new wonder drug?

An ice cube!

Answer to anticipatory question

Medical authorities say that ice is such a powerful anesthetic that surgeons have used it in performing some types of major surgery with patients fully conscious.

In the majority of these cases, the patients sit up in bed immediately after the operation, request food, and then call friends on the telephone. There are no aftereffects or drowsiness because they had no anesthetic by inhalation or by injection.

These are extreme cases, but there are many everyday conditions where ice can be used as a pain reliever.

Answer to anticipatory question

Many old-time remedies used ice or cold water as a basic part of their treatment, but the renewed interest in ice-cube therapy probably stems from a recent report made by doctors at Brooke Army Medical Center in San Antonio, Texas.

Over a two-year period, the Army medics prescribed ice to approximately 5,000 soldiers who complained of various aches and pains when answering sick call. After instructions, most of the men were sent back to their barracks to apply the ice themselves. According to the report, the results were "striking."

Author's question

Answer to author's question

With the latest medical advice being "cool it," you might ask, "Does it really work?" Mrs. Vernon Irby, a Silver Spring, Md., housewife, thinks so. "It was fantastic," she says. "Two ice applications on an aching back had me up and around." Two years ago a similar attack took 10 heat treatments at a hospital to get the same results, she says.

1. What are some of these everyday conditions? (continuous question)

Doctors at Walter Reed Army Medical Center in Washington, D.C., prescribed the home treatment for Mrs. Irby. "They told me to freeze water in orange juice cans and rub the cans on my back," Mrs. Irby said.

Author's question

Another example of an everyday condition and an answer to first continuous question

Have you ever attempted to remove a small sliver from the tip of your finger? It's easy. All you have to do is sterilize the point of a needle in a match flame, then place the tip of the finger on an ice cube until it becomes numb. Now, the sliver can be lifted out without pain.

Author's question

At a doctor's office in Los Angeles, the children will only allow one of his several nurses to give them their immunization shots. Why this favorite nurse? Simple. Before each shot she places an ice cube over the area for about 15 seconds, quickly dries it with tissue, swabs the skin with alcohol, and puts the needle in while the spot is still numb from the ice. The children don't feel a thing.

Sports fans will remember that Sandy Koufax, the Los Angeles Dodgers' great left-handed pitcher, always soaked his aching arm in an ice-bath for at least an hour after each game he pitched. According to Koufax, it worked perfectly.

You would think that the effects of heat would be directly opposite to those of ice. Ironically, however, ice is being used in innumerable cases where heat was once prescribed.

2. Why is ice replacing heat as a treatment? (continuous question and answer)

Doctors agree that both cold and heat penetrate muscles and soothe aches but the ice advocates claim that cold penetrates deeper than heat and thus brings relief from pain much quicker. They say that ice application in these cases must be coupled with exercises, and they agree that the application of ice is usually more uncomfortable than the application of heat.

Answer to anticipatory question

Massive pain quite often accompanies a heart attack, and sometimes the doctor has to inject morphine to prevent severe shock to the patient. But until the doctor comes, almost instant relief can be gained by rubbing an ice cube gently on the chest over the painful area. After ice treatment of this situation, morphine may not even be necessary when the doctor arrives. It should be stressed, however, that the ice treatment merely *eases* the pain—it does nothing whatsoever for what caused the pain in the first place.

Another example of an everyday condition and an answer to first continuous question

If you burn your finger, you probably have been told to rub butter or some other oily substance on the burn. Instinctively, however, you probably will pop your finger into your mouth to cool it.

And your instincts are right, for, ideally, the finger should be soaked immediately in a container of cold water in which ice has been placed. Or, if you prefer, the ice cube can be rubbed gently over the burn until the pain is no longer felt.

While the relief from pain is prompt, more important is the fact that there will be very little swelling, and blisters won't form. Consequently, the burn will heal much more rapidly.

Ice-cube treatment also helps prevent infection, as any part of the body that is refrigerated is not likely to become infected, even if contaminated with dirt.

3. Why does ice cube treatment prevent infection? (continuous question)

While being applied, the ice-cold temperature keeps germs dormant and unable to multiply.

Answer to third continuous question

Ice has another medical virtue.

4. What is it? (continuous question)

Answer to fourth continuous question

It aids greatly in stopping bleeding, not only surface bleeding but that which occurs under the skin—as when an eye is bruised or a shin scuffed. The ugly black-and-blue discoloration is caused by the leakage of blood from torn blood vessels. An ice cube placed over the bruised area constricts the blood vessels, thereby greatly reducing leakage until clotting takes place.

Another example of an everyday condition and the answer to first continuous question

Itching is just one of the many skin conditions that can be relieved by ice.

5. How is itching relieved by ice? (continuous question)

Answer to fifth continuous question

When the skin itches, it is natural for a person to rub or scratch, but the relief is very brief. The itching not only returns but is far more intense. The application of ice often retards the itching.

If the area to be treated is large, crack the ice cubes into small pieces, put them into a large bath towel, and fold over to form a pack which can then be adjusted to the shape of the affected part. Leave the pack in place until the ice melts; the ice can be replaced as often as is necessary. The ice-towel pack is particularly good for such places as the shoulder, in the case of bursitis, or for sprains.

Author's question

Answer to anticipatory question

Does this application to the bare skin ever cause frostbite—which can be dangerous? No—not if applied carefully. Ice, as long as it is mixed with water, is not dangerous because it does not freeze the tissues, it refrigerates them. The difference is slight, but is large enough to be a good margin of safety.

Never add salt to an ice bath or bag. Salted ice does hasten chilling, but it can also cause frostbite.

Author's question

How big a dose of ice can a patient take?

Dr. John Mennell, associate professor of physical medicine at the University of Pennsylvania, recommends a five-to-ten-minute rub with one ice cube.

One word of caution: doctors say that while ice massage relieves many types of pain—including the afterpain of a heart attack—it doesn't necessarily clear up the problem. Ice should never be used without proper diagnosis or knowing what's causing the trouble.

Besides discovering the **answers** to anticipatory questions, your continuous questioning helps you **identify** other concerns that you expect the article to address. You may also have noticed that the author posed questions; writers also recognize the value of questions as a means of stimulating the readers' thoughts.

The opening paragraphs of "In the Eye of the Beholder" are presented below. Notice how the anticipatory questions are answered and how continuous questions are created by careful reading.

IN THE EYE OF THE BEHOLDER

1. Why do I need to know this? (continuous question)	In our May 1980 issue, Esquire celebrated the beauty of athletic women in our cover story, "In Praise of Women's Muscles," by John Casey.
Answer to first continuous question and answer to anticipatory question	This year we wanted to provide an opportunity for a woman to evaluate the male body, and the result is our cover story, "Body Parts" (page 35), by Esquire executive editor Priscilla Flood.
2. Why should I be interested in this? (continuous question) and answer to anticipatory question	You will find the piece to be a personal and detailed description of how the author and her friends experience the physical aspects of the men they encounter.
Answer to second continuous question	Flood believes that one of the factors behind the attention recently paid to the body—the physical-fitness boom that started in the Seventies—was the breakdown of relations between the sexes in the wake of the women's movement. Men and women were uncertain about what to expect from one another, and this uncertainty, Flood theorizes, led to a defensive narcissism: "If I can't get reinforcement from you, I will get it from myself." Now, however, she believes, men and women have more confidence in themselves and are less afraid of celebrating differences between the sexes. It is in this spirit that she conceived the idea for writing "Body Parts," which she hopes will provide some answers to the age-old question, What do women really want?
Why is Esquire celebrating Prince Charles's wedding "with tongue in cheek"?	One of our June photo stories is, appropriately, about brides—or about brides that might have been, as Esquire, with tongue in cheek, celebrates Prince Charles's upcoming wedding ("Ladies Left in Waiting," page 54).
Answer to anticipatory question	The ladies we offer are not presented to diminish the Lady Diana, for she stands on her own merits, nor to criticize the prince, for beauty is in the eye of the beholder;
Answer to third continuous question	we just believe that a man ought to know what he is missing.

As you read these paragraphs, you discovered that the *Esquire* writer introduced two articles, "Body Parts" and "Ladies Left in Waiting," and indicated why they appeared in this issue.

Evaluative Questioning

You ask evaluative questions after you have read the text. Evaluative questions enable you to reflect on the content and to judge its significance.

Upon reflection, a reader of Jack Kemmerer's article might ask these evaluative questions:

1. Was my understanding of the article hampered by a lack of knowledge of the author and the source?
2. Was there sufficient verifiable information to support the author's claims about the use of ice?
3. What are his motives? (What is to be gained by the author in writing the article?)
4. Did the author anticipate the kinds of questions I might ask and attempt to answer them?
5. Of what value is this information to me?

After reading and thinking about the paragraphs of the *Esquire* introduction, you might ask the following evaluative questions:

1. Does *Esquire* give equal time to both sexes in regard to evaluating the male body?
2. Does *Esquire* support the women's movement?
3. What does *Esquire* stand to gain by presenting these articles?
4. What do I stand to gain by reading these articles?

Now read Lillian Smith's short autobiographical story, "When I Was a Child," in its entirety. Frame evaluative questions and see how they compare with those following the story.

WHEN I WAS A CHILD

Lillian Smith

Lillian Smith (1897–1966) was born in Jasper, Florida, and educated at Piedmont College, the Peabody Conservatory of Music, and Columbia University. Her experiences in the South, especially her contact with the peculiar institution of racial segregation, became the principal subject of her writing for such magazines as Saturday Review, New Republic, *and* The Nation. *Her books include* Strange Fruit *(1944),* Killers of the Dream *(1949),* Our Faces, Our Words *(1964), and* The Journey *(1965). "When I Was a Child," an excerpt from* Killers of the Dream, *is Smith's explanation of her family's values, and an account of the racial incident that caused her to question those values.*

I was born and reared in a small Deep South town whose population was about equally Negro and white. There were nine of us who grew up freely in a rambling house of many rooms, surrounded by big lawn, back yard, gardens, fields, and barn. It was the kind of home that gathers memories like dust, a place filled with laughter and play and pain and hurt and ghosts and games. We were given such advantages of schooling, music, and art as were available in the South, and our world was not limited to the South, for travel to far places seemed a simple, natural thing to us, and usually there was one of the family in a remote part of the earth.

We knew we were a respected and important family of this small town but beyond this knowledge we gave little thought to status. Our father made money in lumber and naval stores for the excitement of making and losing it—not for what money can buy nor the security which it sometimes gives. I do not remember at any time wanting "to be rich" nor do I remember that thrift and saving were ideals which our parents considered important enough to urge upon us. Always in the family there was an acceptance of risk, a mild delight even in burning bridges, an expectant "what will happen now!" We were not irresponsible; living according to the pleasure principle was by no means our way of life. On the contrary we were trained to think that each of us should do something that would be of genuine usefulness to the world, and the family thought it right to make sacrifices if necessary, to give each child adequate preparation for this life's work. We were also trained to think learning important, and books, but "bad" books our mother burned. We valued music and art and craftsmanship but it was people and their welfare and religion that were the foci around which our lives seemed naturally to move. Above all else, the important thing was what we "planned to do with our lives." That each of us must do something was as inevitable as breathing for we owed a "debt to society which must be paid." This was a family commandment.

While many of our neighbors spent their energies in counting limbs on the family tree and grafting some on now and then to give symmetry to it, or in reliving the old bitter days of Reconstruction licking scars to cure their vague malaise, or in fighting each battle and turn of battle of that Civil War which has haunted the southern conscience so long, my father was pushing his nine children straight into the future. "You have your heritage," he used to say, "some of it good, some not so good; and as far as I know you had the usual number of grandmothers and grandfathers. Yes, there were slaves, far too many of them in the family, but that was your grandfather's mistake, not yours. The past has been lived. It is gone. The future is yours. What are you going to do with it?" Always he asked this question of his children and sometimes one knew it was but an echo of the old question he had spent his life trying to answer for himself. For always the future held my father's dreams; always there, not in the past, did he expect to find what he had spent his life searching for.

We lived the same segregated life as did other southerners but our parents talked in excessively Christian and democratic terms. We were told ten thousand times that status and money are unimportant (though we were well supplied with both); we were told that "all men are brothers," that we are a part of a democracy and must act like democrats. We were told that the teachings of Jesus are real and important and could be practiced if we tried. We were told also that to be "radical" is bad, silly too; and that one must always conform to the "best behavior" of one's community and make it better if one can. We were taught that we were superior not to people but to hate and resentment, and that no member of the Smith family could stoop so low as to have an enemy. No matter what injury was done us, we must not injure ourselves further by retaliating. That was a family commandment too.

We had family prayers once each day. All of us as children read the Bible in its entirety each year. We memorized hundreds of Bible verses and repeated them at breakfast, and said "sentence prayers" around the family table. God was not someone we met on Sunday but a permanent member of our household. It never occurred to me until I was fourteen or fifteen years old that He did not see every act and thought and chalk up the daily score on eternity's tablets.

Despite the strain of living so intimately with God, the nine of us were strong, healthy, energetic youngsters who filled our days with play and sports and music and books and managed to live much of our lives on the careless level at which young lives should be lived. We had our times of profound anxiety of course, for there were hard lessons to be learned about the body and "bad things" to be learned about sex. Sometimes I have wondered how we ever learned them with a mother so shy with words.

She was a wistful creature who loved beautiful things like lace and sunsets and flowers in a vague inarticulate way, and took good care of her children. We always knew this was not her world but one she accepted under duress. Her private world we rarely entered, though the shadow of it lay at times heavily on our hearts.

Our father owned large business interests, employed hundreds of colored and white laborers, paid them the prevailing low wages, worked them the prevailing long hours, built for them mill towns (Negro and white), built for each group a church, saw to it that religion was supplied free, saw to it that a commissary supplied commodities at a high price, and in general managed his affairs much as ten thousand other southern businessmen manage theirs.

Even now, I can hear him chuckling as he told my mother how he won his fight for Prohibition. The high point of the campaign was election afternoon, when he lined up the entire mill force of several hundred (white and black), passed out a shining silver dollar to each one of them, marched them in and voted liquor out of our county. It was a great day in his life. He had won the Big Game, a game he was always playing with himself against all kinds of evil. It did not occur to him to scrutinize the methods he used. Evil was a word written in capitals; the devil was smart; if you want to win you out-smarted him. It was as simple as that.

He was a practical, hardheaded, warmhearted, high-spirited man born during the Civil War, earning his living at twelve, struggling through bitter decades of Reconstruction and post-Reconstruction, through populist movement, through the panic of 1893, the panic of 1907, on into the twentieth century accepting his region as he found it, accepting its morals and its mores as he accepted its climate, with only scorn for those who held grudges against the North or pitied themselves or the South; scheming, dreaming, expanding his business, making and losing money, making friends whom he did not lose, with never a doubt that God was always by his side, whispering hunches as to how to pull off successful deals. When he lost, it was his own fault. When he won, God had helped him.

Once while we were kneeling at family prayers the fire siren at the mill sounded the alarm that the mill was on fire. My father did not falter from his prayer. The alarm sounded again and again— which signified that the fire was big. With quiet dignity he continued his talk with God while his children sweated and wriggled and hearts beat out of their chests in excitement. He was talking to God—how could he hurry out of the presence of the Most High to save his mills! When he finished his prayer, he quietly stood up, laid the bible carefully on the table. Then, and only then, did he show an interest in what was happening in Mill Town. . . . When the telegram was placed in his hands telling of the death of his beloved favorite son, he gathered his children together, knelt down, and in a steady voice which contained no hint of his shattered heart, loyally repeated, "God is our refuge and strength, a very present help in trouble. Therefore will we not fear, though the earth be removed, and though the mountains be carried into the midst of the sea." On his deathbed, he whispered to his old Business Partner in Heaven: "I have fought the fight; I have kept the faith."

Against this backdrop the drama of the South was played out one day in my life:

A little white girl was found in the colored section of our town, living with a Negro family in a broken-down shack. This family had moved in only a few weeks before and little was known of them. One of the ladies in my mother's club, while driving over to her washerwoman's, saw the child swinging on a gate. The shack, as she said, was hardly more than a pigsty and this white child was living with ignorant and dirty and sick-looking colored folks. "They must have kidnapped her," she told her friends. Genuinely shocked, the clubwomen busied themselves in an attempt to do something, for the child was very white indeed. The strange Negroes were subjected to a grueling questioning and finally grew frightened and evasive and refused to talk at all. This only increased the suspicion of the white group, and the next day the clubwomen, escorted by the town marshal, took the child from her adopted family despite their tears.

She was brought to our home. I do not know why my mother consented to this plan. Perhaps because she loved children and always showed tenderness and concern for them. It was easy for one more to fit into our ample household and Janie was soon at home there. She roomed with me, sat next to me at the table; I found Bible verses for her to say at breakfast; she wore my clothes, played with my dolls and followed me around from morning to night. She was dazed by her new comforts and by the interesting activities of this big lively family; and I was as happily dazed, for her adoration was a new thing to me; and as time passed a quick, childish, and deeply felt bond grew up between us.

But a day came when a telephone message was received from a colored orphanage. There was a meeting at our home, whispers, shocked exclamations. All afternoon the ladies went in and out of our house talking to Mother in tones too low for children to hear. And as they passed us at play, most of them looked quickly at Janie and quickly looked away again, though a few stopped and stared at her as if they could not tear their eyes from her face. When my father came home in the evening Mother closed her door against our young ears and talked a long time with him. I heard him laugh, heard Mother say, "But Papa, this is no laughing matter!" And then they were back in the living room with us and my mother was pale and my father was saying, "Well, work it out, honey, as best you can. After all, now that you know, it is pretty simple."

In a little while my mother called my sister and me into her bedroom and told us that in the morning Janie would return to Colored Town. She said Janie was to have the dresses the ladies had given her and a few of my own, and the toys we had shared with her. She asked me if I would like to give Janie one of my dolls. She seemed hurried, though Janie was not to leave until next day. She said, "Why not select it now?" And in dreamlike stiffness I brought in my dolls and chose one for Janie. And then I found it possible to say, "Why? Why is she leaving? She likes us, she hardly knows them. She told me she had been with them only a month."

"Because," Mother said gently, "Janie is a little colored girl."

"But she can't be. She's white!"

"We were mistaken. She is colored."

"But she looks——"

"She is colored. Please don't argue!"

"What does it mean?" I whispered.

"It means," Mother said slowly, "that she has to live in Colored Town with colored people."

"But why? She lived here three weeks and she doesn't belong to them, she told me she didn't."

"She is a little colored girl."

"But you said yourself that she has nice manners. You said that," I persisted.

"Yes, she is a nice child. But a colored child cannot live in our home."

"Why?"

"You know, dear! You have always known that white and colored people do not live together."

"Can she come over to play?"

"No."

"I don't understand."

"I don't either," my young sister quavered.

"You're too young to understand. And don't ask me again, ever again, about this!" Mother's voice was sharp but her face was sad and there was no certainty left there. She hurried out and busied herself in the kitchen and I wandered through that room where I had been born, touching the old familiar things in it, looking at them, trying to find the answer to a question that moaned in my mind like a hurt thing. . . .

And then I went out to Janie, who was waiting, knowing things were happening that concerned her but waiting until they were spoken aloud.

I do not know quite how the words were said but I told her that she was to return in the morning to the little place where she had lived because she was colored and colored children could not live with white children.

"Are you white?" she said.

"I'm white," I replied, "and my sister is white. And you're colored. And white and colored can't live together because my mother says so."

"Why?" Janie whispered.

"Because they can't," I said. But I knew, though I said it firmly, that something was wrong. I knew my father and mother whom I passionately admired had done that which did not fit in with their teachings. I knew they had betrayed something which they held dear. And I was shamed by their failure and frightened, for I felt that they were no longer as powerful as I had thought. There was something Out There that was stronger than they and I could not bear to believe it. I could not confess that my father, who had always solved the family dilemmas easily and with laughter, could not solve this. I knew that my mother who was so good to children did not believe in her heart that she was being good to this child. There was not a word in my mind that said it but my body knew and my glands, and I was filled with anxiety.

But I felt compelled to believe they were right. It was the only way my world could be held together. And, like a slow poison, it began to seep through me: *I was white. She was colored. We must not be together. It was bad to be together. Though you ate with your nurse when you were little, it was bad to eat with any colored person after that. It was bad just as other things were bad that your mother had told you. It was bad that she was to sleep in the room with me that night. It was bad. . . .*

I was suddenly full of guilt. For three weeks I had done things that white children are not supposed to do. And now I knew these things had been wrong.

I went to the piano and began to play, as I had always done when I was in trouble. I tried to play Paderewski's *Minuet* and as I stumbled through it, the little girl came over and sat on the bench with me. Feeling lonely, lost in these deep currents that were sweeping through our house that night, she crept closer and put her arms around me and I shrank away as if my body had been uncovered. I had not said a word, I did not say one, but she knew, and tears slowly rolled down her little white face. . . .

And then I forgot it. For more than thirty years the experience was wiped out of my memory. But that night, and the weeks it was tied to, worked its way like a splinter, bit by bit down to the hurt places in my memory and festered there. And as I grew older, as more experiences collected around that faithless time, as memories of earlier, more profound hurts crept closer and closer drawn to that night as if to a magnet, I began to know that people who talked of love and Christianity and democracy did not mean it. That is a hard thing for a child to learn. I still admired my parents, there was so much that was strong and vital and sane and good about them and I never forgot this; I stubbornly believed in their sincerity, as I do to this day, and I loved them. Yet in my heart they were under suspicion. Something was wrong.

Something was wrong with a world that tells you that love is good and people are important and then forces you to deny love and to humiliate people. I knew, though I would not for years confess it aloud, that in trying to shut the Negro race away from us, we have shut ourselves away from so many good, creative, honest, deeply human things in life. I began to understand so slowly at first but more and more clearly as the years passed, that the warped, distorted frame we have put around every Negro child from birth is around every white child also. Each is on a different side of the frame but each is pinioned there. And I knew that what cruelly shapes and cripples the personality of one is as cruelly shaping and crippling the personality of the other. I began to see that though we may, as we acquire new knowledge, live through new experiences, examine old memories, gain the strength to tear the frame from us, yet we are stunted and warped and in our lifetime cannot grow straight again any more than can a tree, put in a steel-like twisting frame when young, grow tall and straight when the frame is torn away at maturity.

Sample evaluative questions:

1. Is it important that the incident took place during the author's childhood?
2. Why did the author forget the incident for thirty years? Does this have anything to do with her motive for writing the story?
3. Are Smith's parents hypocrites? Does she see them as such?
4. Why does she change from using "I" to "we" near the end of the story?
5. Is the fact that this story is part of a book, *The Killers of a Dream,* significant to its meaning?
6. Are there universal truths in this story that go beyond the subject of racial segregation?
7. How does the author want me to react to the story?

Evaluative questions must always be based on the ideas discovered during anticipatory and continuous reading. Of course, these questions may lead to answers that concern broader issues, but they should be stimulated by and related to what has been read.

Using these three types of questions before, during, and after careful reading ensures your active participation in discovering ideas when reading. With practice, a questioning attitude and the formulation of questions will become automatic.

Exercise

1. As you read the following article (1) survey the article and underline the statements that stimulate you to ask a question, (2) write down that question, and then (3) write down the answer to each question. Each answer should be based on the ideas you discover while reading.

CASTING COMMERCIALS: IT WAS EASIER FINDING SCARLETT O'HARA

Joan Walker

It's along about this time of the year, what with reruns popping up all over the dial, that viewers are more grateful than ever for the commercials. Some experts think—and with a certain justification— that the commercials are better than the shows at the height of the season. They really are, in rerun time. There are, of course, several reasons for the often high quality of commercials. For one thing, they often cost more than the programs they accompany. A one-minute commercial has been known to cost more than $100,000. With that kind of money, some quality's bound to creep in. An even more important reason, perhaps, is the infinite care that goes into the casting of commercials. The producers don't pluck those actors off the sidewalk. It wasn't any more difficult to find Vivien Leigh to play Scarlett O'Hara for David O. Selznick than it was to find Jan Miner to play Madge the Manicurist for Palmolive Liquid.

Take a large agency like Ted Bates. Here, roughly, is what can happen when they have to cast a commercial. First the producer tells the casting office what he has in mind. Say he announces that he wants an attractive blonde woman, between 28 and 35, and she has to be warm and animated. Okay. The casting people draw up a dream list of their favorite seven or eight warm, animated, attractive, 30ish blondes. It includes actresses the casters have been impressed with on or off Broadway or in the flicks or in summer stock or in other commercials (but not, of course, in a commercial for a conflicting product). Dream list drawn up, the casters call the actresses' agents. It turns out that the top candidates are all in Europe or on the coast or otherwise unavailable. (It is sometimes hard to talk Hollywood-based people into doing commercials. California is series-oriented— Hollywood is where most series are made—and a producer of a series is not interested in hiring actors who are already starring in commercials. If he did, he would automatically be cutting down on the number of potential sponsors for his series, and very few producers are that suicidal. Sometimes, if an actor is in a commercial that is being run on the air, he can't even get a job making a pilot film for a series.)

The casters then dredge up a new list; the agents suggest more candidates; and, finally, 20 or 30 warm, animated blondes of the right type arrive for a pre-screening. If, out of those 20 or 30, five or six look promising, all is well: The five or six read their lines, and the best reader gets picked. But, if none of them read the copy in just the right warm, animated way, then the casting office calls a bunch of new agents and starts all over again. (There are almost 100 agents in New York City who handle people for commercials.) When the casting office does pick The One to its satisfaction, it presents her for approval. It presents her to the producer who will make the commercial, the writer (or writers), the director, the art director, the account executive, sometimes the account supervisor, and do not forget the client himself. All of them have veto power, and the whole routine can start all over again.

It must be remembered that this routine I've outlined was just for a warm, lively, attractive blonde of a certain age. While not a dime a dozen, women fitting that description—even women fitting that description who can read—are around town. When the needs are more esoteric that that—which they often are—the casters are in more trouble. Just a glance at the files in the casting office at N. W. Ayer gives an idea of how complicated casting can be. Under "Female" come the following categories: Ingenue; Young Leading Lady; Foreign; Singers; Characters; Model; Kook; Negro; Spokeswoman, and Specialty (this would include subcategories like Jugglers, Clowns, Dwarfs, and Twins). Scali, McCabe, and Sloves—a newish, up-and-coming agency—not long ago found itself needing, for a Volvo commercial, a little old lady who looked weak but who could slam a car door until the car shook. The agency people looked at 18 or 20 little old ladies in California. It turned out that there weren't any strong weak-looking ones out there. The search had to be shifted to the East, where the perfect answer was found at last: Estelle Winwood. Another time, for another Volvo commercial, the agency needed someone to play a Volvo salesman. He had to look better than the average American car salesman, but not *too* much better or he wouldn't be believable. A balding Old World type whose car-salesman personality would emerge—now that's esoteric.

Casting for children is always tough, because of both the children and their relatives. N. W. Ayer found itself a while back—and it is still shuddering at the thought—needing seven one-year-old babies. Seventy-two one-year-old babies turned up. They couldn't come alone, so, needless to say, Ayer got 72 mothers too. *And* almost that many grandmothers. *And* 102 big brothers and sisters. All of them wanted to be discovered for television commercials. As everyone knows, there's a great deal of money to be made appearing in commercials. There is, in this town, one eight-year-old girl who earned an income in six figures last year making television commercials.

Finding exactly the right actor or actress, no matter what the age, is not easy. What is even more difficult is finding exactly the right non-actor or non-actress. These ordinary real people—"the realzies," they call them at Ted Bates—are the ones who use a certain product, like it, and are willing to deliver a testimonial to that effect. First they have to be tracked down. You can't call an agent for a realzie. There are several ways to find them, all tedious. One is to stand at a counter in a drugstore waiting for someone to come in and ask for the product in question. Whoever does has to then be vaguely attractive (an ugly user is no help), cannot have any speech defects, and must not freeze on camera. You would be amazed at the number of willing, attractive, articulate people who are rendered speechless by a camera. Realzies are definitely the worst.

2. Read the following article and list the evaluative questions it raises.

GUN CONTROLS: ON TARGET?

In the time it takes to read this article, someone in the U.S. will die as a result of an incident involving firearms. In fact, every day in the U.S., approximately 50 people die from firearms—through murder, accidents, and suicide.

By helping keep guns out of the hands of the wrong people, gun control laws could lower these shocking figures. Professor Marvin Wolfgang of the University of Pennsylvania, an expert on criminal homicide, says: "Violence and instruments of violence breed violence. Legislation which makes more restrictive the manufacturing sale and distribution, and licensing of firearms is, I think desirable in almost any form."

Effective gun regulations on a nationwide basis would make it difficult for criminals to purchase firearms. For example, a 1965 study in Massachusetts (a state with strict gun controls) showed that 85 percent of the weapons used in crimes had been purchased out-of-state! Federal gun control laws will enable police to solve gun crimes by quickly tracking down the gun's owner.

The United States' rate of murders *by guns* (the number of gun murders per 100,000 population) is far above the rates of nations with strong gun control laws. Compare the U.S. rate of 2.7 with rates of .03 in the Netherlands, .04 in Japan, .05 in Britain, and .12 in West Germany, all of which have tight gun control laws.

The Second Amendment to the U.S. Constitution reads: "A well-regulated militia being necessary to the security of a free state, the right of the people to keep and bear arms shall not be infringed." Notice that the Amendment connects the right to bear arms with the needs of a state militia. This clause was written when the U.S. depended on its citizen-soldiers answering an immediate call to arms.

Thus the U.S. Supreme Court has ruled that previous gun control laws *are* constitutional since they don't interfere with "the preservation of efficiency of a well-regulated militia."

Federal gun control laws will not infringe upon the privilege of law-abiding citizens to own guns. But they will deny that privilege to criminals, just as driving privileges are denied to those who habitually disobey driving laws.

chapter 3
Discovering Ideas When Writing

Both reading and writing are processes which seek to transmit meaning from one person to another. When you read, you attempt to determine the meaning of the words on the page. But when you write, you first must discover your *own* ideas: you cannot communicate until you know what you want to say.

Many experienced writers begin with only a general idea of what they want to say. Then while writing they refine and focus their thinking, often by reading what they have written. Their own preliminary thoughts made visible on a piece of paper stimulate further and deeper investigation of the subject.

This chapter addresses the very first stage of composing: starting to define an approach to a topic.

The most troublesome moment in the writing process occurs when the writer confronts a blank piece of paper. This moment provokes anxiety even for the most experienced writer, and it can be absolutely terrifying for the novice, particularly when the moment comes shortly before the due date for a paper or report.

This anxiety is both natural and unavoidable. It results from the challenge of composing which requires a number of steps, from idea generation to rough draft to rewriting. The first step, idea generation, is the most difficult because it is the starting point. Once there are some words on paper, the writer has something to work with, a framework in which to explore ideas and to think about ways of expressing them. This first step, though never easy, can be made more manageable if it is approached with a clear understanding of the composing process.

Beginning with Questions

As you saw in Chapter 2, reading demands that you ask yourself questions so that you can understand the material, anticipate the flow of ideas, and then evaluate what you have read. Composing, too, depends on questioning, although the type and pattern of questions here are different.

To compose, you must first decide what you want to write about. Your goal is to develop a number of ideas that define your attitude toward a topic and that are complex and interesting enough to enable you to explore the topic fully.

Professional interviewers use questions to entice their respondents to talk about a particular issue. In effect, an interviewer and respondent both do what a single writer must do. You can learn how to discover ideas, then, by studying how a good interviewer leads his or her subject into a topic. The following excerpt from an interview of Terrel Bell, the secretary of education, was conducted by Jim Lehrer for public television's "MacNeil-Lehrer Report":

> LEHRER: Mr. Secretary, welcome.
>
> SEC. TERREL BELL: Thank you.
>
> LEHRER: First, what do you see as the major failures of our education system?
>
> SEC. BELL: Well, I think our major failures are on the teenage level. Our teenagers are just not reaching the levels of accomplishment that, by measures that we have, that we had expected. The college entrance examination scores, for example, have been declining now for 12 consecutive years. We simply have to do something about that. I'm concerned about the fact that we've stopped teaching, or the enrollments have tapered off considerably in teaching, foreign languages in a country, in a world, that's shrinking, and in a nation where our international commerce is expanding. You can get a college degree in the United States without knowledge and competence in any language but English. And so on the higher education level, we surely need to do something about that as well as increase instruction on the secondary school level. I'd have to say that the achievement measures that we have on elementary school children are going up. But something happens on the teenage level, and in our high schools.
>
> LEHRER: What do you think it is that happens?
>
> SEC. BELL: Well, I don't want to be too simplistic about a complex question. But I believe that we've lost some of the rigor and discipline that we used to have in our secondary schools.
>
> LEHRER: What do you mean by discipline? Define discipline in your context.
>
> SEC. BELL: Yes. I would refer to that in a broader context than just behavior. I would use "discipline" as it relates to the standards that you have, the requirements that you place upon students, and the students' ability themselves to discipline their minds and

to pursue serious subject matter in a way so that they attain mastery.

LEHRER: What's your impression or your feeling as to why this discipline has not been there? What has caused it to go away?

SEC. BELL: Well, I think it's part of the total times that we're in. I think it relates to the home. I think it relates to the fact that we've been so concerned about the bottom level of the education ability span that we've been neglecting—

LEHRER: "Bottom level" meaning the people coming from disadvantaged circumstances?

SEC. BELL: Yes. And slow learners and handicapped children. I don't think we ought to abandon that, but I think we've been so obsessed with it that we have not challenged our able students or even the students that are in the mid-range of ability.

LEHRER: When you say "we"—"we" haven't challenged—who do you mean?

SEC. BELL: Well, I'm speaking about the academic community, and I have to include myself in that. All of us that labor in the vineyard of education, I think, need to be seriously concerned about this, and soberly resolving to do something about it.

LEHRER: Where do you see the major responsibility? I mentioned at the beginning that, you know, there's everybody's talking about whose fault it is that all these bad things are happening, and the kids can't read and write, and all that sort of thing. Where, very specifically, would you place some blame? Or responsibility, if not blame?

SEC. BELL: Well, I think that the local officials that set the standards and the requirements, and the state structure, has to carry most of the responsibility because the Tenth Amendment has delegated that to that source. Now, many would say, well, what about all the federal regulations that have been bothering us, and what about the federal priorities and requirements that come on, that they have to meet the rights of low-income and disadvantaged and minority and the handicapped children? So I know that federal intervention has had something to do with it.

A careful examination of the beginning of this interview demonstrates how Lehrer leads Bell *into* the subject. His questions are designed to build on the previous answers and to narrow the focus of the discussion. The following diagram illustrates this process. The key words Lehrer uses in his first seven questions are in bold type, followed by the important words or concepts from Bell's responses:

1. **failure** teenagers; foreign language; elementary OK
2. **what happens** rigor and discipline lost
3. **discipline** not behavior, but requirements and student's ability
4. **why** home; concern about the bottom
5. **bottom** haven't challenged able or mid-range students
6. **who hasn't challenged** academic community
7. **responsibility** local officials; federal intervention

The questioning in this interview falls into two categories: (1) probing and (2) clarification. Lehrer's first question is really a statement of the topic for discussion: What is the major failure of our education system? The secretary's response is broad and unfocused; he lists two areas of concern and one in which he sees no problem.

The secretary is, in effect, thinking out loud, and his first answer is a good model of how a topic can be approached in preparation to write about it. The secretary responds to the topic or question generally, touching on areas of interest or concern. Lehrer's next question demands a deeper probe into the topic: he wants to know what happens after elementary school.

Secretary Bell's response shows a narrowing of his thinking about the topic, and so he replies that "rigor and discipline" have been lost. Lehrer asks that he focus more closely, by requesting a clarification of the term *discipline*. The secretary's answer leads Lehrer to a probing question, *Why* has discipline, as defined in the previous answer, been lost?

The answer to the "why" question again urges Bell to refine his ideas: He expresses two areas of concern, and in a probing question, Lehrer concentrates on one of them—the attention paid to the "bottom" range of students and the neglect of the better students. After Bell's response, Lehrer seeks another clarification. Who, he asks, has not challenged the better student, and the secretary offers two answers—local officials and federal intervention.

Lehrer's first seven questions fall into the following pattern:

1. Statement of topic.
2. Probe.
3. Clarification.
4. Probe.
5. Clarification.
6. Clarification.
7. Probe.

This pattern illustrates how questioning works both to generate ideas and to narrow a focus on a topic so that the ideas generated will dig deeper into a subject instead of spreading out over its surface. Good questioning is a process in which questions build from the answers to previous questions, sometimes demanding a pause to clarify an idea and sometimes inviting a step further into the topic.

Generating Ideas Through Questions

The Lehrer-Bell interview shows how questions can lead to an exploration of a topic. In order to write about a topic, you must first decide what you want to say, and you can do that by asking yourself questions.

When you ask yourself questions, you should try to push yourself more and more into the topic, as Lehrer did in his interview. This inward movement can be achieved by building questions on previous answers. And as the process continues, try to phrase questions that either probe or seek clarification.

For example, suppose that your topic is federally guaranteed student loans. Your first question should establish an outline of the topic:

Question: What do I know about federally guaranteed student loans?

Answer: I know that such loans are offered to students, that they carry a low rate of interest, and that they have been in the news recently.

Consider what you can ask yourself next. At least three directions are possible: (1) the loans are federally guaranteed; (2) they carry a low rate of interest; and (3) they have been in the news. Each of these possibilities can be the basis for a question that will approach the topic.

For example, if you focus on the first choice, you could concentrate on the word *federal* and ask yourself, "Why should the federal government guarantee loans for students?" That would be a probing question, and it would push you deeper into the topic. Your answer could be that the federal government has both the resources and the obligation to attempt to make higher education accessible to as many students as possible. Or you might answer that the federal government should not be involved in this kind of program because it will add a level of unnecessary bureaucracy and because it might intervene in an area in which the individual states should be free to develop their own loan programs, or not, if they so choose.

The second choice could result in a different approach to the topic and could generate a question such as "Why are these low rates of interest important?" This would be a probing question. Or perhaps a clarification question would be in order, such as "Exactly how much lower are these low rates?"

Finally, the third choice might lead you to inquire, "Why have these loans been in the news?" Clearly, the answer to this question depends on factual knowledge. You would have to know that the current administration has proposed limiting the loan program and raising the minimum income standards for eligibility. This focus would probably soon invite a clarification question like "What exactly are the changes being considered?"

Following one line of questioning as a model for this process, we shall use the first choice, the one pertaining to the federal government's participation in student loan programs. (The first question, labeled T, establishes the topic; the others are designated either P for probe or C for clarification.)

1. *Question:*   What do I know about federally guaranteed student loans? **T**

   Answer: I know that such loans are offered to students, that they carry a low rate of interest, and that they have been in the news recently.

2. *Question:*   Why should the federal government guarantee loans to students? **P**

Answer: The federal government has both the resources and the obligation to make higher education accessible to as many students as possible.

3. *Question:* Why does the federal government have an obligation in this area? **P**

   Answer: Because our society needs an educated population.

4. *Question:* Isn't education accessible to everyone? **C**

   Answer: The accessibility of education depends on one's income.

5. *Question:* How so? Isn't it true that many public institutions charge only a small tuition? **P**

   Answer: A small tuition might be too much for some people; moreover, tuition is only part of the problem. People have to eat while they go to school.

6. *Question:* Well, then, why don't they work? **P**

   Answer: Many do, but sometimes they still need more money.

7. *Question:* How much more? **C**

   Answer: Maybe a couple thousand dollars for living expenses.

8. *Question:* Why should the government give money to these students? **P**

   Answer: Because in a democratic society, the government should assist the disadvantaged.

9. *Question:* What do you mean by *assist?* **C**

   Answer: Well, in this case, to give money to people who would not otherwise have it.

10. *Question:* It could be argued that the government should restrict itself to providing equal access, but not equal opportunity, couldn't it? **P**

And so forth.

The purpose of this questioning is to generate ideas to form the basis for writing about a topic. You do not have to write down the questions and answers, as in the model above, but it would probably be helpful to jot down your ideas as you think about the topic. Actually seeing ideas in words usually stimulates further thought and ideas.

Distinguishing Between Facts and Opinions

Ideas, as the term is used, express statements. Statements can reflect either fact or opinion. A fact is a statement that can be proved true or false according to objective criteria. But an opinion represents an individual's belief that something is or is not true; therefore, an opinion cannot be tested according to external standards. It is the property of the individual who holds it. Both kinds of ideas are necessary and useful, and distinguishing between them is an essential writing skill.

Discovering your ideas, then, also means distinguishing between facts and opinions. Of course, factual ideas should be accurate, and opinion ideas should be understood as open to debate. Depending on your purpose, you can confine yourself to factual ideas (informative purpose), work on the level of opinions (expressive purpose), or blend the two (persuasive purpose). Whatever your purpose, the first step is to distinguish between facts and opinions as you generate ideas.

Examine the model questions and answers concerning federally guaranteed student loans. Some of the ideas generated through this questioning are factual, and others are opinions:

Facts

- Federally guaranteed student loans carry a low rate of interest.
- Some college students do work.
- These loan programs have been the subject of recent debate.
- Many public institutions charge a small tuition. (The factual nature of this statement depends on the definition of *modest*. Such a definition is, of course, subject to debate. A more purely factual statement would be "Many public institutions charge a lower tuition than do similar private institutions.")

Opinions

- The federal government has both the resources and the obligation to make higher education accessible to as many students as possible.
- Our society needs an educated population.
- The accessibility of education depends on one's income.
- A small tuition might still be too much for some people.
- These college students still need additional money for living expenses.
- In a democratic society, the government should attempt to assist the disadvantaged.
- This assistance can take the form of giving money to people who would not otherwise have it.

As you can see, most of the ideas generated through questioning fall into the category of opinions. This disproportion is predictable for at least two reasons: most ideas *are* opinions; that is, relatively few statements of ideas are purely factual. In thinking about a topic, you may often seek an approach to that topic that interests you, and such an approach will demand determining how you feel, and thus feelings are, in this sense, the same as opinions.

If your questioning process works well, you will acquire more ideas than you can conveniently use. But too much material is far better than not enough. Depending on which purpose you choose, you might have to do some research to gather enough factual material for an informative purpose, continue working toward a narrower focus for an expressive purpose, or try to blend available factual information to support your opinions for a persuasive purpose.

Hierarchy of Questions

Although everyone, in some way or other, uses a question-and-answer procedure to generate ideas, this process is seldom consciously organized. A question produces an answer that might invite another question, and so on, but the ordering of these questions and answers is random. Therefore, the ideas produced do not fall readily into a pattern of thought, and the organization of individual ideas into a pattern is as important as generating the ideas themselves.

This organization can be imposed on the discovered ideas, or perhaps more efficiently, you can organize the discovery procedure itself to produce ideas that form a pattern.

Suppose, for example, that you want to describe an orange. You could first ask yourself what type of description you want to make. Perhaps you would like to describe the orange's physical composition. You would then arrange your questions into a logical sequence:

- What shape does an orange have?
- Beginning from the outside, what is its first physical component?
- After the orange is peeled, what does the inside of the peel look like, as compared with the outside?
- What substance covers the inner fruit?
- What shape do the sections of the fruit have?
- What is inside each section?

These questions produce a series of ideas that describe the orange in an orderly manner, from the outside in. You could develop similar series of questions to describe the taste of the orange, perhaps by asking yourself what it tastes like and what it does not taste like. Or you could classify the kinds of foods that contain oranges and order your questions from those things, such as orange juice made directly from the fruit, to those things flavored by oranges, such as cakes.

The description of a physical object like an orange necessarily demands questions that lead to factual statements. More abstract subjects, though, require a somewhat different patterning of questions because such subjects will usually include both factual information and opinions. These subjects can be organized by either proceeding from the most specific to the more general, or vice versa, from the more general to the most specific. In either case, the more specific questions and answers will probably be more factual, and the more general will usually be opinions. Consider an examination of the quality of television programming:

- Specific

  Facts: What do I know about television programming? Which shows have I watched recently? What kinds of shows were they?

  Opinions: Were they good? If good, how? If bad, how? Were they popular shows?

- General

  Opinions: Can I generalize on the basis of these shows? *or* What do I think about television programming? Why do I think it is good or bad? In what ways are the shows good or bad? Which shows, or types of shows, fall into categories of good or bad?

- Specific

  Facts: Which show best represents my conclusion about television programming? How long has it been on the air? How popular is it, as measured by the rating services?

As you can see, ideas lead to other ideas. The more you think about a topic, the more you will question your own statements, and the more you will discover about both the assumptions behind them and the conclusions to which they lead. Moreover, the questioning process will lead you to distinguish between facts and opinions and also to discover your purpose. Organizing your questions can more efficiently provide a pattern for ideas. Generating and patterning ideas are, thus, a necessary first step.

Exercises

1. List five questions that will elicit factual answers about each of the following:
   a. Inflation.
   b. Fast-food restaurant.
   c. The Beatles.
   d. Handguns.
   e. Cigarette smoking.
2. List five questions that will elicit opinions about each of the following:
   a. The 1960s.
   b. The Middle East crisis.
   c. Labor strikes.
   d. Nuclear energy.
   e. Automobile safety.

Note: Exercises 3 through 6 require writing an essay. You first should write a draft, and then revise it according to the following suggested guidelines:

1. Is my focus clear; that is, have I identified one approach to the topic?
2. Have I explored the topic so that I can draw on details from my own experience and knowledge?

3. Have I distinguished between facts and opinions, and have I used each in accordance with my purpose?
4. Have I eliminated all mechanical errors of spelling and punctuation?

3. Imagine that you are writing a letter to an automobile insurance company about obtaining a policy for a newly purchased car. Think of what you want to know. Write five questions that would elicit this information. Identify those questions that are probes and those that are clarifiers. Then write the letter.
4. Suppose you want to describe a movie to a friend. List five questions you could ask yourself to determine what you want to say about the movie. Identify those questions that evoke facts and those that produce opinions. Then write your review of the film.
5. Select an ordinary physical object. Examine it closely, and then outline some questions that will help you describe it. Finally, write your description.
6. Think of ten questions for each of the following. Write the questions as they occur to you and then separate them into facts and opinions. Define a purpose (expressive, informative, or persuasive), and use your answers to these questions as a basis for an essay on the topic.
   a. Imported automobiles.
   b. National defense.
   c. Magazine advertising.
   d. Professional athletes or entertainers.
   e. Responsibility for severely handicapped infants.

part TWO

Purpose

chapter 4
Reading to Discover the Author's Purpose

When you read, your thinking works on three levels: decoding the written symbols on the page, distinguishing the form of the written message, and discovering the purpose of the writing. Decoding is the simplest level of this process, as it is only translating visual images into words. On a more sophisticated level, distinguishing form demands recognizing how these individual words are shaped into a complete message. Finally, discovering purpose permits you to understand how that message relates to you.

For example, the letters *l o v e* are visual symbols that can be decoded to form the word *love*. This word, however, can appear in various types of writing, such as the following:

A love poem

An essay about the love of liberty

A love letter

A letter to the editor about a politician's love of power

Each of these forms provides a different structure for the various concepts suggested by the word *love*. Because the form shapes the meaning of the idea, recognizing the form enables you to understand the writer's intended meaning.

Closely associated with the form of a piece of writing is its purpose, as certain forms are appropriate to certain purposes. Purpose, as we have defined it, identifies an emphasis in writing among three possible choices: the writer, the subject matter, or the audience. Moreover, because each purpose anticipates a certain response, you as a reader, or as part of the audience, should know what response is expected of you.

For example, you may be the audience for a love letter in which the writer declares that he or she will love you eternally. Or you may read a chapter in a psychology textbook about the complex love between a child and a parent. Finally, you may read an editorial in a newspaper that declares that patriotic citizens should show their love of country in a moment of crisis. Purpose, then, controls how something is written and how it is read, and this chapter discusses and gives strategies for determining purpose and its relationship to the reader's response. This information and these strategies will help you read with the fullest comprehension possible. Further, recognizing purpose in your own reading will assist you in defining the purpose you wish to serve when you write.

Defining the Author's Purpose

The author's purpose can be defined as the writer's intent, which is to anticipate a particular response from the reader. When the writing is effective, that is, if its purpose is clearly communicated, the reader will respond as the author intended.

Broad categories of purpose can be identified according to the author's emphasis:

- Does the writer emphasize personal attitudes, values, or feelings so as to establish his or her view of the subject?
- Does the writer concentrate on the subject so as to present it objectively?
- Does the writer stress a point of view, attitude, value, feeling, or course of action that the reader should agree with or aspire to?

Although distinct categories of purpose can be identified, these categories are not mutually exclusive. For example, in persuasive writing, a writer may use personal attitudes, feelings, values, or credentials to attract the audience's sympathy and attention. Likewise, a combination of facts and opinions also can be used in writing to persuade. Therefore, you should understand that these categories of purpose are not absolute and you should be careful to seek out the *predominant* purpose or central intent of a work when expression, information, and/or persuasion are combined.

Recognizing the Author's Purpose

Knowledge of the author's purpose helps determine which of the following is predominant:

1. Personal attitudes, values, or feelings (expressive mode).
2. A direct, objective presentation of information or events (informative mode).
3. A point of view or course of action that the reader should adopt (persuasive mode).

The reader's response is influenced by the purpose, and each purpose anticipates a particular response:

1. The expressive mode requires the reader to recognize the author's own view of the subject.
2. The informative mode enables the reader to learn factual information, recreate images, or follow a course of events.
3. The persuasive mode requests the reader to accept or reject the author's position through careful examination of the evidence (facts, opinions, credentials) offered to support that view of the subject.

Although it is possible to find all of these purposes in nearly all writing, the following list indicates the most frequent places for each purpose:

Expressive	*Informative*	*Persuasive*
Newspaper or magazine columns	Textbooks	Editorials
Essays	Encyclopedias	Political essays
Autobiographies	Instruction manuals	Book, movie, or
Personal letters	Technical journals	play reviews,
	Historical accounts and biographies	Advertisements

Examples of these purposes in various works are followed by a discussion of each.

Expressive Mode

I was a man living in a never-never land somewhere far beyond the constraints my grandparents had known but far short of true freedom. I knew no black people—young or old, rich or poor—who didn't feel injured by the experience of being black in America. Though some went mad, most coped with the special problems that race presented to them. I had coped by translating my anguish into words, by trying to change the minds and the hearts of people. I believed it was possible to communicate with white people about race and thereby make things better. . . .

During those days when I was pounding out this book in Bobby Clark's apartment, I was approached by Murray Gart, the editor of the *Washington Star*. Murray was engaged in a stubborn struggle to keep that great old paper alive, and he wanted to know if I would come and help him. Though he never said it, I understood that he was searching for greater credibility and readership in Washington's large black community, and he thought I might be able to help. . . .

So we negotiated. I would write long pieces for the paper and, aside from him, would have only one editor, my good and respected friend, Eileen Shanahan, a fine journalist and one of the toughest feminists in the business. I would be called associate editor, but I would be more like a writer in residence. I thought the capital needed two papers and that the struggle to keep a good newspaper alive was a noble one. . . .

When I moved back to Washington, I got an apartment in Anacostia, a poor black section of town. After so many years of a thoroughly integrated life, it was curious but comforting to get up in the morning and see only black people in my building and at the places where I went to have my clothes cleaned or shoes repaired. Some people thought my living there was something of a gimmick or a conceit, but it wasn't. The rent was cheap, the view was fabulous, and the constant proximity to ordinary black people was psychologically nourishing.

I wrote some things in the *Star* that I liked—about the city and about black people—and was really warming to my tasks when Time Incorporated, the *Star*'s parent company, decided to cut its losses and close the paper down. I was thoroughly depressed, because the *Star* was a fine paper with many fine journalists working on it. Weak though we were, the *Washington Post* had to keep an eye on us, and I am convinced that the competition made the *Post* a better paper. . . .

This autobiographical account of one event in Roy Wilkins's life allows him to express his feelings ("anguish," "psychologically nourishing," "depressed") about a decision he made and its outcome. His purpose is expressive because he relates the personal impact that the decision had on his life at that time.

The following poem is written in the expressive mode:

A BIRTHDAY

My heart is like a singing bird
    Whose nest is in a watered shoot;
My heart is like an apple-tree
    Whose boughs are bent with thick-set fruit;
My heart is like a rainbow shell
    That paddles in a halcyon sea;
My heart is gladder than all these
    Because my love is come to me.

Raise me a dais of silk and down;
    Hang it with vair and purple dyes;
Carve it in doves and pomegranates,
    And peacocks with a hundred eyes;
Work it in gold and silver grapes,
    In leaves and silver fleurs-de-lys;
Because the birthday of my life
    Is come, my love is come to me.

Christina Rossetti's poem expresses her reaction to a new-found love. She uses figurative language to express her joy: "My heart is like an apple-

tree . . .," ". . . is like a rainbow shell . . .," ". . . is gladder than all these
. . ." and her purpose is to convey the wonderful change in her life: "Because the birthday of my life Is come. . . ."

Informative Mode

The favorable geographic factors and the presence of diverse races
who shared with each other their own peculiar cultural and social
experiences gave to Egypt an advantage over many other lands and
stimulated the early development of a civilization there. By the time
of the new Stone Age the inhabitants of Egypt had settled down to
a sedentary life of agriculture. There is much evidence to bear out
the belief that they were cultivating wheat, millet, barley, and flax.
They had also domesticated many animals, including goats, sheep,
donkeys, and cattle. Shortly, they began to reclaim land and to develop a system of irrigation. Their resourcefulness and self-sufficiency
are amply demonstrated in the high degree of skill which they
achieved in weaving linen and other textiles, in making tools, and in
building houses. As they entered the age of metal, they displayed
exceptional skill in fashioning objects of art and implements in copper
and bronze.

Even before 3000 B.C. there was a large industrial population in
Egypt. Men were engaged in mining, metallurgy, brickmaking, ma-
sonry, carpentry, tanning, weaving, and shipbuilding. The rather clear-
cut division of labor encouraged specialization and promoted efficiency in production. Craftsmen working in their own shops, on the
estates of the great landlords, or in the royal workhouses produced
works of such utility and beauty that any age would be proud to claim
them.

Sculpture and painting are seldom highly developed except in
areas where the social and cultural experience of a people has en-
dured for a long period of time and where economic and political life
make for both stability and freedom. It would be too much, therefore,
to expect that Egyptian sculpture and painting were what modern
critics would judge as advanced. They did, however, serve a useful
purpose for Egyptians as religious and historical materials. The
sculpture was hardly more than crudely cut outlines of subjects, while
painting lacked perspective and shading. In architecture the Egyptians
made remarkable advances in the precision-like constructions of
houses, royal palaces, and pyramids. These works gave clear evidence of a thorough knowledge not only of architecture but physics,
engineering, and geometry as well.

Egyptians, again drawing on the diverse experiences of their several forebears, organized the kind of political state that evolved from
the simple to the complex, from the local city-states to a powerful
national unit. As prosperity came to Egypt and as the inhabitants
discerned the advantages in larger political units, small villages began
to cooperate in order to bring about more effective methods of irrigation and to pool their resources for the general welfare. As cities

began to unite, political organization shifted from a kinship to a territorial basis, and there came into existence the large city-states, generally called "nomes." As the rulers of nomes extended their influences to other areas, the process of national unification was well under way. By 4000 B.C. the nomes had become so unified as to form an upper and lower kingdom. Gradually a complete system of government had evolved with powerful officials who maintained their position both by reason of heredity and military strength.

It was near the end of the fourth millennium B.C. that Egypt was unified under one ruler, the Pharaoh. There emerged a conception of him that at once strengthened his position and made possible the almost irrevocable cohesion of the country. He was regarded as the descendant of a god and therefore divine. He wielded absolute authority over the social, religious and economic life of his people. He was, moreover, the defender of the realm and the dispenser of justice. There were well-conceived notions of impartial justice, the administration of which was guaranteed by the Pharaoh. Under him was a hierarchy of officials, secular and religious, who executed his decrees and commands.

Just as there emerged a central political organization, there also evolved, in due time, a kind of national religion, at the head of which was, of course, the Pharaoh. The principal god of the country was the principal god of the city from which the Pharaoh came. Finally, the sun god, Ra, and later Amon-Ra, stood at the center of the Egyptian pantheon with many lesser deities playing subordinate roles. The elaborate hierarchy of priests administered the souls of the living and the dead. Intricate rites were performed in the temples and at the pyramids, the burial places of members of the royal family. The priests not only played an important role in systematizing and directing Egyptian religious life, but also wielded considerable influence in secular life. Whenever the opportunity presented itself, the priests would ally themselves with members of the nobility to reduce the power of the Pharaoh and thereby enhance their own position. That the opportunity seldom came was due to the fact that the Pharaoh usually maintained a sufficiently firm hand to prevent the rise of any group that could successfully challenge his authority.

In this example, the author describes the geographic, industrial, cultural, political, and religious characteristics of the emerging Egyptian civilization. He uses a chronological progression ("before 3000 B.C.," "by 4000 B.C.," "it was at the end of the fourth millennium B.C.") to relate the sequence of events in the description. His purpose in this passage from his book is to tell the reader about the specific factors that influenced the beginnings of Egyptian civilization.

A second example of the informative mode comes from the area of psychology:

Research on continuity in the life span calls upon approaches that deal with events of personal history.

1. Retrospective Analysis. In this approach techniques such as interviews and autobiography are employed to tap the person's recollections about past events. These data suffer primarily from the subjective character of recall, because a person reports only what he can remember or is willing to state. Retrospective analysis is the method used in psychoanalysis where its limitations are to a considerable degree overcome by lengthy and intensive effort to produce exhaustive information. This material can be examined for consistency and for clues to cross-check its accuracy. In either case continuity is examined by reconstructing personal history.

2. Cross-sectional Analysis. In this strategy an investigator taps pertinent information from samples of individuals of different ages. By comparing these samples, it is possible to ascertain average, or typical, trends that cut across the age span. For example, we might devise a test to measure attitudes toward the mother and administer it to groups of 6-, 8-, 10-, 12-, 14-, and 16-year olds. The results can reveal how such attitudes vary with age. The chief limitation of this technique is that it reveals only a general trend without taking into account the development of particular persons. It is just as important to know what happens in the person's life history, as it is to know tendencies for people in general. The cross-sectional approach has been very widely used in modern child psychology, because it lends itself well to controlled, systematic sampling and to the rapid, simultaneous comparison of one age group with another.

3. Longitudinal Analysis. Here the investigator chooses subjects of a specified age and periodically reexamines them—that is, he follows them during a given span of years. Clearly, its chief limitation is the very time-consuming and expensive process demanded; furthermore, we see that technical difficulties interpose themselves through changes in science over the years, with the result that either theory or method may alter. Nevertheless, the investigator must stick to the procedures with which he began.

The great advantage of this approach lies in the possibility of combining the study of organization with continuity, because the same persons are involved at each point in time.

Here the author's purpose is to describe objectively three types of analysis that can be used to study life-span continuity and the advantages of each. It is a typical example of objective, subject-centered textbook language.

Persuasive Mode

Two thousand Americans will die of cancer by the end of the century because of radiation from nuclear energy, the National Academy of Sciences estimates.

A terrible human toll.

Two thousand Americans die of cancer caused by smoking cigarettes every 10 days. Two million Americans will die of lung cancer by the end of the century. Eighty percent will be because of cigarettes.

The Three Mile Island accident that has triggered huge protests against nuclear energy released about 1.7 millirems of radiation, which equals the risk of death involved in smoking one-seventh of a cigarette.

These figures are estimates and projections, some informed and some not so well informed. But the indisputable fact is that smoking cigarettes will take a toll in human suffering and death a thousand times greater than the toll from radiation from nuclear energy.

Where are our perspectives, our values? Why don't protesters march up to the gates of tobacco companies and wave placards and sing protest songs and try to block the gates? For some reason, it just isn't fashionable.

And Joan Baez and Judy Collins haven't come up with any songs about a million people dying from smoking cigarettes.

This writer compares the dangers of nuclear radiation and the dangers of cigarette smoking in an effort to persuade the reader to protest the latter. The language used conveys the author's disgust and is part of the author's attempt to convince the audience to protest cigarette smoking.

A final example of the persuasive mode:

Success means many wonderful, positive things. Success means personal prosperity: a fine home, vacations, travel, new things, financial security, giving your children maximum advantages. Success means winning admiration, leadership, being looked up to by people in your business and social life. Success means freedom: freedom from worries, fears, frustrations, and failure. Success means self-respect, continually finding more real happiness and satisfaction from life, being able to do more for those who depend on you.

Success means winning.

Success—achievement—is the goal of life!

Every human being wants success. Everybody wants the best this life can deliver. Nobody enjoys crawling, living in mediocrity. No one likes feeling second-class and feeling forced to go that way.

Some of the most practical success-building wisdom is found in that Biblical quotation stating that faith can move mountains.

Believe, really believe, you can move a mountain and you can. Not many people believe that they can move mountains. So, as a result, not many people do.

On some occasion you've probably heard someone say something like, "It's nonsense to think you can make a mountain move away just by saying 'Mountain, move away.' It's simply impossible."

People who think this way have belief confused with wishful thinking. And true enough, you can't wish away a mountain. You can't wish yourself into an executive suite. Nor can you wish yourself into a five-bedroom, three-bath house or the high-income brackets. You can't wish yourself into a position of leadership.

But you can move a mountain with belief. You can win success by believing you can succeed.

The author's purpose in this passage is to convince the reader that success "is the goal of life" and that "you can win success by believing you can succeed." He uses synonyms for success ("winning," "achievement," "prosperity") that are emotionally charged and have a positive connotation, in order to persuade his audience to adopt his point of view.

Questioning: A Strategy for Determining the Author's Purpose

As indicated in Chapter 2, questioning is a valuable tool in determining the author's purpose and the reader's response.

Expressive Mode

Material-centered
1. Does the author refer to himself or herself by using "I" or "me"?
2. Does the author use sentimental or figurative language?
3. Is the subject introduced through the author's experience with it?
4. Does the author refer to the subject and conclusions or outcomes in terms of personal growth or change for better or worse?

Reader-centered
5. Can I identify and/or sympathize with the author's values, attitudes, feelings, or beliefs regarding the subject?

Informative Mode

Material-centered
1. What is the main idea of the work?
2. What are the details?
3. Are facts important to the work?
4. Is the language straightforward and unemotional?

Reader-centered
5. Am I supposed to visualize or recreate images in my own mind as I read?
6. Should I be aware of a particular order or sequence in the presentation of the subject?
7. What is (are) the idea(s) or event(s) I am supposed to remember about the subject?

Persuasive Mode

Material-centered
1. Are opinions or facts or both offered as support for the subject?
2. Is the information about the subject complete?
3. Is the information one-sided?
4. Is the author qualified to write about the subject?
5. Does the author anticipate and answer questions that the reader might raise about the subject?
6. Does the author stand to gain anything by writing the work?
7. Does the author use emotionally charged language?

Reader-centered
8. Does the work cause me to feel happy, sad, angry, anxious, indignant or in some way arouse my emotions?

9. Does the author suggest that I should feel, think, believe, or act in a certain way?
10. Do I agree, disagree, accept, reject, like, or dislike what I have read because of the emotion(s) it provokes?

Consider the following examples:

Expressive Mode

> When I flew home from Ireland, I couldn't write the story, could not confront the fact of my own mortality. In the end, I dragged out some words and made the deadline but at an ugly price. My short temper lengthened into diatribes against the people closest to me, driving away the only sources of support who might have helped me fight my demons. I broke off with the man who had been sharing my life for four years, fired my secretary, lost my housekeeper, and found myself alone with my daughter Maura, marking time.
>
> As spring came, I hardly knew myself. The rootlessness that had been such a joy in my early thirties, allowing me to burst the ropes of old roles, to be reckless and selfish and focused on stretching my newfound dream, to roam the world on assignments and then to stay up all night typing on caffeine and nicotine—all at once that didn't work anymore.
>
> Some intruder shook me by the psyche and shouted: "Take stock! Half your life has been spent. What about the part of you that wants a home and talks about a second child"? Before I could answer, the intruder pointed to something else I had postponed: "What about the side of you that wants to contribute to the world? Words, books, demonstrations, donations—is this enough? You have been a performer, not a full participant. And now you are 35."
>
> To be confronted for the first time with the arithmetic of life was, quite simply, terrifying.

1. *Question:* Does the author refer to himself or herself by using "I" or "me"?

   Answer: Yes.

2. *Question:* Does the author use emotional language?

   Answer: Yes. Examples include "fight my demons," "ugly price," "diatribes against people," "stretching my newfound dream," and "terrifying."

3. *Question:* Is the subject introduced through the author's experience with it?

   Answer: Yes. "When I flew from Ireland, I couldn't write the story, could not confront the fact of my own mortality."

4. *Question:* Does the author refer to the subject and conclusions or outcomes in terms of personal growth or change for better or worse?

Answer: Yes. "To be confronted for the first time with the arithmetic of life was, quite simply, terrifying."

5. *Question:*   Can I identify and/or sympathize with the author's values, attitudes, feelings, or beliefs about the subject?

Answer: Yes. A recent experience, my mother's death, made me identify with the author's crisis and feelings of uncertainty about life.

Author's Purpose: To express her strong emotional response to an incident in Ireland that frightened her and caused tremendous upheaval in her life.

Informative Mode

In both urban and rural settings the Iranian family exercises a far greater claim upon the individual than is generally found in the West. In the Iranian family unit, described as patriarchal by ethnographer Haas (1946), there exists great deference to parents, a high level of mutual accountability, and close association in both work and leisure. Children through young adulthood reside with parents, at least until marriage, except for the possible interludes of university education or military service. A highly elaborated nomenclature for relatives throughout the extended family attests to the importance of every member. In addition to the relationships by blood or marriage, each family has its cautiously selected additional friends whose allegiance is visibly demonstrated. The interdependence of family and select friends leads to distinct "in-group" behavior (Triandis, 1972).

The solidarity of the family is symbolized by the high wall that typically surrounds each private dwelling. The same wall that assures privacy from the outer world effects a sharing of life and space within. The average household density of five persons (Swan, 1968), nearly twice that of the average home in the United States, accentuates the closeness of life and sharing. Regularly the entire family of two or three generations gather together in a single room for either joint or separate activity.

1. *Question:*   What is the main idea of of the work?

Answer: The Iranian family has more influence on its members than the American family does.

2. *Question:*   What are the details?

Answer: Iranian family is patriarchal.

Great respect for parents.

Mutual accountability between parent and child.

Children home with family until marriage or college or military service.

Every family member is important.

Friends also part of extended family, and loyalty is expected.

High walls around houses symbolize family solidarity and privacy.

Average household contains five persons; twice that of United States.

Two to three generations gather for joint or separate activities.

3. *Question:* Are facts important to the work?

   Answer: Yes. Sources are cited for each detail (Haas, Triandis, Swan).

4. *Question:* Is the language used straightforward and unemotional?

   Answer: Yes.

5. *Question:* Am I supposed to visualize or recreate images in my own mind as I read?

   Answer: No.

6. *Question:* Should I be aware of a particular order or sequence of events in the presentation of the subject?

   Answer: Yes.

7. *Question:* What is (are) the idea(s) or event(s) I am supposed to remember about the subject?

   Answer: See the answers to Questions 1 and 2.

Author's Purpose: To provide an objective, carefully researched description of an individual member of an Iranian family, in comparison with a member of an American family.

Persuasive Mode

The foremost problem with compassion these days is that it has become hidden behind something far lower and simpler, behind mere sentimentality. Who hasn't witnessed the indifference and even cruelty of students toward their classmates, then seen those same students tearful and distraught over the loss of the class gerbil? A significant part of the educator's task in dealing with compassion thus becomes a matter of bringing home the differences between true compassion and mere sentiment.

Unlike compassion, sentimentality makes us feel good. We feel warm all over and lumpy in the throat. We can get rid of it with a good cry. Through it we enjoy a glow of feeling without incurring a debt of obligation. Unlike compassion, sentimentality is often easy and pleasant.

Also, sentimentality is promiscuous—tears for all causes. While compassion would urge pity for those unjustly harmed, sentimentality says: Harm nothing. True compassion has an inkling of justice in it, and of commitment. Sentimentality knows only of feelings and self. Compassion finds fitting objects in the destruction of greatness, in the blindness of fate and nature to nobility, in unjust destruction of the brave and innocent. It runs deep. It understands tragedy. Sentimentality, on the other hand, engages tragedy only on the level of soap opera. It is content to wade in the shallows.

I've made this contrast of compassion to sentiment in order to alert us to what passes for compassion these days, with the hope that our students can be raised up, educated, from mere sentimentality to true compassion itself. The difference may be rendered more vivid in the classroom by fairly straightforward juxtapositions of literary or artistic works. Compare, say, the sentimentality of Walt Whitman's "O Captain! My Captain!" with the far deeper movements in his "Vigil Strange I Kept on the Field One Night." The former pushes us to cry without there being any developed ground for it. "Vigil Strange," on the other hand, moves the informed soul to suffer profound pity, to experience compassion's tragic core. Similarly at Christmas time one might read O. Henry's "Gift of the Magi" (which has all the depth of a greeting card) following Dickens' "Christmas Carol." Or compare one of Keane's pictures of teary, doe-eyed children with a good photographic print of Michelangelo's Pieta. Or take Shel Silverstein's hollow work, *The Giving Tree,* to set off against Tom Dooley's *Night They Burned the Mountain.* Or take *Love Story,* in print or film, and contrast it with *The Diary of Anne Frank* in the same medium. The point here, of course, is not to ridicule any particular writers or artists. It is, rather, to bring home a difference, to sharpen perceptions, and refine reactions.

Now compassion, like love, is a virtue of action as well as of emotion. It is not only something felt but something done. Thus, compassion stories like the parable of the Good Samaritan and the folktale of Grandfather's Corner aim not so much at moving us inwardly as teaching us outwardly, of informing our deliberate actions rather more than our inner sensibilities.

Still, the two are intimately connected. The aim is not so much to learn about compassion as it is to learn compassion itself, to move out of the grandstands and onto the playing field. In this regard, for example, *King Lear* is better than *The Merchant of Venice,* even though the latter is all about compassion. For *Lear* engages the soul as well as the intellect in a way that *The Merchant of Venice* rarely does. Moral education is not a spectator sport.

Through all this we should recognize the fact that compassion is not an unproblematic virtue. Although it has healthy intuitions about justice, like its sister virtue courage, it sometimes wells up from emotive springs insufficiently tempered by right reason. It is a feeling that needs to be educated and formed. Yet, where else other than in the classroom can moral sense, reason, and thoughtful discussion better be examined, considered, and combined?

1. *Question:*   Are opinions or facts or both offered to support the subject?

   Answer: The author's opinions are used exclusively.

2. *Question:*   Is the information about the subject complete?

   Answer: No. It lacks facts or proof to support his suggestion that compassion be taught in the classroom.

3. *Question:* Is the information one-sided?

   Answer: Yes. It does not indicate any opposing argument and stresses only the positive aspects of compassion.

4. *Question:* Is the author qualified to write about the subject?

   Answer: Can't be sure.

5. *Question:* Does the author anticipate questions the reader might raise about the subject and answer them?

   Answer: To some degree, by using examples to point out the difference between compassion and sentiment. However, he doesn't consider alternatives to the classroom as places where compassion might be investigated or taught.

6. *Question:* Does the author stand to gain anything by writing the work?

   Answer: Not apparent from essay.

7. *Question:* Does the author use emotional language?

   Answer: Yes. Examples include "debt," "obligation," "promiscuous," "commitment," "destruction of greatness," "blindness of fate," "nobility," "brave," "unjust," "sentimentality," "teary," "engages the soul," "moral education is not a spectator sport," "healthy intuitions," "emotion springs insufficiently tempered by right reason."

8. *Question:* Does the work cause me to feel happy, sad, angry, anxious, indignant or in some way arouse my emotions?

   Answer: Yes. The author appeals to my emotions by using certain examples (cruelty of children to others, as compared with their love of animals; examples of literature that have strong emotional themes) to persuade me to take greater responsibility for the moral education of school-age children.

9. *Question:* Does the author suggest that I should feel, think, believe, or act in a certain way?

   Answer: Yes. I should believe that compassion "is a feeling that should be educated and formed" and that the classroom is the best place to teach it.

10. *Question:* Do I agree, disagree, accept, reject, like, or dislike what I have read because of the emotion(s) it provokes?

   Answer: Yes. I agree and accept the author's ideas and recommendations (see the answer to Question 3).

Author's Purpose: To persuade the audience to see the difference between compassion and sentiment and to believe that the classroom is a place where "moral sense, reason, and thoughtful discussion [can] be examined, considered, and combined."

These questions will help you analyze various modes of expression and discover the author's purpose. They are broad enough, however, to accommodate variations in subject and writing style, and so, some will not always be answered affirmatively. Use them in evaluating your response to what you read and in determining the author's purpose.

Prejudging the Author's Purpose

Some words of caution. Sometimes you may anticipate an author's purpose before reading the work itself because you may be familiar with the individual's reputation, point of view, position, or occupation. Celebrities, activists, political figures, and artists are often associated with subjects or causes on which they have taken a stand, and therefore, what they believe or endorse may be expected to affect their writing. Ralph Nader, Gloria Steinem, Jane Fonda, Jerry Falwell, Jesse Jackson, and Aleksandr Solzhenitsyn all are examples of people whose ideas have gained popular notice because of their dedication to a cause. For example, Ralph Nader is closely associated with consumer advocacy; Jane Fonda is well known for her stand against nuclear warfare; and Aleksandr Solzhenitsyn is a noted writer whose works protest the oppression of the Soviet people.

You may decide to read the works of these people or others like them because the thoughts they convey are considered significant and acceptable. On the other hand, the recognition they have achieved through their position on a subject or cause may make you decide not to read a particular piece, or to read it with a closed mind. Whether you agree or disagree with the author, your intellectual responsibility remains the same: to read and evaluate the work as objectively as possible. Otherwise, your own bias, be it negative or positive, will interfere with your ability to comprehend and evaluate the work fairly. Obviously, it is not always possible to be totally objective, but you should try to formulate your attitudes, values, and beliefs with a knowledge and understanding of varying points of view, including those opposing your own.

Exercises

1. Read the following passages. Using the sets of questions in "Questioning: A Strategy for Determining the Author's Purpose," determine the author's purpose.

> A. Why do approximately 6,000 students come to Hofstra for its two Summer Sessions? That is a sizeable educational community, however dispersed over day, late afternoon and evening courses and it does not include enrollment at the Hofstra Commack Center, nor the summer programs in France, Italy, Spain and Taiwan.
>
> The paramount answer lies in the quality and diversity of Hofstra's academic offerings—more than 475 courses and some 30 specialized workshops and special programs, taught by regular Hofstra faculty, augmented by distinguished visiting and adjunct professors.
>
> But there are other reasons as well. Partly it is the campus itself,

with many inducements to al fresco studying or idling—grassy quads, shady trees, benches. Partly it is a library that is both pleasant and extensive. In addition, it is exhibitions in the Emily Lowe Gallery and the David Filderman Gallery, or tennis, handball, touch football or jogging on the playing fields. Certainly, it is also the opportunity to make new friends.

There is Hofstra's location, suburban yet close to Manhattan, less than an hour away by car or train, with more to see and do than in any comparable big city in the world. An hour's driving can bring you to and from northernmost Westchester County or towns to the east in Long Island's Suffolk County, all via main roads and parkways.

For those with time to spare, Long Island itself is a major attraction, stretching between Long Island Sound and the Atlantic Ocean. You can finish a class and in half an hour be swimming at Jones Beach or be at another of the six state parks on the Island. There are noted arboretums and gardens, at least eight museums and many art galleries. Sports and recreation opportunities are as complete as summertime can make them. And the summer calendar of events, cultural and entertaining, on the Island and in New York City is bountiful indeed.

B. Two blocks, of two rooms each, one room behind another. Between these blocks a hallway, floored and roofed, wide open both at front and rear: so that these blocks are two rectangular yoked boats, or floated tanks, or coffins, each, by an inner wall, divided into two squared chambers. The roof, pitched rather steeply from front and rear, its cards met and nailed at a sharp angle. The floor faces the earth closely. On the left of the hall, two rooms, each an exact square. On the right a square front room and, built later, behind it, using the outward weatherboards for its own front wall, a leanto kitchen half that size.

At the exact center of each of the outward walls of each room, a window. Those of the kitchen are small, taller than wide, and are glassed. Those of the other rooms are exactly square and are stopped with wooden shutters.

From each room a door gives on the hallway. The doors of the two front rooms are exactly opposite: the doors of the rear rooms are exactly opposite. The two rooms on either side of the hallway are also connected inwardly by doors through their partition walls.

Out at the left of the house, starting from just above the side window of the front room, a little roof is reached out and rested on thin poles above bare ground: shelter for wagon or for car.

At the right of the house, just beneath the side window of the front room, a commodious toolbox, built against the wall. It is nailed shut.

The hallway yields onto a front porch about five feet long by ten wide, reaching just a little short of the windows at either side, set at dead center of the front of the house. A little tongue of shingles, the same size, is stuck out slightly slanted above it, and is sustained on four slender posts from which most of the bark has been stripped.

Three steps lead down at center; they are of oak: the bottom one is cracked and weak, for all its thickness. Stones have been stacked beneath it, but they have slid awry, and it goes to the ground sharply underfoot. Just below and beyond it is a wide flat piece of shale the color of a bruise. It is broken several ways across and is sunken into the dirt.

C. At 6:30 A.M., while silk-stocking Manhattan is asleep, East Harlem is starting to bustle. The poor are early risers. They have the jobs others don't want: the early-hour jobs, the late-hour jobs. Many rise early because it is a rural habit.

Along about 7:30 the streets are filled with fast-moving people: men, women, and swarms of children of all sizes. The parochial school children can be see in clusters, with their togetherness identity tag—a school hat, a blouse, a uniform.

You may be able to buy a *New York Times* at the corner news-stand in the morning, but you probably will not be able to buy a cup of coffee. The poor drink their coffee and eat their breakfasts, such as they are, at home. Few eat out.

Some will stand at the bus stops, but most will crowd into the downtown subways that speed them to jobs in commerical or silk-stocking areas: to serve the affluent, or work in their stores or small industrial shops. Many of the Negro women will go to domestic service; and the Puerto Rican women, to their sewing machines in the garment shops.

Later in the day, if it is warm, the men who have no jobs will come out and stand on the sidewalks and talk together. They will watch the street and the passers-by and kibitz with one another. The old people, and from time to time the housewives, will sit at the window and join the watchers. And those with leisure may call them idle. Later, when the children return from school, the side-walks and streets will jump with activity. Clusters of men, sitting on orange crates on the sidewalks, will play checkers or cards. The women will sit on the stoop, arms folded, and watch the young at play; and the young men, flexing their muscles, will look for some adventure. Vendors, ringing their bells, will hawk hot dogs, orange drinks, ice cream; and the caressing but often jarring noise of honk-ing horns, music, children's games, and casual quarrels, whistles, singing, will go on late into the night. When you are in it you don't notice the noise, but when you stand away and listen to a taped conversation, the sound suddenly appears as a background roar. This loud stimulation of the senses may produce some of the emotionalism of the poor.

East Harlem is a busy place, night and day, filled with the joyous and troubled lives of residents—rather than the heavy commercial traffic of mid-Manhattan. New York's street life is unique. So much action, so much togetherness. The critics who lament its passing have a point. The middle class who disdain life conducted so openly in the streets might compare its satisfactions to the sometimes parched and estranged quality of their own backyards.

D. As I worked my way into other books and plays and films, it became clearer and clearer to me how fortunate I had been to have had mother who said, "Buddy, did you really write this—I think it's wonderful!" and a father who shook his head no and drove me to tears with his, "I think it's lousy." A writer, in fact all of us in life, needs that mother force, the loving force from which all creation flows; and yet the mother force alone is incomplete, even misleading, finally destructive, without the father force to caution, "Watch. Listen. Review. Improve."

Sometimes you find these opposing forces personified in your editors, your associates, your friends, your loved ones. But finally you must counterpoise these opposites within yourself: first, the confidence to go forward, to do, to become; second, to temper rampant self-approval with hardheaded, realistic self-appraisal, the father discipline that barges into your ivory tower and with a painful truth jars your reverie of creative self-glorification.

Those conflicting but completmentary voices of my childhood echo down through the years—wonderful, lousy, wonderful, lousy—like two powerful, opposing winds buffeting me. I try to navigate my little craft so as not to capsize before either. Between the two poles of affirmation and doubt, both in the name of love, I try to follow my true course.

E. About 1700 B.C., a strong ruler, Hammurabi, came to power in Sumer and conquered the upper Tigris-Euphrates Valley. Hammurabi was more than a great military leader. He turned out to be an able organizer and a wise and just statesman as well. He is best known for the *code*, or collection of laws, that was drawn up under his direction. In it he speaks of himself as the father of his people, their "pastor, savior, and good protecting shadow."

Hammurabi's code of 282 laws controlled all aspects of Babylonian life. Argriculture was carefully regulated. For example, men who failed to cultivate their fields or to maintain the irrigating canals and ditches were punished. Some laws concerned commerce and industry, and included provisions regarding wages, hours, and conditions of work. There were laws dealing with property rights, contracts, and bankruptcy. Others dealt with marriage and divorce. The laws were enforced by judges, under the supervision of the kings' advisers and officials. There were severe penalties for trying to bribe a judge or a witness.

The laws of Hammurabi gave some degree of justice to everyone—a real advance over the political and social customs of the rest of the ancient world. The idea of punishment was basically "an eye for an eye; a tooth for a tooth." If a man caused another to lose an eye, then his own eye was put out. If a son struck his father, his hand was cut off.

Justice was not equal for all people, however. If a wealthy man destroyed the eye of a poor man, he did not lose his eye but merely paid a fine. A thief who could not repay what he had stolen was put to death. If he had money, he had only to repay more than he had stolen.

chapter 5
Purposeful and Purposeless Writing

When you read, you try to discover the author's purpose for writing so that you can understand the response expected of you. Similarly, when you write, you should define a purpose to control and focus your ideas.

The writing process begins with discovering ideas, but these ideas will not be of much use until you decide how you want to treat them. Without a clear purpose in mind, your ideas will probably slide away from you in several different directions, and because your thinking is unfocused, you will have difficulty thinking of appropriate details to flesh out your ideas. On the other hand, once you have established a purpose for your writing, you will know what you expect from your reader. You will be able to make your ideas work for you because you can make them serve the purpose you have decided on.

How Purpose Improves Writing

As a classroom assignment, students were asked to imagine themselves as participants in an automobile accident and to write letters to various people after the accident. For example, some students wrote to an insurance company and others wrote to a close relative. All worked from the same set of facts concerning the accident. In one variation of this exercise, the two "drivers" were imagined to be a sixty-year-old woman and a teenaged boy. One student in this class assumed the role of the woman and wrote the following letter:

> Dear Susan,
>   How are you? I'm OK, but you'll never guess what happened to me last night.
>   Well, last night I had to take Fluffy to the vet, the poor thing. All

her fur was falling out, and she looked absolutely terrible, just like a drowned rat.

Anyway, Fluffy and I were on the way home from the vet's office, in the rain no less. Now, you know how I hate driving in the rain. It's even worse than when it's foggy.

So here I am going along, driving slowly because I was so nervous. And poor Fluffy was so pathetic looking, staring out the window. Dr. French did say, though, that she'd soon be as good as new.

Back to last night. Do you remember that light on Nichols Road? You know, the one that always turns red just as you get to it?

Well, Fluffy and I knew it would turn red, so we started to slow down, and the next thing I knew . . . wham! Somebody crashed into me from behind.

It was some teenager in a Fire-eagle, or something. You know, one of those hot rods all the kids drive.

Well, nobody was hurt, thank God, but poor Fluffy was shaken up very badly. I must say that the young man who hit me was very nice and polite. He couldn't apologize enough. So while he went to call a police officer, I did my best to calm Fluffy.

To make a long story short, the police came, and now I guess whatever happens is up to the insurance companies.

Nobody was hurt, and my car wasn't too badly damaged, but I'm afraid that nice young man's Fire-eagle will never be the same.

So what's new with you?

Love,
Mary

When asked to identify the purpose of this letter, the class had no difficulty determining that it was expressive. Clearly, the letter focuses on the writer (and her cat). Because the student who wrote this letter knew the purpose he wanted to serve, he was able to structure his ideas effectively. As part of the assignment the following ideas had been provided:

One driver was a teenaged male.

The other driver was a mature woman.

The accident occurred on a rainy day.

The traffic light had just begun to change.

Everybody in the class began with these facts with which to start writing. But the author of the "Fluffy" letter was able to add a number of new ideas. Because the purpose of the letter was expressive—because its emphasis was on the writer and her feelings—this student took advantage of this and described the letter writer's feelings about the accident and her cat. Moreover, the student was able to control his language and style to produce an engaging and amusing tone.

As part of this exercise, each student in the class was asked to assume that he or she had received one of the letters and then to write a response.

Dear Mary,

I was very sorry to hear about your accident. Thank goodness no one was hurt, including Fluffy. Glad to hear that your old, priceless DeSoto wasn't damaged very badly. I hope that you hear from the insurance companies soon and that they pay your claim without too much trouble.

Love,
Susan

The student who wrote this response worked conscientiously: she responded to each of the main points of the Fluffy letter, although she did ignore the young man and the details of the accident. The letter, though, is colorless. It is caring, but in a bland, almost formal way: it simply does not communicate as effectively as does the Fluffy letter.

Although differences in the writer's personalities or abilities can explain, to some degree, the variations in the letters, there is another important point of comparison: the second letter seems to lack the purpose of the first. It repeats the facts, almost in an informative way, and the expressions of concern do not reveal much of the person behind them. Although the class did identify the purpose of the second letter as expressive, they had a little more difficulty because the purpose was not strongly defined.

Deciding on Your Purpose

Purposeful writing is more interesting and comprehensible to your reader and also more fun for you to compose. Deciding on a purpose for your writing, then, becomes an essential step in writing.

To identify your purpose, you must understand the nature of your writing task. This, in turn, depends largely on your perception of your audience's expectations and on the effect you intend your writing to create. Whether your audience will shape your purpose or your purpose will shape your audience is difficult to determine. Let us examine how the interaction between purpose and audience works in a particular situation.

Suppose that you see a movie you really like. You are engaged by the actors who capture your sympathy; you are held in suspense by the plot which nails you in the last scene; you are impressed by the cinematography that makes lights and shadows of color hint at the relationships among the characters; and you are moved by the background music which announces and then modulates each change of mood.

You go home and want to share this marvelous experience with someone; that is, you want to communicate. You have a subject—the film—and you are the writer (or speaker). To communicate, you need both an audience and a purpose. Either the audience or the purpose can be the most important, or they can be combined.

For example, if you are so excited by this movie that you just have to tell someone about it, you could pick up the telephone and dial the first number that occurs to you. In such a circumstance, your purpose is the most important, and that purpose is expressive: you want to communicate how moved you are and how the film has made you aware of feelings and ideas. The center of your interest in communication is, in short, yourself. Your audience will be whatever sympathetic listener you can find.

If, on the other hand, you want to share your enthusiasm with a particular person, someone whom you respect, and someone who, as a film buff, will particularly enjoy hearing about this movie, then your purpose and audience will coincide. Your purpose still will be expressive because you want to relate your perceptions of the film. But your audience will be equally important, and because you know this person will be symphathetic to your excitement and be interested in hearing what you have to say, your expressive purpose will blend quite naturally with your selection of this person as your audience.

But if the first person you meet after leaving the theater is another friend, one who considers film a decadent and corrupt art form, who has stopped going to movies, and who always argues loudly for the superiority of the printed word—if this person is your audience, he or she, then, will determine your purpose. Against all odds and moved by your desire to tell someone about this film, you may well decide to attempt to *persuade* this friend that going to see this movie would be worthwhile and might even change his or her opinion about the possibilities of film.

In the first instance, your purpose is primary and your audience secondary; in the second, your purpose and audience blend; and in the third, your audience's feelings and expectations determine your purpose. The interaction between audience and purpose is complex: each, to a certain degree, is dependent on the other. Discovering your purpose for writing requires understanding this subtle relationship.

Beginning with a Need

You write in response to some need, and so the first step in determining your purpose is to identify this need. For example, establish the motivation for writing in the following circumstances:

> *Situation 1:* You are angry about traffic jams.
>
> *Situation 2.:* You have just learned something fascinating about a popular singer.
>
> *Situation 3.:* You have just seen your favorite team lose its tenth consecutive game.

Consider Situation 1 in more detail. You are angry about traffic jams, because you feel that your time is being needlessly wasted. Somebody should do something—mandate carpools, improve mass transportation, improve highways—something. Ask yourself:

1. Do I want to find an outlet for my frustration?
2. Do I want to make somebody understand the situation?

3. Do I want to try to improve the situation?
4. Do I expect to care about my frustration?
5. Do I want somebody to share my anger—to empathize?
6. Do I want to warn people about the dangers of commuting on the route I take?
7. Do I want to figure out the causes and reasons for the situation?
8. Do I want to propose possible solutions?

Now try to match a purpose to each question (express a feeling, inform, persuade). It is likely that Questions 1, 4, and 5 will yield an *expressive* purpose, that Questions 2 and 7 will produce an *informative* purpose, and that Questions 3, 6, and 8 will result in a *persuasive* purpose.

For example, Question 1 clearly identifies as your purpose the need to release your emotions; that is, your emphasis is on yourself, on the expression of your frustration. The second question, on the other hand, invites attention to the subject matter. Your communication is motivated by your desire to present the situation as objectively as possible, and therefore you will be writing for an infomative purpose. Finally, the third question answers your need to do something about the situation. In order to effect change, you need help; that is, you must convince others (your audience) to change their minds or to act to improve the conditions that cause the traffic jam. Such an attempt to influence your audience serves a persuasive purpose.

Try the same approach to Situation 2: you have just learned something fascinating about a famous country singer. Specifically, you have discovered that this person, who has recorded one hit after another and affects a down-home style of speech and dress, was born in the Bronx, New York and never was near a cow or anything else pertaining to the countryside until he was old enough to vote. Ask yourself the following questions:

1. What do I feel about this discovery? Am I angry or amused or indifferent?
2. Do I think the singer's success is based on deceit or fraud?
3. Do I believe that the singer's background is irrelevant, that good music will attract its own audience?
4. Do I want to smash all of my records of this performer?
5. Do I want to demand my money back from the record company?
6. Do I intend to write a letter to this performer and suggest that he tell the truth about his background?
7. Do I want to analyze why a singer's appearance helps sell records?
8. Do I believe that all star performers reflect the society in which they live?
9. Do I feel like including this discovery with other bits of evidence that feed my conviction that I will try to avoid sacrificing my principles for success?

The likely responses to these questions, as for those concerning the traffic jam situation, will produce different motivations for writing, which fall into the three types of purpose: expressive purpose (Questions 1, 4, and 9), informative purpose (Questions 2, 7, and 8), and persuasive purpose (Questions 3, 5, and 6).

To illustrate, let us examine each of these groups:

Expressive purpose: Question 1 clearly demands expression of the writer's feelings; Questions 4 demands the release of anger; and Question 9 demands the confirmation of a personal value.

Informative purpose: Question 2 seeks a cause-and-effect relationship; that is, it is an explanation of reality focused on the subject; Question 7 seeks the same kind of explanation in a larger context; and Question 8 seeks the same thing from a still broader perspective.

Persuasive purpose: Question 3 invites the statement of a position that could influence an audience, in this case, to disregard surface distractions and concentrate on substance; Question 5 obviously invites a response from the audience; and Question 6, in a more personal way, asks the same as Question 5 does.

Finally, let us study the possibilities of the third situation: you have just seen your favorite team lose its tenth consecutive game. You are a faithful fan who watches nearly every game, and you have suffered through several losing seasons. You find yourself more depressed after each loss: Ask yourself:

1. Do I want to write a letter to the president of the club and demand that the coach or manager be fired?
2. Do I believe that the players are overpaid and unmotivated?
3. Do I want to tear up my season ticket?
4. Do I want to consider shifting my loyalties to a winning team?
5. Do I want to warn a younger person about the dangers of becoming involved with a losing team?
6. Do I want to explain my periodic depression to the people with whom I live?

Again, the possible responses can be grouped into the three categories:

Expressive (Questions 3 and 4): Focus on you.

Informative (Questions 2 and 6): Focus on subject matter.

Persuasive (Questions 1 and 5): Focus on audience.

Questions 3 and 4 pertain to your personal feelings concerning your team, and the actions suggested by the questions will have no impact beyond that on yourself. If, on the other hand, these actions are intended to stimulate a reaction by the team's owner, then the purpose will be persuasive. For example, a couple of years ago, some long-suffering supporters of the New York Giants football team rented an airplane and flew it over the stadium during a home game to display a banner that proclaimed their disappointment. This well-publicized incident was designed to pressure the team's management to improve the team's performance.

Questions 2, and 6 focus on the subject matter and could well lead to an informative purpose. Responses to these questions may be, for Question

2, an objective analysis of the team's problems and, for Question 6, an explanation of your behavior to those who care about you.

Questions 1 and 5 clearly concentrate on your audience. In the first case, you would be making a gesture similar to those fans who rented the plane to fly over the stadium; that is, you would hope to exert some pressure on the team's management. The fifth question is more personal in intent but still persuasive, because you would hope to influence another so that he or she could avoid the problems you face as a loyal supporter of a losing team.

Making Sure of Your Purpose

The questions and possible responses in the preceding section seem to point to particular purposes and audiences. But if the questions had been answered differently, they would have produced different purposes and perhaps a different sense of audience.

For example, tearing up a season ticket to express your disgust at your losing team would become an attempt at persuasion if the ticket tearing occured in the team's executive offices in front of one of those people you felt was responsible for the team's incompetence. Similarly, the letter you could write demanding the dismissal of the coach or manager, although clearly persuasive, as seen from one point of view, could also be expressive. In explaining why you think the coach or manager should be relieved of his responsibilities, you might also project your personal feelings, and in so doing, you would be serving an expressive purpose.

In short, although one purpose should dominate a piece of writing, it is not always possible, or even advisable, to ignore secondary purposes. The important thing is to have one purpose clearly in mind and then permit the other purposes to support the main one.

Problems arise when you can find no clear purpose or when you seem to give equal importance to more than one purpose. These problems can produce purposeless writing or ambiguous purpose, in which no one purpose clearly controls the writing. Moreover, writing that lacks a purpose or has no one definite purpose is ineffective, because clear purpose and sense of audience control the manner in which the writing takes shape. Each purpose is best served by a particular kind of presentation: Expressive writing is subjective; that is, it communicates feelings, and the language that communicates an expressive purpose should be personal. Informative writing, on the other hand, by concentrating on the subject matter, should be objective, and therefore the language in such writing should be factual and unemotional. Finally, a persuasive purpose is an attempt to influence an audience, and its language should be forceful, even colorful, as in expressive writing, but structured into a logical argument that seeks to attain a certain degree of objectivity.

To illustrate how these different purposes and audiences control the shape of the writing, let us examine the same topic treated expressively, informatively, and persuasively. Assume that the topic is proposed legislation that would limit smoking in public places. An expressive piece, written by a smoker, might resemble the following:

> The proposed legislation to limit smoking in public places infringes on my rights as a citizen and as a taxpayer. I am outraged that the government would assume that it could tell me where I can and cannot smoke.
>
> Smoking may be hazardous to my health, but it is my privilege to decide both whether I want to expose myself to this risk and, if so, where I might choose to confront this danger. I resent any attempt to limit my choice in this matter.
>
> The government simply does not have the right to tell me where I can smoke, any more than it can tell me where I can eat or drink. If I can eat food in a restaurant and have a drink before my meal, then certainly I can have a cigarette in the same place with my after-dinner coffee. If the first two are matters of choice for me, then so, too, should be the third.
>
> My lungs are my business. The government should attend to what properly concerns it. It seems to me that the government has enough problems without intruding on areas where it does not belong. It is more important for the government to worry about the red in the federal budget than the black residue in my lungs.

Although this piece has some persuasive qualities—particularly the criticism of the government, the statement of individual rights, and the irony in the last paragraph concerning the redness of the budget as compared with the blackness of the smoker's lungs—there is no real attempt to convince the reader to do or think anything specifically about the issue. Rather, the focus in on the writer's feelings of anger at what he or she perceives as governmental interference. This focus is obvious in that the issue is treated personally and subjectively, but it is important only insofar as it relates to the writer. The writer, too, invites empathy from the reader, expecting or hoping that he or she will share this anger or at least try to understand it as a legitimate expression of one person's reaction to the subject.

Informative writing, on the other hand, focuses on the subject matter so that a piece written on the same topic with this purpose would be different in detail and in language. An informative purpose demands that the writer's personality and feelings *not* intrude into the writing and that the audience be permitted to come to its own conclusions:

> The decision last week by the state legislature to consider a bill that would limit smoking in public places follows years of heated debate and controversy. On one side of the question are the smokers who feel that their rights would be limited by the proposed legislation, and on the other are the nonsmokers who believe that their right to breathe unpolluted air is being ignored.
>
> The legislation specifically applies to public buildings, such as governmental offices, and to places where the public gathers, such as restaurants and other places of entertainment. In the first category,

the bill would permit smoking only in entranceways and rest rooms. For the second, smoking would be permitted only in certain sections of the establishment.

Proponents of the legislation claim that there is now medical evidence to link disease to the inhalation of "second-hand" smoke. According to this view, a nonsmoker can be subjected to the same medical risks as the smoker can, just by being in a smoke-filled room and breathing in some of this atmosphere. Opponents dispute the validity of the medical evidence and see the more important issue as that concerning individual freedom. Some even go so far as to say that their rights to smoke in public places are protected under the First Amendment's guarantees of freedom of expression.

The issue is certainly complex. Also involved are the owners of the establishments, particularly restaurants, who feel that their businesses will suffer if people cannot enjoy a cigarette with their meals. Supervisors of government employees wonder about the effect on the morale of their workers if smoking is prohibited at work stations, whereas these same supervisors now have to respond to complaints from nonsmokers that they cannot work comfortably under the current conditions.

Finally, just about everybody agrees that the law would be almost impossible to enforce. Police officials have said that they have little enthusiasm for ticketing offenders, and more importantly, they believe that their police officers could better spend their time on more serious problems. As in the case of Prohibition, the issue is highly charged emotionally, and it leaves all concerned parties with feelings of anger and impotence.

This informative piece differs significantly from the expressive one. It is much more factual because it explains exactly what the proposed legislation includes. It is objective because it attempts to identify the feelings and beliefs of both sides of the issue and because it does not favor one position over the other. Its language is controlled and neutral: words such as *feel*, *believe*, and *claim*, clearly identify what follows as opinions about which the writer offers no personal judgments. Little, if anything, in the piece arouses an emotional reaction in the reader.

However, the purpose of a persuasive piece dictates that the writing convince the audience to take a position on the issue. In order to accomplish this purpose, the writer probably would appeal to the reader's emotions by means of a logically developed argument:

The current controversy concerning the limiting of smoking in public places is a conflict between individual rights: those of the smoker to poison himself or herself and those of the nonsmoker to breathe uncontaminated air.

Nobody would deny that in the final analysis, an individual has the right to risk cancer, emphysema, or heart disease by smoking cigarettes. Even if such a right were denied and smoking were made illegal, as suicide now is, it would be impossible, and probably inadvisable, to attempt to prohibit smoking entirely. The person who wants to jump off a bridge is not about to be deterred because the act is illegal. And the individual who insists on smoking will not throw away his or her cigarettes only because a governmental body has declared that smoking is now against the law. In either case, the government should do no more than warn its citizens against the hazards of the actions, whether the quick death of jumping off a bridge or the slow and hideous assault on one's health caused by smoking.

Nonetheless, the government does have the responsibility to protect innocent citizens from the harmful actions of others. Just as the government, through its laws, prohibits attacks on persons or the theft of their goods, so too should it ensure that no one should have to work, or relax, in an impure environment. The government should not try to control what occurs in private residences, but it should and must eliminate hazardous conditions in those places over which it properly does have control. The proposed legislation demands that government assume the responsibility for protecting innocent victims against the wrongful actions of those who callously disregard the rights of their neighbors.

This piece does make a logical argument: it states that the conflict is over rights on both sides but that the more important consideration is the health and well-being of innocent victims. It asserts that this concern is of more significance than are the rights of the smoker who can still indulge his or her habit in private. Moreover, the piece works on the readers' emotions by comparing smoking with suicide and by suggesting that exhaling smoke in a public place is similar to other illegal attacks on innocent people. Finally, emotionally charged language such as "callously disregard," "hideous assault," and "poison himself or herself" adds a strong persuasive element to the writing.

The sense of audience for each of these examples is the same, in that the writer supposed that his or her piece would be read by anybody interested in the issue. The next chapters will show how the sense of audience can be broken down into a number of categories, but we should note here that even when the audiences are similar, each purpose assumes different responses. The expressive piece expected that the audience would share the writer's feelings of outrage; the informative one assumed that the audience wanted an unbiased and objective presentation of the subject; and the persuasive one supposed that the audience would be receptive to having its opinions and feelings on the topic influenced by an admittedly partisan presentation.

Discovering your purpose in writing will ensure that you have a clearly defined reason for communicating. By identifying your purpose, you will understand what approach you want to take to a particular topic. This identification also includes a sense of audience so that you will know not only why you are writing but to whom. And as the three previous examples indicate, purpose and sense of audience combine to shape your writing and to control your choice of language and structure.

Exercises

1. Identify the purpose and audience most suitable for the following:
   a. Breaking up a relationship.
   b. Speaking on a nuclear power plant.
   c. Discussing the economy.
   d. Studying for a test.
   e. Selecting a major area of study.
2. Answer the questions following each topic and determine what kind of purpose each answer would produce.

   Topic: A local teacher's union has voted to authorize a strike.

   a. Do I want to join the picket line?
   b. Do I want to tell the union leader that this action is wrong?
   c. Do I want to explain the issue to my school-age children or brother or sister?
   d. Do I want to write to the president of the school board and demand a speedy resolution?
   e. Do I want to analyze the impact of federal budget cuts on the situation?
   f. Do I want to tear up my application for a job in this district?

   Topic: You have just finished reading a controversial book.

   a. Do I want to tell a friend about this book?
   b. Do I want to burn my library card in front of the library?
   c. Do I want to figure out why this book is a best-seller?
   d. Do I want to advise a friend to read this book?
   e. Do I want to find out more about this author?

   Topic: For the fifth time in a row your weekend plans have been rained out.

   a. Do I want to ask my boss to change my days off?
   b. Do I want to study the weather patterns for the past ten years?
   c. Do I want to check my horoscope for the next month?
   d. Do I want to discuss with my friends the desirability of finding indoor activities?
   e. Do I want to take out my frustration on an inanimate object?
   f. Do I want to begin studying yoga or transcendental meditation?
3. Define a purpose for one of the topics in Question 2, state it, and write an essay based on it. Indicate the response you expect from your audience.

   After you have written the essay, read it to see how well the essay communicates its purpose, by asking yourself the following questions:
   a. Do I emphasize my personal attitudes, values, or feelings concerning the subject?
   b. Is the language often abstract and subjective?
   c. Do I want the reader to share and/or understand these attitudes, values, or feelings?

d. Is the subject matter important insofar as it shows how I have changed my thinking or behavior?

If you can answer these questions affirmatively, you will have established a clear expressive purpose.

e. Do I concentrate on the subject matter?
f. Do I present the subject matter objectively?
g. Do the details in the essay focus on the subject matter?
h. Is the language straightforward?
i. After I read the piece, do I remember the subject matter more clearly?

If you can answer these questions affirmatively, you will have established an informative purpose.

j. Do I present attitudes, beliefs, or a course of action for the reader to accept?
k. Do I offer opinions and factors to support these attitudes, beliefs, or course of action?
l. Do I emphasize one point of view on an issue?
m. Do I use emotional language?
n. Do I present myself as qualified to discuss the issue?
o. Do I anticipate questions of those readers who might not agree with me?

If you answer these questions affirmatively, you will have established a persuasive purpose.

Note that if your answers to these questions are a mixture of positive and negative, you may not have established a clear purpose, and you should probably rethink your approach to the topic.

4. Make up your own questions for the following topics. Then answer the questions, define a purpose for one of the topics, and write an essay guided by this purpose. Finally state the response you expect from your audience.

a. You just missed winning a door prize by one digit.
b. Your boss refuses your request for a raise.
c. The concert you want to attend is sold out.
d. You find that the cost of gasoline is limiting your social life.
e. Your favorite entertainer admits to abusing drugs.

After you have written your essay, check it for purpose, as outlined in Exercise 3.

part THREE

Audience

chapter 6
Reading for an Audience

Thus far, we have discussed the audience as the recipients of communication. Furthermore, we have shown that a particular purpose anticipates a particular response from the intended audience and that audience sometimes helps determine purpose. But the idea of audience needs to be explored more fully because it governs the writing process in several important ways.

Simply stated, not every piece of writing suits every reader. When you browse through a library or a bookstore, you probably spend most of your time in certain sections and ignore others. For example, you might check out the science fiction titles and pass by the collection of gardening books, or vice versa. You might pick up a photography magazine and discover that its presentation was too technical for you, or you might scan an organic cookbook only to find that it contained recipes for dishes you would not consider eating. In all these instances, you would be a possible audience for these publications, but you might not fit the profile of the *intended* audience.

Similarly, when you are choosing a book to recommend to a friend or to give to someone as a gift, you must decide whether it is appropriate for that person. Your decision is governed by a variety of factors, including the person's age, education, and interests. Each of these factors either adds to or detracts from the value of the book to this person.

Writers almost always have in mind a certain audience to whom they direct their material. Sometimes this audience is determined by the publication for which a writer works. Magazines, for example, usually appeal to a certain segment of the population, and therefore magazine writers shape their material to appeal to the kind of person who would be likely to read the magazine. This intended audience can range from one person to the population at large, with many possibilities in between:

Type of Writing	*Audience*
Personal letter	A friend or relative
Business letter	A consumer or an officer of a company or corporation
Technical journal	A defined group of professionals or craftspeople (doctors, accountants, carpenters, and the like)
Newsletter	Members of an organization
Newsmagazines	General public
Novels	General public

This list could be expanded, but the point is that each type of writing assumes a particular audience, and this assumption controls the writer's approach to the topic, choice of vocabulary, level of formality, complexity of sentence structure, tone, and style.

The following passages are examples of materials written for specific audiences.

> The college believes that liberal admissions requirements are an essential part of its philosophy, and in that context we have maintained for many years a Full Opportunity Admissions program.
>
> Full Opportunity means that we will offer acceptance in an appropriate program at the college to all applicants residing in Suffolk County who have graduated from high school the prior year; and, to applicants who are high school graduates and who were released from active duty with the Armed Services of the United States within the prior year.
>
> Each applicant must be a graduate of an approved high school or hold the New York State High School Equivalency Diploma. Selection of applicants for admission is based upon high school performance, objective test data, program elected, and subjective criteria such as interest, maturity, and motivation as these factors are evaluated by teachers, counselors or employers acquainted with the applicant.
>
> In addition to the above requirements, all high school applicants must meet the special high school course requirements listed on the chart located in this section of the catalog.

This is a formal document addressed to students who might apply to this college. It clearly explains its Full Opportunity Admissions program and its acceptance requirements for interested applicants.

> These are "well made," clearly constructed plays in the realistic tradition of the preceding decades. Cause and effect are the basis of the plot and events in the play. Cause and effect also dictate the acting. What motivates the character (the cause) has to be discovered, identified, and used to initiate and justify the character's actions and attitudes. Realistic acting is required, so that the audience will be convinced that they are seeing real people, characters that sound and behave like people in life. In these plays the actors' emotional

lives should be realistic and internalized. The performance should have some details but not be cluttered. Motives, behavior, gestures, and rhythms should be explored and selected during rehearsals so that the performance, though designed by the actor, will flow naturally without calling attention to technique or deliberate theatricality.

The suggestions offered in regard to character motivation, performance objectives, and technical language indicate that actors are the intended audience for this passage.

The crab apple tree, cold-hardy and beautiful of bloom, is among the most popular of landscaping trees. With fall tree-planting time approaching, these beauties are worth a look if your yard needs some dressing up.

There are so many varieties of crab apples that selecting the best type for your property may be a many-weekend project. But planting it will take only a few hours from one weekend day. First, sit back and spend some time in contemplation.

The author of these paragraphs is writing for an audience interested in the landscaping and tree-planting aspects of gardening.

You say you've played so much Pac Man you get an ache in your jaw every time you gulp a dot? You say you can't tell Inky from Pinky from Blinky from Clyde (the four gumdrop monsters, in case you just got out of a chess marathon)? You want a new kick? Well, you're not alone. In the last five months the most coin-fed machine in the land has been another Japanese creation, the whimsical Donkey Kong.

The game begins when a hulking ape named Donkey Kong ("Donkey" is a rough transliteration of the Japanese word for "stupid") carries a maiden to the top of a skyscraper under construction. Grasping a four-way joystick, the player guides a workman named Mario up ramps and ladders as the damsel bellows for help, and Donkey Kong rolls or hurls barrels into Mario's path. With a button, the player can make Mario jump over these safely. Each time Mario jumps, the machine emits a humorous "sproing!" If Mario succumbs to the various perils, he tumbles into a heap and a halo appears over his head. If he reaches the heroine, D. K. merely grabs her again (fracturing a heart that appears over her head) and carries her higher to a new configuration of beams. It's not every game that's funny and Sisyphean, too.

This passage is intended for sophisticated video game enthusiasts. Even though Donkey Kong might be played by youngsters, the description provided here includes vocabulary ("whimsical," "transliteration," "configuration," "Sisyphean") suitable for a more mature audience.

Knowledge of the human body develops from an understanding of its anatomy and physiology. Through the study of anatomy one learns the structural parts of the body, and through the study of physiology one learns how these parts function. These parts are not just single components working independently of each other, but rather a vast interrelated network of parts working together to maintain homeostasis of the living organism.

This knowledge grows out of a basic understanding of modern cell biology, inorganic and organic chemistry, atomic physics and basic algebra. Since most beginning students in the health careers (toward whom this book is focused) do not possess adequate backgrounds in all of these areas, one of the primary purposes of this book is to start with basic exercises and build from them into more complex studies. As evident from the listing in the Table of Contents, the approach of this book is quite unique in stressing the necessary basics to full comprehension of physiological principles. Most books assume some previous background in the sciences; this book was written especially for those lacking this background and yet contains a general review for those with some background.

Although the contents have been arbitrarily divided into discrete exercises to illustrate individual principles for the purpose of organized study, it should always be kept in mind that none of the bodily systems or bodily functions operates in isolation. Therefore, one should frequently review each system's effect on others as part of the total organism. This awareness is illustrated by an attempt to group interrelated topics and systems into larger units.

The writer of this commentary makes clear the audience for which he is writing: students in the health careers.

Dear Ann:

I was touched by your reference to your late father, Abe Friedman from Sioux City, Iowa. I knew him and he was a wonderful man. It was typical of him to feed every panhandler who stopped him on the street. He performed so many acts of charity and kindess quietly, never seeking praise or thanks. Truly a prince of a man.

I clipped something from your column a few years ago, and it would be ever so appropriate to run it again. Your dear father lived by these words.

You don't know me but I remember you and your twin sister as youngsters. My, but you were cute!

No Name, Just a Voice from the Past (Spencer, Iowa)

Letters like this that apppear in advice columns are personally directed to the columnist. If the columnist chooses to print the letter, it is because its subject matter may be of general interest and is, in turn, broadly directed to those who follow the column.

Until I got to the Continent, I was under the impression American collectors had a monopoly on exploiting the romance of Prince

Charles and Lady Diana. How could I have been so naive.?

It all concerns the plethora of pictorial paper produced, first for the royal wedding, then the 21st birthday of the princess and the arrival of the child. A fellow of the Royal Philatelic Society who attended the LIBA-82 exhibition in Liechtenstein summarized it succinctly, " . . . never before have so many adhesives been issued to capitalize on popular current events . . . all within a matter of months." The same sentiments were paraphrased by German, Austrian and Scandinavian visitors. A Swiss suggested that "now it wouldn't be too surprising if we got material when Prince William got his first tooth, took his first step, contracted the measles, etc., etc."

Even though you may be familiar with some members of the royal family, this passage is written especially for philatelists.

As you can see, determining the audience for whom a work is intended can be achieved through careful inspection of the details in the writing.

The next section of this chapter will help you learn to evaluate what you read in order to discover the audience for whom it is intended.

Questions for Evaluating Audience

1. *Question:* What is the source or origin of the work?

   Answer: Knowing the source or origin of reading matter can be an invaluable tool in determining its intended audience. Publications often address a specific audience, and therefore recognizing the type of publication in which a work appears helps identify its audience. For example, an article on divorce that appears in *Parents* magazine and one that appears in *Cosmopolitan* magazine will differ in focus because of the diverse needs, concerns, and possibly values of each magazine's readership. Likewise, a book written for children about the same subject will have a very different presentation from one written for a graduate sociology course at a university. Books, newspapers, magazines, journals, and the like can and usually do address the assumed needs of particular and very different audiences, even though their goal is the same: to communicate—through the printed word. Being aware of the source or "place" where reading material appears is one way in which you can identify the target group for whom it was written.

2. *Question:* Who is the author?

   Answer: If you know who the writer is, you may know something about his or her reputation and credibility. This information will allow you, first, to decide whether to consider the work seriously and, second, to decide whether the author's values, goals, interests, or attitudes appeal to you. You might not agree with or support the writer's ideas, but you would know something about the author based on other works he or she has published, the attention given to those works by critics and others, general style, and so on, which may help you assess the intended audience.

3. *Question:*   What type or level of vocabulary is used in the work?

   Answer: One of the easiest ways to detect the suitability of reading material for a particular audience is to take note of its vocabulary. Consideration of vocabulary in determining intended audience includes the *type* of vocabulary, the author's use of specialized language or jargon, and the *level* of vocabulary, the author's use of difficult or obscure words. The following examples may help clarify the difference between type and level of vocabulary:

> The singer's warm caressing tone colored with great emotion can embrace a lyrical phrase in the most masterful tenor. Given fullest expression, it can take on a brillant open-throated clarity as it soars above the staff.

>> These sentences use the specialized language of music ("tone," "lyrical phrase," "tenor," "open-throated clarity," "staff").

> The singer's voice can be vibrant, almost buoyant in quality and expression. The sound it makes can bring exultation to the listener, dispelling the vicissitudes of life now somehow swept away by the sweet intoning of the chanteuse.

>> The words in these sentences ("vibrant," "buoyant," "exultation," "dispelling," "vicissitudes," "intoning," "chanteuse") make it necessary for its audience to have a wider vocabulary in order to comprehend the writer's message.

4. *Question:*   How complex are the sentences?

   Answers: Sentence complexity refers to the difficulty of the syntax (pattern of grammatical relations of words, phrases, and clauses in sentences). Wide reading and/or formal education may be necessary in order to understand the works of authors who write in a complex style. The introduction to Ralph Waldo Emerson's *Nature* is an excellent example of sentence complexity:

> Philosophically considered, the universe is composed of Nature and the Soul. Strictly speaking, therefore, all that is separate from us, all which Philosophy distinguishes as the NOT ME, that is, both nature and art, all other men and my own body, must be ranked under this name, NATURE. In enumerating the values of nature and casting up their sum, I shall use the word in both senses;—in its common and in its philosophical import. In inquiries so general as our present one, the inaccuracy is not material; no confusion of

thought will occur. Nature, in the commmon sense, refers to essences unchanged by man; space, the air, the river, the leaf. Art is applied to the mixture of his will with the same things, as in a house, a canal, a statue, a picture. But his operations taken together are so insignificant, a little chipping, baking, patching, and washing, that in an impression so grand as that of the world on the human mind, they do not vary the result.

Although there is some fairly difficult vocabulary, it is understanding the grammatical patterns in the flow of words, phrases, and clauses that enables you to understand the meaning.

5. *Question:* What is the tone of the work?

Answer: The tone of the work, also part of the writer's style, refers to how the author "sounds" to the reader. Word choice helps the reader determine whether the writer's tone is critical, objective, reassuring, personal, or any number of other possibilities. A writer's tone can "talk down to", "talk at" or "talk to" an audience. Writers make the tone of their work fit the response they desire and that response helps determine the audience.

A second excerpt from Emerson provides an example of what is meant by tone:

I greet you on the recommencement of our literary year. Our anniversary is one of hope, and, perhaps, not enough of labor. We do not meet for games of strength or skill, for the recitation of histories, tragedies, and odes, like the ancient Greeks; for parliaments of love and poesy, like the Troubadours; nor for the advancement of science, like our contemporaries in the British and European capitals. Thus far, our holiday has been simply a friendly sign of the survival of the love of letters amongst a people too busy to give to letters any more. As such it is precious as the sign of an indestructible instinct. Perhaps the time is already come when it ought to be, and will be, something else; when the sluggard intellect of this continent will look from under its iron lids and fill the postponed expectation of the world with something better than the exertions of mechanical skill. Our day of dependence, our long apprenticeship to the learning of other lands, draws to a close. The millions that around us are rushing into life, cannot always be fed on the sere remains of foreign harvests. Events, actions arise, that must be sung, that will sing themselves. Who can doubt that poetry will revive and lead in a new age, as the star in the constellation Harp, which now flames in our zenith, astronomers announce, shall one day be the pole-star for a thousand years?

This portion of a Phi Beta Kappa address at Harvard University in 1837 uses a personal, encouraging, and altogether hopeful tone that is most obvious even when it appears in print. The word *we* brings the audience closer to the writer.

The challenge the *we* of the paragraph must face and the hope of "a new age" make the writer's voice a positive one.

6. Question: What is the author's attitude toward the subject?

Answer: The author's attitude toward the subject can, like tone, be determined by word choice and is also an aspect of style. The way the author describes or relates to the subject matter can be defined as attitude. The writer's attitude can be positive, negative, ironic, nostalgic, or whatever. Tone and attitude are closely related because they are stylistic descriptions based on the audience's judgments. Attitude, however, pertains to the author-subject relationship, whereas tone refers to the author-reader relationship. Identifying the writer's attitude toward the subject can help determine appropriate audience because it (attitude) affects who reads the work and how he or she will respond to it. Edgar Allan Poe's "Annabel Lee" offers several examples of word choice used to convey attitude:

It was many and many a year ago,
  In a kingdom by the sea,
That a maiden there lived whom you may know
  By the name of ANNABEL LEE;
And this maiden she lived with no other thought
  Than to love and be loved by me.
I was a child and she was a child,
  In this kingdom by the sea,
But we loved with a love that was more than love—
  I and my ANNABEL LEE—
With a love that the winged seraphs of heaven
  Coveted her and me.
And this was the reason that, long ago,
  In this kingdom by the sea,
A wind blew out of a cloud, chilling
  My beautiful ANNABEL LEE;
So that her high-born kinsmen came
  And bore her away from me,
To shut her up in a sepulchre
  In this kingdom by the sea.
The angels, not half so happy in heaven,
  Went envying her and me—
Yes! — That was the reason (as all men know
  In this kingdom by the sea)
That the wind came out of the cloud by night,
  Chilling and killing my ANNABEL LEE.
But our love it was stronger by far than the love
  Of those who were older than we—
  Of many far wiser than we—

And neither the angels in heaven above,
   Nor the demons down under the sea,
Can ever dissever my soul from the soul
   Of the beautiful ANNABEL LEE:
For the moon never beams, without bringing
    me dreams
   Of the beautiful ANNABEL LEE;
And the stars never rise, but I feel the bright
    eyes
   Of the beautiful ANNABEL LEE:
And so, all the night-tide, I lie down by the side
Of my darling — my darling — my life and my
    bride,
   In the sepulchre there by the sea—
   In her tomb by the sounding sea.

7. *Question:*   What is the author's purpose?

   Answer: Understanding the author's purpose helps determine the appropriate audience. As explained previously the author's purpose influences the reader's response. Because the author hopes to have the reader respond in a certain way, he or she shapes the work accordingly. Writers use the expressive mode to elicit empathy, the informative mode to describe or create mental images, and the persuasive mode to convince. You should try to decide which mode the author is using, which in turn should help you decide both the appropriate audience and the appropriate response.

        Try to decide what audience and response the author of the following passage intended:

A SUNDAY IN LONDON

Washington Irving

In a preceding paper I have spoken of an English Sunday in the country and its tranquilizing effect upon the landscape; but where is its sacred influence more strikingly apparent than in the very heart of that great Babel, London? On this sacred day the gigantic monster is charmed into repose. The intolerable din and struggle of the week are at an end. The shops are shut. The fires of forges and manufactories are extinguished; and the sun, no longer obscured by murky clouds of smoke, pours down a sober, yellow radiance into the quiet streets. The few pedestrians we meet, instead of hurrying forward with anxious countenances, move leisurely along; their brows are smoothed from the wrinkles of business and care; they have put on their Sunday looks and Sunday manners with their Sunday clothes, and are cleansed in mind as well as in person.

And now the melodious clangor of bells from church towers summons their several flocks to the fold. Forth issues from his mansion the family of the decent tradesman, the small children in the advance; then the citizen and his comely spouse, followed by the grown-up daughters, with small morocco-bound prayerbooks laid in the folds of their pocket handkerchiefs. The housemaid looks after them from the window, admiring the finery of the family and receiving, perhaps, a nod and smile from her young mistresses, at whose toilet she has assisted.

Now rumbles along the carriage of some magnate of the city, peradventure an alderman or a sheriff; and now the patter of many feet announces a procession of charity scholars, in uniforms of antique cut, and each with a prayerbook under his arm.

The ringing of bells is at an end; the rumbling of the carriage has ceased; the pattering of feet is heard no more; the flocks are folded in ancient churches, cramped up in by-lanes and corners of the crowded city, where the vigilant beadle keeps watch, like the shepherd's dog, around the threshold of the sanctuary. For a time everything is hushed; but soon is heard the deep, pervading sound of the organ, rolling and vibrating through the empty lanes and courts, and the sweet chanting of the choir making them resound with melody and praise. Never have I been more sensible of the sanctifying effect of church music than when I have heard it thus poured forth, like a river of joy, through the inmost recesses of this great metropolis, elevating it, as it were, from all the sordid pollutions of the week, and bearing the poor, world-worn soul on a tide of triumphant harmony to heaven.

The morning service is at an end. The streets are again alive with the congregations returning to their homes, but soon again relapse into silence. Now comes on the Sunday dinner, which, to the city tradesman, is a meal of some importance. There is more leisure for social enjoyment at the board. Members of the family can now gather together, who are separated by the laborious occupations of the week. A schoolboy may be permitted on that day to come to the paternal home; an old friend of the family takes his accustomed Sunday seat at the board, tells over his well-known stories and rejoices young and old with his well-known jokes.

On Sunday afternoon the city pours forth its legions to breathe the fresh air and enjoy the sunshine of the parks and rural environs. Satirists may say what they please about the rural enjoyments of a London citizen on Sunday, but to me there is something delightful in beholding the poor prisoner of the crowded and dusty city enabled thus to come forth once a week and throw himself upon the green bosom of nature. He is like a child restored to the mother's breast; and they who first spread out these noble parks and magnificent pleasure grounds which surround this huge metropolis have done at least as much for its health and morality as if they had expended the amount of cost in hospitals, prisons, and penitentiaries.

1. *Question:*   What is the source or origin of the work?

   Answer: "A Sunday in London" is an essay taken from *The Sketch Book*, a collection of essays published in 1820. It contains some of Irving's earliest and finest works and was published in both the United States and England. In 1815 Irving went to England on business and remained abroad for nearly twenty years. He wrote the essay as a tourist in London.

2. *Question:*   Who is the author?

   Answer: Washington Irving was one of the most successful authors of his time. Born in New York in 1783, Irving began writing at age twenty-three and collaborated on the series of *Salmagundi* papers, on the social life of New York City in the early 1800s. His other works include *Knickerbocker's History of New York*, *Bracebridge Hall*, and *Tales of a Traveller*.

3. *Question:*   What type of level of vocabulary is used in the work?

   Answer: Irving uses some fairly difficult words ("Babel," "intolerable din," "repose," "countenances," "obscured," "melodious clangor," "comely," "morocco-bound," "magnate," "peradventure," "alderman," "vigilant beadle," "sanctuary") and metaphors ("smoothed from the wrinkles of care," "the gigantic monster is charmed into repose," "like a child restored to the mother's breast").

4. *Question:*   How complex are the sentences?

   Answers: Most of the sentences Irving uses are complex ("The few pedestrians we meet, instead of hurrying forward with anxious countenances, move leisurely along; their brows are smoothed from the wrinkles of business and care; they have put on their Sunday looks and Sunday manners with their Sunday clothes, and are cleansed in mind as well as in person.", "The housemaid looks after them from the window, admiring the finery of the family and receiving, perhaps, a nod and smile from her young mistresses, at whose toilet she has assisted."; "The ringing of bells is at an end; the rumbling of the carriage has ceased; the pattering of feet is heard no more; the flocks are folded in ancient churches, cramped up in by-lanes and corners of the crowded city, where the vigilant beadle keeps watch, like the shepherd's dog, around the threshold of the sanctuary.").

5. *Question:*   What is the tone of the work?

   Answer: The essay's tone is personal, though somewhat formal. Irving's "speaks" to his readers as equals with whom he wishes to share his observations. His preference for *I* and *me* indicates the personal tone of the essay. The complexity of the language assumes that the readers can understand his ideas, even though they are expressed rather elegantly.

6. *Question:* What is the author's attitude toward the subject:

   Answer: The "sacred influence" of the English Sunday in London is a subject about which the author is most positive ("but where is its sacred influence more strikingly apparent than in the very heart of that great Babel, London?") and stands in direct contrast with his obviously negative attitude toward week-day London ("The intolerable din and struggle of the week . . ."). Irving's attitude is conveyed by his word choice, sometimes metaphorical or symbolic: "the melodious clangor of bells from church towers summons their flocks to the fold.", "Never have I been more sensible of the sanctifying effect of church music than when I have heard it thus poured forth, like a river of joy, through the inmost recesses of this great metropolis, elevating it, as it were, from all the sordid pollutions of the week, . . ."; ". . . to me there is something delightful in beholding the poor prisoner of the crowded and dusty city enabled thus to come forth once a week and throw himself upon the green bosom of nature."; ". . . and they who first spread out these noble parks and magnificent pleasure grounds . . . have done at least as much for its health and morality as if they had expended the amount of cost in hospitals, prisons, and penitentiaries."

7. *Question:* What is the author's purpose?

   Answer: Irving expressively describes his reaction to the striking contrasts of Sunday and weekday London so that his purpose is to underscore the importance of spiritual well-being in an industrialized society. Irving refers to the Bible, the church, spiritual rebirth, and health symbolized by the one day of the week that is devoted to such matters. ("that great Babel, London," "this sacred day," "cleansed in mind as well as in person," "flocks to the fold," "each with a prayerbook under his arm," "church music . . . like a river of joy . . . bearing the poor world-worn soul on a tide of triumphant harmony to heaven," "the green bosom of nature").

This essay is written for an educated audience that may or may not have been to London. The sophistication of the work, especially its use of symbolism and contrast make it suitable for well-educated readers. Although written over 180 years ago, it still has relevance today.

Exercises

1. Identify the audience for each of the following passages, and state the reason(s) for your choice, according to some or all of "Questions for Evaluating Appropriate Audience."

   A. You've heard it all before about Southern California rock: mellow, bland, stuporous, banal, sun-damaged, pseudo-country, with nice harmonies and appealing melodies that sound especially good if you're the kind of over-ripe avocado-head who not only eats quiches, but drinks spritzers made with "Perry-Ay." And that's only talking about the Eagles.

But something's changed. I'm not sure whether to credit the medfly, Reaganomics, Mt. St. Helens, or the cancellation of "Lou Grant." But Southern California rock is rocking harder, getting more topical, more literate, more expansive. A number of recent albums— some from people responsible for instilling my bias in the first place— show that there's not only more energy in Southern California than I thought imaginable, there may even be intelligent life.

B. There are two Americas. One is the America of Lincoln and Adlai Stevenson; the other is the America of Teddy Roosevelt and the modern superpatriots. One is generous and humane, the other narrowly egotistical; one is self-critical, the other self-righteous; one is sensible, the other romantic; one is good-humored, the other solemn; one is inquiring, the other pontificating; one is moderate, the other filled with passionate intensity; one is judicious and the other arrogant in the use of great power.

We have tended in the years of our great power to puzzle the world by presenting to it now the one face of America, now the other, and sometimes both at once. Many people all over the world have come to regard America as being capable of magnanimity and farsightedness but no less capable of pettiness and spite. The result is an inability to anticipate American actions which in turn makes for apprehension and a lack of confidence in American aims.

C. Like a sultan in command of an oddly assorted harem, Raul Julia stands on the stage of Broadway's 46th Street Theater surrounded by women: beautiful, fat, statuesque, elegant, earthy, young, and not-so-young women. In the hit musical "Nine," he plays Guido Contini, a world-famous Italian film director, and he is the only adult male on the stage. The rest of the cast consists of four little boys, who play the young Guido and his schoolmates, and those 22 wildly diverse actresses, who play the many women in the life of this philandering international celebrity.

In Paul Mazursky's ambitious new film, "Tempest," which opened recently in New York, Julia plays a grizzled Greek peasant who lives, with a herd of goats, in a cave on an isolated island. As Kalibanos— a variation on Caliban in Mazursky's interpretation of Shakespeare's "The Tempest"—Julia plays a character so starved for female companionship that he makes comical, oafish passes at the 15-year-old daughter of his American employer.

The worldly Italian director and the primitive Greek goatherd take their place among a rich assortment of Julia characterizations: a German cutthroat in the New York Shakespeare Festival's "Threepenny Opera" revival, an elegant Englishman in the Broadway production of Harold Pinter's "Betrayal," the most famous of all Transylvanians in "Dracula." It is all the work of a 41-year-old Puerto

Rican who says that when he arrived in New York in 1964, freshly graduated from the University of Puerto Rico, "I was very confident. I came here ready to do everything."

D. You've come a long way, sister. The gym classes you skipped at school now form a significant part of your adult entertainment. You are working hard, playing hard, making yourself hard and strong. The sports for which you were once only a cheerleader now serve as your after-work recreation and, thanks to Title IX, part of your school-age daughter's curriculum. Spurred by feminism's promise of physical, domestic and economic freedom, you have done what few generations of woman have dared or chosen to do. You have made muscles—a body of them—and it shows. And you look great.

As a comely by-product of the fitness phenomenon, women have begun literally to reshape themselves, and with themselves, the American notion of female beauty. At home or on the beach or by the office water cooler, a new form is emerging. It may be slimmer than before, but it is surely stronger. It may be massive or petite, but it is always graceful. The face, stripped of its old layers of makeup, looks more natural. The frame, deprived of some adipose tissue, looks more sinuous. It is a body made for motion: for long, purposeful strides across the backcourt, through the mall, into the boardroom. It is a body that speaks assurance, in itself and in the woman who, through will power and muscle power, has created it. It is not yet, and may never be, for everybody, but for many men this feminine physical assurance can be galvanizing; there can be an allure to equality.

E. We have waited for more than 340 years for our constitutional and God-given rights. The nations of Asia and Africa are moving with jet-like speed toward gaining political independence, but we still creep at horse-and-buggy pace toward gaining a cup of coffee at a lunch counter. Perhaps it is easy for those who have never felt the stinging darts of segregation to say, "Wait." But when you have seen vicious mobs lynch your mothers and fathers at will and drown your sisters and brothers at whim; when you have seen hate-filled policemen curse, kick and even kill your black brothers and sisters; when you see the vast majority of your twenty million Negro brothers smothering in an airtight cage of poverty in the midst of an affluent society; when you suddenly find your tongue twisted and your speech stammering as you seek to explain to your six-year-old daughter why she can't go to the public amusement park that has just been advertised on television, and see tears welling up in her eyes when she is told that Funtown is closed to colored children, and see ominous clouds of inferiority beginning to form in her little mental sky and see her beginning to distort her personality by developing an unconscious bitterness toward white people; when you have to concoct an answer for a five-year-old son who is asking: "Daddy, why do white people treat colored people so mean?"; when you take a cross-country drive and find it necessary to sleep night after night in the uncomfortable corners of your automobile because no motel will accept you; when you are humiliated day in and day out by nagging signs reading "white" and "colored"; when your first name becomes "nigger," your middle name becomes "boy" (however old you are) and your last name becomes "John," and your wife and mother are never given the respected title "Mrs."; when you are harried by day and haunted by night by the fact that you are a Negro, living constantly at tiptoe stance, never quite knowing what to expect next, and are plagued with inner fears and outer resentments; when you are forever fighting a degenerating sense of "nobodiness"—then you will understand why we find it difficult to wait. There comes a time when the cup of endurance runs over, and men are no longer willing to be plunged into the abyss of despair. I hope, sirs, you can understand our legitimate and unavoidable impatience.

F. There was once a town in the heart of America where all life seemed to live in harmony with its surroundings. The town lay in the midst of a checkerboard of prosperous farms, with fields of grain and hillsides of orchards where, in spring, white clouds of bloom drifted above the green fields. In autumn, oak and maple and birch set up a blaze of color that flamed and flickered across a backdrop of pines. Then foxes barked in the hills and deer silently crossed the fields, half hidden in the mists of the fall mornings.

Along the road, laurel, viburnum and alder, great ferns and wildflowers delighted the traveler's eye through much of the year. Even in winter the roadsides were places of beauty, where countless birds came to feed on the berries and on the seed heads of the dried weeds rising above the snow. The countryside was, in fact, famous for the abundance and variety of its bird life, and when the flood of migrants was pouring through in spring and fall people traveled from great distances to observe them. Others came to fish the streams, which flowed clear and cold out of the hills and contained shady pools where trout lay. So it had been from the days many years ago when the first settlers raised their houses, sank their wells, and built their barns.

Then a strange blight crept over the area and everything began to change. Some evil spell had settled on the community: mysterious maladies swept the flocks of chickens; the cattle and sheep sickened and died. Everywhere was a shadow of death. The farmers spoke of much illness among their families. In the town the doctors had become more and more puzzled by new kinds of sickness appearing among their patients. There had been several sudden and unexplained deaths, not only among adults but even among children, who would be stricken suddenly while at play and die within a few hours.

There was a strange stillness. The birds, for example—where had they gone? Many people spoke of them, puzzled and disturbed. The feeding stations in the backyards were deserted. The few birds seen anywhere were moribund; they trembled violently and could not fly. It was a spring without voices. On the mornings that had once throbbed with the dawn chorus of robins, catbirds, doves, jays, wrens, and scores of other bird voices there was now no sound; only silence lay over the fields and woods and marsh.

On the farms the hens brooded, but no chicks hatched. The farmers complained that they were unable to raise any pigs—the litters were small and the young survived only a few days. The apple trees were coming into bloom but no bees droned among the blossoms, so there was no pollination and there would be no fruit.

The roadsides, once so attractive, were now lined with browned and withered vegetation as though swept by fire. These, too, were silent, deserted by all living things. Even the streams were now lifeless. Anglers no longer visited them, for all the fish had died.

In the gutters under the eaves and between the shingles of the roofs, a white granular powder still showed a few patches; some weeks before it had fallen like snow upon the roofs and the lawns, the fields and streams.

No witchcraft, no enemy action had silenced the rebirth of new life in this stricken world. The people had done it themselves.

This town does not acutally exist, but it might easily have a thousand counterparts in America or elsewhere in the world. I know of no community that has experienced all the misfortunes I describe. Yet every one of these disasters has actually happened somewhere, and many real communities have already suffered a substantial number of them. A grim specter has crept upon us almost unnoticed, and this imagined tragedy may easily become a stark reality we all shall know.

chapter 7
Writing for an Audience

The preceding chapter pointed out that different types of writing aim at different audiences, which likewise determine the writer's style, vocabulary, tone and the like. For example, the textbook for an economics class assumes that its audience will have certain characteristics, for example, that its readers can handle a fairly sophisticated vocabulary and syntax. If it is an introductory text, it will more carefully explain technical terms than it would if it were more advanced. In addition, the writer of the introductory text could reasonably decide that not all of the book's readers will have a compelling interest in economics, and therefore, he or she might try to engage the reader's attention through interesting and relevant examples. On the other hand, the author of an advanced text would probably figure that the book's audience is interested in economics, and so he or she would feel less pressure to attract the reader's attention.

Similarly, any time you write, you make certain assumptions about your audience, assumptions concerning your credibility, your audience's interest in what you have to say, its previous knowledge of and concern for your topic, your audience's educational level, and sometimes such things as their political or moral beliefs. In addition, your purpose defines the response you expect from your audience.

These concerns can be divided into two categories: assumptions that derive from your perception of your audience, and those that reflect expectations based on your purpose. The first group includes knowing that you are writing something that will be read. As obvious as this statement seems to be, many inexperienced writers do not consciously identify an audience, and therefore they write in a vacuum. Because a sense of audience, along with purpose, controls every part of your writing, from vocabulary and sentence structure to general approach to topic, not carefully identifying an audience places you at a considerable disadvantage.

Assumptions About Audience

As an obvious example of how audience controls writing, consider the difference in vocabulary and sentence structure that would be necessary to communicate to an eight-year-old, on the one hand, or a college graduate, on the other. If you were writing a letter to the eight-year-old, you would probably choose your words carefully so as not to exceed the child's vocabulary. You would also simplify your sentences so that the child would not get lost in complicated syntax. But if you were writing about the same topic to a college graduate, you would limit neither your vocabulary nor your sentence complexity. You would assume that the college graduate could understand a sophisticated level of writing. To illustrate, suppose you were describing an airplane trip to your eight-year-old niece or nephew:

> We left on a bright and sunny day. The plane seemed very big, bigger than a school bus, and it carried three times as many passengers.
>
> I was nervous before the plane took off. I didn't really believe that it would get off the ground. Then it started to roll down the runway, going faster and faster. The next thing I knew the plane was pointing up. I looked out of the window and saw the ground falling away from me. At first, I could see the cars on the street and the houses. In a few seconds, though, I could see only clouds.
>
> After a while, I relaxed and enjoyed the rest of the flight. It was a little bumpy at times, like riding over a rough road. But I think you will enjoy flying when you get the chance.

The reading level of this description is simple enough to be understood by the child to whom it was written; it has a fairly simple vocabulary and its sentences are short.

However, shaping writing to a certain reading level is only one of the assumptions about audience that a writer must make. In this case, the writer made several other important decisions about his or her audience:

1. The eight-year-old probably has not flown in an airplane.
2. He or she would be interested in how big the plane is.
3. He or she would be interested to learn that an adult was nervous before take-off.
4. The physical excitement and visual experience would appeal to the youngster's imagination.

In responding to these assumptions, the writer compared the size of the airplane to something familar to the child—a school bus. The nervousness was communicated with a humor that the child could appreciate, and it was combined with a child's sense of amazement that planes really do fly. The visual phenomena were presented clearly and concretely.

Now compare this description with one written with a college graduate as the intended audience, and see if you can identify the assumptions made concerning the audience:

> The flight home was smooth and uneventful, if you ignore a couple of moments when we encountered—as the pilot said, in that irritatingly confident drawl—"a little weather up ahead," which was followed by sudden drops in altitude that had me falling well ahead of my stomach and then ascents in which we joined company again, both the worse for wear. Each time, my hand would reach for that little bag in the pouch behind the next seat, my heart thumping and my rational self insisting that next time I would take a bus. Or walk. Or stay put.
>
> Anyway I survived, although I was a little green around the edges when I got off the plane. Most of the other passengers seemed to have been able to ignore the rough spots and looked at me with a kind of condescension. Or maybe that is just my paranoia speaking.
>
> Afterwards I stared at that huge plane sitting on the runway. It appeared to me to be both monstrous and yet somehow frail, like a giant pterodactyl with a huge wing span too large for its own body. I marveled at the engineering, I suppose, and then turned my eyes thankfully to the ground beneath my feet.

In thinking about the assumptions that shaped this piece of writing, perhaps you identified some of the following:

1. The audience would be literate enough to handle sophisticated vocabulary and sentence structure.
2. The college graduate had flown before.
3. Because the audience would be familiar with commercial flights, the writer could refer to such things as the pilot's tone of voice and "that little bag."
4. The audience would know something about psychology.
5. The audience would know something about geological periods.
6. The audience knows the writer—perhaps a friend or relative who would appreciate the piece's self-mocking tone.

These two descriptions could have been based on the same plane flight, though the different audiences led to different purposes; the first is informative, the second expressive. The informative piece provides information, whereas the expressive one invites a sharing of the experience.

Audience Familiarity with Subject

Among the assumptions a writer makes about an audience is an estimation of the reader's familiarity with and interest in the subject matter. For example, suppose you were taking an essay examination in a psychology class and encountered the following question:

> Whether human behavior is most influenced by nature or whether it derives more from nurture is an issue that divides contemporary social scientists. Take a position in the nature/nurture debate and

support your views with appropriate references to the readings discussed this semester.

The writer of the question, the instructor who made up the exam, clearly assumed that his or her students would recognize the term *nature/nurture* and would know that the first part refers to the idea that behavior is inborn and the second part to the theory that it is shaped by an individual's environment. The instructor can and should make this assumption because the students were required to read material that used these terms. Therefore, one of the first decisions a writer must make about his or her audience is based on the following question: How much can I expect my audience to know about my subject matter?

Often, as in a classroom situation, this question is fairly easy to answer. In fact, whenever you write for a well-defined audience, you can make confident assumptions concerning your audience's knowledge of the subject matter. Suppose you are writing a story for your school newspaper about the football game won by the school team the past weekend. In your story, you want to explain the victory by emphasizing that defense more than offense was responsible:

> Our *eleven* triumphed 7–0 over State U this past Saturday because our defense completely stymied the other team's offense.
>
> *Blitzing linebacker* Joe McNulty had a field day, three times *sacking* Don Maloney, State's fine quarterback, and *cornerback* Willie Montrose *picked off* two errant *passes* when Maloney's *protection* gave him sufficient time to *set up* and throw. Whatever State tried, even an unusual *flanker reverse*, did not succeed in denting our formidable defense.
>
> This was fortunate because our offense was not having a very good day, often being stopped by *fumbles* or simply poor execution at crucial times. In the fourth quarter, though, we managed a sustained drive, helped along by a thirty-yard *screen pass* to *halfback* Bones Branmeyer. The touchdown at the end of that drive accounted for all the points that either team could score in this tightly contested struggle.

Because this story would appear on the sports page of the school newspaper, you could assume that your audience would be both familiar with and interested in the subject matter. Therefore, you could use language appropriate to and understood by fans of football. Such fans would know what a *blitzing linebacker* or a *screen pass* are and in fact would understand all the italicized words in the story. In the same way, a review of a play or concert could be based on the assumption that your audience would know theatrical words such as *denouement* or musical terms such as *cadenza*.

These examples apply to a well-defined audience who, because of some special situation, circumstance, or shared interest, would be familiar with your subject matter. These assumptions permit you to use the specialized language that a particular subject matter such as sports demands, but they also exclude people who are not familiar with the subject. The opposite extreme occurs when you can assume that your audience knows very little about the subject. In such a case, you must either not use any specialized vocabulary or explain any such terms. If, for example, you wanted to describe the beauty of the Brooklyn Bridge to an audience who knew very little about bridges generally, and less about the Brooklyn Bridge specifically, you would have to describe it in a way that would be accessible to the general reader:

> The Brooklyn Bridge, once called the "eighth wonder of the world" but now often overshadowed by more modern and spectacular bridges, remains one of the most interesting structures built to join two land masses separated by a body of water.
>
> Although it is not now the longest suspension bridge—a bridge that hangs over the area it transverses with no support from underneath—it is still the most fascinating. It was designed by an engineer who understood both the forces of stress and aesthetic principles. Its bold solid granite towers seem to be forever in tension with the graceful cables that curve over the river and hold the roadway above the water. Part of the beauty of the bridge results from the difference between the massive, impenetrable towers and the graceful, almost airy cables through which the sun and wind can pass freely. And the catenary curve of the cable—that natural arc of a cable strung between fixed points—only adds to the contrast between stone, rigid and vertical, and wire, graceful and curving.

The writer of this description assumed that that his or her audience knew very little about suspension bridges and therefore defined key terms such as *suspension* and *catenary* so that the audience might be able to visualize the description of the bridge.

Writing requires making assumptions about the audience's knowledge of and interest in a subject. Just as important, though, is understanding how the audience and the purpose interact.

Audience and Purpose

The three purposes each assume or expect a different kind of response from the audience, and these expectations control, to a significant degree, the manner in which a writer approaches a subject, the choice of language, and the method of developing ideas.

The words used to present ideas can focus on the writer, the subject matter, or the audience. For example, imagine that the student government at your school has just contracted to pay a popular band $10,000 for a one-night concert. Suppose too that this band is your favorite and you want to express your excitement at the oopportunity of attending the concert. The basic information you would want to communicate would be as follows:

> The Why will appear on March 23.
> I will buy a ticket for that concert.

However, assuming that your purpose is expressive, you will want to present this information with a focus on yourself. You would, therefore, choose language that would project a sense of yourself:

> The *fabulous* band The Why will make March 23 an *extraordinary* night, one I will never forget.

Besides centering on you as the writer, as is natural in expressive writing, your choice of words will help you express your values and interests. Specifically, *fabulous* and *extraordinary* are words that communicate a value judgment; and all value judgments are subjective and thus may not be shared by everyone else. For example, a friend might say:

> I wouldn't attend a performance of that *presumptuous* and *derivative* band if they were giving away the tickets. That night will go down in history as completely *dull*.

This friend's opinions concerning the band contradict yours, and the language reflects this. But not only does an expressive purpose dictate the choice of words that will communicate your feelings, it also forces you to use language that will evoke a particular kind of response in your audience. Strongly subjective words such as those in the examples above invite the reader to share the writer's emotions, whether those emotions project a positive or negative attitude.

Also, because expressive writing is highly subjective, it permits a considerable variation in level of formality. The examples above were written in a fairly formal style and with a formal vocabulary. But the first statement could have been phrased in even more colloquial language:

> The Why is just an *outrageous* band. I wouldn't *blow the chance* to see that concert.

Or the second, statement:

> The Why just doesn't *cook*, not even *simmer*. I'd just as soon *crash* at a convention of accordion players.

Colloquial language is found more in conversation than in writing, and moreover, it frequently identifies the speaker as a member of a particular peer group in which such language is used. You should be aware that when you use colloquial words in either speech or writing, you are telling your audience that you want to be seen as belonging to the peer group identified with that particular colloquial vocabulary.

Although an expressive purpose invites subjective and sometimes colloquial language, an informative one demands a much more detached and objective style. Since the focus of informative writing is on the subject, the language used to present the subject to the audience ordinarily does not project the writer's personality, but informative writing need not be dull because of its emphasis on objectivity: rather its colors should be those which naturally emanate from the subject rather than those which are added by the writer. Accordingly, an informative statement concerning the appearance of The Why should be able to describe the qualities of the band without interjecting or imposing the writer's own feelings:

> The Why, who over the past few months have attracted a *devoted* following, will bring its particular brand of *energetic* musical performance to our theater on March 23. The group's lead singer, Rickie Ogleby, recently said that a concert should be not only a musical experience but also a spiritual happening that *generates good karma*.

Words such as *devoted, energetic,* and *generates* add texture to the statement that this particular group will perform in concert on such and such a date, but they are words pertaining more to the subject than to the writer: they more fully explain the subject to the audience without adding any bias or prejudice from the writer. Note that the last word occurs in a statement attributed to the leader of the band; thus the writer takes no responsibility for the accuracy of the assertion that attending a performance of The Why approximates a spiritual experience for the audience.

In persuasive writing, the audience is the focus of the writer's attention, as the goal of such writing is to convince the audience to think or behave differently. People can be persuaded to do or believe something through logical argument or appeals to their emotions.

As a writer with a persuasive purpose, you will want to consider how your audience will react to what you have to say. You should begin by assessing its present feelings on the subject: Does my audience have a particular view on this issue?

The answer to this question will determine the finer points of your approach. For example, if you wanted to send a letter to the college newspaper in which you argued that spending $10,000 on The Why was an unthinkable waste of student money, you would want first to judge the group's popularity with the student body. Assuming that the group was, in fact, very popular and that a majority of the students would welcome the opportunity to attend the concert, you would know that you could not attack the group itself, for by so doing you would alienate your audience and make it unreceptive to your views.

An alternative approach would have to be found, one that would win your audience to your side and make it sympathetic to your argument. In this case, you could concentrate on the amount of money being spent for the concert, assuming that students would have a vested interest in how their money is spent. Keeping these two factors in mind—your reader's desire to attend the concert and their concern about spending their money wisely—you could write a statement such as the following:

> Although The Why is a popular band, and well worth seeing, the concert is just too expensive.

Another consideration in presenting a persuasive argument is establishing your credibility. In effect, you have to ask yourself the following question: Why should my audience believe me? In other words, you must present yourself as being in a position to make a considered and informed judgment on the issue:

> Although The Why is a popular band, one that I particularly like, even more than The What, the concert is just too expensive.

By observing that you also like the band and in fact know enough about it to compare it with another popular group, you establish both your shared interest with your audience and your credentials as an informed observer.

Finally, people like to be given an alternative when they are told they should not do something. Therefore, besides stating that $10,000 should not be spent on a one-night concert, it would be useful to suggest other ways to use the money.

> Although The Why is a popular band, one that I particularly like, even more than The What, the concert is just too expensive. Because of all the problems on campus, all the clubs and activities that need money, we should decide whether it is better to spend such a large amount for one night's entertainment, or to spread out the money over the year. I think the second option would be a much better choice. For a few dollars, we all can buy The Why's latest album, and the $10,000 can fund such continuing activities as the newspaper, the student book exchange, and a film series, and it could even provide a start for other ideas that now have no funding at all.

This argument has considered the audience first: it accepts the student's desire to attend the concert; it establishes the writer's credentials; and it offers alternative ways to spend the $10,000.

It could, however, be made stronger by adding an emotional level of persuasion, which could be done by introducing words that engage the audience's sympathy:

> Although The Why is a *compelling and exciting* band, one that I follow *devotedly*, even more than The What, the concert is *outrageously* expensive. When we consider all the *pressing* problems, the *worthwhile* but *starving* clubs and activities that *deserve* money, we should decide whether it is *ethically* correct to *squander* such a large amount of money on one night's entertainment or to spread out our *hard-earned* money over the year and get its *full value*. For a few dollars, we all can buy The Why's latest album, and the $10,000 can *respond to the needs* of such *valuable* activities as the newspaper, the student book exchange, and the film series, and it can even provide a start for other ideas now *languishing* for lack of funding.

The italicized words provide an added appeal to the audience's sensibilites by working on an emotional rather than a purely logical level of persuasion. Such appeals to emotion instead of reason should always be made cautiously and within a logical argument that is valid by itself. A purely emotional argument, however, does not often persuade because it ignores the audience's need to be moved by rational concerns.

Strategies for Considering Audience

Your concerns as a writer preparing material for an audience can be summarized in the following questions:

1. How can I describe my audience in terms of age, interests, life experiences, and education?
2. Is my audience defined by a shared interest in my topic?
3. What previous knowledge of or interest in my topic can I assume?
4. What is my purpose, and how does it interact with my audience?
5. What response do I want from my audience?

Your answer to Question 1 will control your choice of words and style. You will want to write at a level appropriate to your audience's ability to comprehend your material. You will also try to relate your material to the experiences and interests of your audience.

In regard to Questions 2 and 3, if you are writing for an audience that shares your interest in your topic, you will be able to use technical or specialized vocabulary, and you can assume a familiarity with the subject matter, which will relieve you of having to explain references to ideas or people that would be familiar to an informed audience. For example, you would not have to tell a football fan who Joe Namath is or a musician who Leonard Bernstein is or a film buff who Ingrid Bergman is, and so on.

Remember when answering Questions 4 and 5 that an expressive purpose invites empathy from your audience; an informative one attempts to educate your audience; and a persuasive one seeks to change your audience's beliefs and/or actions. An expressive purpose is best served by a language and a style that project a sense of your personality. Expressive writing is subjective and can be either formal or informal. An informative purpose demands a more objective approach, one that reduces your visibility as the writer. Persuasive writing, because it asks for a more dramatic response, requires the most thorough analysis of your audience, including how it can best be approached, and how it can be made sympathetic to your position so that it will accept your opinion.

A Word on College Writing

Many college writing assignments will present difficulties because you are asked to write for an undefined audience. Essay questions, for example, often do not specify an audience, nor do assigned papers. Therefore, you must assume that the instructor who asked the essay question or assigned the paper is the audience.

Determining your audience for college writing assignments includes the following factors:

- Your reader is a person who, although he or she teaches a certain subject, occasionally thinks of other things.
- You as a person do matter.
- You will write better if you write naturally.

These assumptions in turn suggest certain corollaries:

- Because a college classroom is a fairly formal place, your writing should be more formal than informal.
- Nonetheless, a reasonable formality does not demand writing that seems to have been composed by a corpse.

Your purpose is crucial to your approach to essays or papers. Most often, you will be asked to write either informatively or persuasively. Expressive writing is less frequently required and sometimes is not accepted as it permits such a subjective approach to the material.

Exercises

1. Imagine you are writing about one of the following.
   a. A camping trip.
   b. A new job.
   c. An interesting or useful book.
   d. Unusual weather.
   e. Winning a lottery.
   Choose a member of your family or a close friend to whom you will send this piece of writing and answer the following questions:

   - What assumptions about your audience can you make in terms of age, experience, education, and interest in your topic?
   - What purpose will this piece of writing serve?
   - What response can you expect from your audience?

   Write an essay on your topic to the audience you have identified and for the purpose you have determined.
2. Suppose your boss asks you to write a newsletter for the employees of the company for which you work. What assumptions about your audience would help you decide what material should be included in the newsletter? What purpose do you think would be most appropriate? Write a sample piece for the newsletter.
3. Write two short essays (about two paragraphs) on the same topic. Address one of the essays to an audience that would be familiar with your

topic and the other to one that would know very little about it. Analyze the differences between the two in vocabulary and assumed familiarity with the subject matter.

4. Make up an essay question for any course you are currently taking. Key the question to material you have recently been assigned to read.

5. Choose one of the following for an essay directed to members of your class:
   a. Tuition costs.
   b. The physical condition of your campus.
   c. The registration procedure.
   d. Student-sponsored activities.
   e. The value of your degree.

   Analyze your audience's anticipated response to this topic if it were treated expressively, informatively, and persuasively.

   Write an essay for one of the three purposes.

   Decide whether your language and approach to the topic are shaped by your audience and purpose.

   Write a different version of this essay, directed to your instructor as a representative of the college. Analyze this essay in the same way as the one you wrote for your peers.

   For each of the essays you have written, check your sense of audience by asking yourself the following questions:

1. Have I identified my audience's familiarity with my subject?
2. Have I established my credibility by demonstrating my awareness of my audience's concerns about the subject?
3. Is my vocabulary appropriate for my audience? Have I used specialized language for an audience that is familiar with my subject and more general language for an audience that is not?
   Is my level of formality suitable for the intended audience?
4. Is my sentence structure appropriate for my intended audience?
   Are my sentences tightly structured to achieve a formal level of writing or more loosely patterned to communicate a conversational or informal level?
5. What tone do I communicate to the audience?
   Does my tone accurately project my attitude toward the subject matter and audience?
6. What attitude toward my subject have I expressed?
   Am I judgmental, either positively or negatively, toward my subject? Does this attitude serve my purpose?

After you have examined your writing for its sense of audience, revise it as necessary so that your finished essay recognizes your audience's relationship to your subject matter and serves your purpose in writing the essay.

part FOUR

Strategies and Forms

chapter 8
Reading: Examples and Comparison and Contrast

Our discussions of purpose and audience have shown you how they determine the approach to a topic and govern both the selection of details and the style of the writing. In brief, purpose and audience help identify a *controlling idea* and the specifics that will develop it.

All writing establishes a relationship between a generalization—a controlling idea—and specific details. This relationship can be developed in a variety of forms which structure the details into a pattern that explains and expands the controlling idea. Whether the writing is expressive, informative, or persuasive, the writer decides which organizational pattern is most appropriate for the subject, the purpose, and the intended audience.

This section introduces you to strategies for identifying the organizational patterns that develop the controlling ideas of the materials you read and write.

Determining Form

Organizational techniques create a relationship between the controlling idea and the specific details that clarify and expand it. The writer establishes the controlling idea as part of his or her decision about the purpose and appropriate audience for the work. Once decided, the idea needs to be developed. The details chosen to develop that idea require a pattern that will show their relationship to one another and to the controlling idea, the purpose, and the audience.

As the reader, you need to identify the controlling idea, and to recognize, when possible, the relationship between each of the details that develop the controlling idea.

Questions for Determining Controlling Idea, Form, Purpose, and Response

The following questions are an excellent means of identifying the controlling idea and the relationship among details, whether they are stated or implied.

Controlling Idea
1. Who or what is the subject of the work?
2. What aspect(s) of the subject is (are) discussed in the work?
3. What does the author want you to understand and remember, in general, about the aspect(s) of the subject discussed in the work?

Form
4. How are the ideas presented? Are they examples or illustrations, comparisons and/or contrasts, causes and/or effects, a series of actions or events, classifications, or definitions (or qualities and characteristics of same)?
5. How do they develop the controlling idea?

The answers to these questions will give you the author's general and specific ideas, the latter in terms of their type and relationship to one another and to the general idea of the work. Two additional questions can be asked to determine the purpose and the desired response:

Purpose
6. Does the work emphasize the author (expressive mode), the subject (informative mode), or the audience (persuasive mode)?

Reader's Response
7. How does the author want the reader to respond to the work?

The answers to these questions will help you recognize the author's ideas, their development, and their relationship to the author's purpose dand to the reader's response. Each will help you evaluate the reading materials presented in this chapter, which focus on two organizational patterns: example and comparison and contrast.

Examples

Examples are a series of instances that typify, or represent, concrete events or occurrences. As they are used here, examples also include abstract or hypothetical thoughts, ideas, or experiences. When concrete, examples usually prove or show the truth of the general idea, and when abstract they usually clarify the general idea by showing evidence of logical thought. Only sometimes are they related to one another, and when they are, they are more easily remembered. Nonetheless, they always develop the author's controlling idea with concrete or abstract evidence.

Consider the following paragraphs:

> There is a noticeable change in the fashion industry's edict concerning the hemline. No more is it mandated that a certain length must be worn for a woman to be in fashion. In the 1960s, for example, the miniskirt, rising several inches above the knee, was "in" whereas the early 1970s called for a woman to drop her hemline to just above her shoes and later to midcalf. The earlier Victorian era mandated

floor-length hemlines, a trend that lasted into the early years of the twentieth century.

But the woman's true liberation from one, and perhaps very un-flattering, hemline to a variety—any of which she may call her own—arrived in the 1980s. The long and leggy young woman can show off her gams with the revived mini (long enough to cover the subject and short enough to be interesting), or one less fortunate may cover her legs to the degree that satisfies: floor-length, ankle-length, calf-length, knee-length, or somewhere in between. Take your pick.

In these paragraphs, the author's controlling idea is that fashion no longer requires a certain hemline, and it is stated in the beginning sentences of the first paragraph and restated in the first sentence and last two sentences of the second. Examples develop that idea in both paragraphs by giving concrete instances of mandated hemlines in recent and past history. The relationship between these ideas is chronological and because of that relationship, is easily remembered. These examples prove that the woman of the 1980s has choices that were at other times unavailable to her. The author's purpose is to inform, and so the emphasis is on the subject. It is written in a positive, lighthearted tone and is intended for the fashion conscious.

When used to develop a central thought, examples can also be abstract. Consider the examples in the following paragraphs concerning the golf ball:

Most games that involve the use of a ball can be described, but seldom explained. Consider the ball itself.

We begin with the golf ball, white until soiled, hard as a rock, the surface uniformly pitted with mini-craters, in size about that of a meatball. This ball is stroked with a slender, wandlike shaft, about the length of a cane, the bottom end tipped with a blade, variously tilted, or a fistlike wooden knob. A mystical belief that the club, not the player, directs the ball, and the ball, not the player, determines its direction, is common among most players. With their needs in mind, a ball is promised that will correct the mistakes made by the club. A ball could more easily be drawn to the hole by a magnet, but the excitement generated among the spectators is based on the role in the game that chance plays. No thrill equals the sight of a peerless player missing a nine-inch putt. Golf balls not stroked are often given to babies, found in car seats, stored in raincoat pockets, or left where they can be stepped on.

Golf is played in the open, preferably on grass, over a course cunningly strewn with obstructions. Bunkers, sand traps, trees, streams, ponds, and spectators, along with rain, sleet, cold, and lightning, make the game of golf what it is. What it is was not known to many golfers until they saw the game on TV. The mock-ups used by the commentators made clear a fact that many golfers found puzzling. What they were doing was walking up and down, back and forth. Most ball games seem to have in common the going back and forth, rather than going any place.

The very smallness of the ball may substantially contribute to the high moral tone of the game. What is there to fight over? Each player has several balls of his own. Although equipped with sticks that would make good clubs, the golf player refrains from striking his opponents, making loud slurring remarks, or coughing or hissing when another player is putting. It is not at all unusual to hear another player described as a great gentleman.

In this game alone the opinion of an official is accepted in a depressed, sportsmanlike manner. The player does not scream and curse, as in baseball, or stage riots, as in football, but accepts without comment or demonstration the fickle finger of fate. Law and order prevail on the links, if viewed on prime time. The game was once played for the health of it, by amateurs (a term currently applied to unemployed track stars); now the lonely, single golfer is burdened with the knowledge that he does for nothing what others are paid for. This condition is technically described as a handicap.

Some players hit the ball and stand, dejected, waiting for it to land; others turn away and leave it up to the caddy. Some enjoy the pain they give to others, some like to torture themselves. Although the physical challenge is substantial—miles and miles of walking, hours of waiting, the possibility of heatstroke or of being struck by lightning—the crucial element is mental. If not in a seizure of torment and self-doubt, the player must pass hole after hole daydreaming, or wondering why he has so many clubs to choose from. A loss of concentration on the easy holes will invariably cost him the hard ones. In summary we can say that the smallness of the ball is no measure of the effort it takes to stroke it or of the reward it brings.

This excerpt from a longer article, titled "Odd Balls," states its controlling idea in the first paragraph. The golf ball is first considered as one whose use is hardly ever explained, although it is described. The author offers examples of mystical beliefs about the way the game is played and scored and attitudes toward it, which again describe but do not explain the ball's use in the game. Though unrelated, the examples serve as evidence of the author's logical investigation into the golf ball. This informative piece seems intended for those familiar with the game of golf and interested in abstract speculations about it. It appears that the readers are expected to empathize or share the author's feelings about the subject.

The following excerpt from an article called "Southpaw Stigma" uses examples to develop several paragraphs organized around the controlling idea of its first paragraph:

Just because "left" isn't "right" doesn't mean it's wrong. Yet, there's a stigma about "left"—left-handed jokes, left behind, left over, left out, in left field.

As a group, lefties are really all right. After all, if the right-handed majority had been forced to deal with fearful parents, overzealous if well-meaning teachers, and even some pediatricians (all three who constantly insisted you be "other" handed), chances are you'd be a bit edgy, stubborn, and nonconformist, too.

Lefties in our society have a lot to deal with. They are governed by both written and unwritten "bills of rights." Even the vocabulary works against them. For instance, there's no fair shake in an allegedly neutral word like *ambidextrous*, which translates literally as being "right-handed on both sides." (Certainly a one-sided view.)

But left is a negative in several languages. Australians occasionally call left-handed folks "mollydookers," which means "woman handed." *Gauche* is French for "left"; *sinister* derives from Latin; *mancino* means "deceitful" in Italian; *linkisch* implies awkwardness in German; *na levo* means "sneaky" in Russian; and *zurdo* is Spanish for "malicious." All of these are, at best, left-handed compliments to a person who is not right-handed.

Only the Greeks have a good word for the left-handed: *aristera*, which translates as "those fit to govern." To prove the point, left-handed leaders include Tiberius, Alexander the Great, Queen Victoria, and, among presidents of the United States, Harry S. Truman, James Garfield and Gerald Ford.

Left-handedness bears the brunt of many superstitions and myths. Some researchers contend that left-handers are brain damaged as a result of oxygen deficiencies at birth, predisposed to be alcoholics or suicidal, prone to reading disabilities; better (or worse) in athletics, and have "different ears for music." But overall, such myths just don't hold up under scientific scrutiny. . . .

Do psychologists have a good definition for left-handedness? Is there a clear understanding of why people are left-handed as opposed to right-handed? Are left-handed people significantly different from others? Do parents need to worry and try to change their children's handedness? No, no, no, and NO, respectively.

It is probably not a bad idea, then, to try to put a stop to the stigma that surrounds southpaws and to conclude that those who are other than right-handed should be left alone!

Beginning in the fourth paragraph, the author offers examples to show that left is a negative word in several languages. That idea is expressed in the paragraph's topic sentence, which concerns an aspect of the controlling idea: there is a stigma attached to being left-handed. Designed to persuade its readers to drop the negative attitude they may have toward left-handedness (last paragraph), the author offers examples that typify the meaning of *left* in Greek: "those fit to govern" (paragraph 5), examples of myths and superstitions surrounding left-handedness (paragraph 6), examples of questions that indicate lack of knowledge of or unncessary worry about left-handedness (paragraph 7), in order to convince the readers to think positively about the subject. Written for those who are left-handed or are concerned about others who are, the author wishes to have the readers believe as he does.

Comparison and Contrast

The similarities and/or differences between and among things or ideas are highlighted in the organizational pattern of comparison and contrast. This pattern clarifies each thing individually and in relation to other things compared and/or contrasted with it. Sometimes writers will point out only the similarities and ignore the differences between and among things, or vice versa. At other times, both likenesses and differences will be explored. When this is done, writers may organize their work so that the similarities and the differences are discussed separately. This approach is referred to as the *block method*. Should authors choose to discuss both together, they may use the *alternating method* which allows them to match qualities or characteristics for each item and discuss all the items to be compared and contrasted in terms of that quality. Either way, the specific ideas presented to develop the controlling idea all concern the similarities and differences of two or more things.

The paragraphs below show comparison and contrast as a method of development:

> The free exit of people from the Soviet Union is prohibited. The Soviet Union has a problem with people leaving the country, which it calls "defection."
>
> The free entry of opiates into the United States is prohibited. The United States has a problem with opiates coming into the country, which it calls "trafficking in dope."
>
> The United States recognizes that its citizens have an inalienable right to leave their country. The United States therefore has no such problem as "defection."
>
> Similarly, if the United States recognized that its citizens also have an inalienable right to self-medication (a right of which they were deprived in 1914), there would be no illegal inflow of heroin into the country. The United States would therefore have no such problem as "trafficking in dope."

Here the author uses similiarities and differences between the Soviet Union and the United States (Soviet Union: free exit of people; United States: free entry of opiates) and the problems they create (Soviet Union: defection; United States: trafficking in dope) within each country. He then explains that in the United States if the inalienable right to self-medication were recognized, as is the inalienable right of a citizen to leave the country, the problem of drug trafficking would be solved. Although not directly stated, you can see that the controlling idea is that laws that deny rights to citizens in dissimilar countries cause crimes in both. The author serves his informative purpose by using specific ideas to show points of likeness and differences in the laws and problems of the countries cited.

Below is another example of comparison and contrast as a method of development:

> Salamanders are superficially similar to lizards, in that they have four legs and a long tail, but the resemblance ends there. Lizards

thrive in tropical or arid regions, whereas most salamanders are confined to moist or aquatic environments in the temperate zones. Lizards have dry, scaly skin; salamanders have moist, slimy skin that supplements their breathing. In fact, one group, known as the woodland salamanders, have no lungs but breathe entirely through their skin.

Lizard eggs have leathery shells and are laid on the land; most salamanders lay gelatinous eggs in the water or in moist places such as under moss or rotting logs. In futher contrast to lizards, salamanders have no claws and are not poisonous, and only a few can bite hard enough to get your attention.

The likenesses and differences between lizards and salamanders are concretely described. The author's purpose is to inform the reader of the likenesses and differences in lizards' and salamanders' physical shape, habitat, description, and skin function (first paragraph) and laying of eggs, presence or absence of claws, and bite (second paragraph). Comparison and contrast allows the writer to distinguish the two reptiles and more clearly describe each.

A final example of the use of comparison and contrast is an excerpt from Arthur Schlesinger's "Shooting: The American Dream."

Now in the third quarter of the twentieth century violence has broken out with new ferocity in our country. What has given our old propensity new life? Why does the fabric of American civility no longer exert restraint? What now incites crazy individuals to act out their murderous dreams? What is it about the climate of this decade that suddenly encourages—that for some evidently legitimatizes—the relish for hate and the resort to violence? Why, according to the Federal Bureau of Investigation, have assaults with a gun increased 77 percent in the four years from 1964 through 1967?

We talk about a legacy of the frontier. No doubt the frontier has bequeathed us a set of romantic obsessions about six-shooters and gunfighters. But why should this legacy suddenly reassert itself in the nineteen sixties? Moreover, Canada and Australia were also frontier societies. Canadians and Australians too have robust, brawling traditions; they too like to strike virile poses. Indeed, the Australians exterminated their aborigines more efficiently than we did our Indians. But Canadians and Australians do not feel the need today to prove themselves by killing people. The homicide rate in Canada and Australia is one quarter that of the United States.

We talk about the tensions of industrial society. No doubt industrial society generates awful tensions. No doubt the ever-quickening pace of social change depletes and destroys the institutions which make for social stability. But this does not explain why Americans shoot and kill so many more Americans than Englishmen kill Englishmen or Japanese kill Japanese. England, Japan and West Germany are, next to the United States, the most heavily industrialized countries in the world. Together they have a population of 214 million people. Among these 214 million, there are 135 gun murders a year. Among the 200 million people of the United States there are 6,500 gun murders a year—about *forty-eight times* as many. Philadelphia alone has about the same number of criminal homicides as England, Scotland and Wales combined—as many in a city of two million (and a city of brotherly love, at that) as in a nation of 45 million. . . .

The National Rifle Association suggests that, if a person wants to commit a murder and does not have a gun, he will find some other way to do it. This proposition is at best dubious and it does not apply at all to the murder of political leaders. No one has ever tried to assassinate a President with a bow and arrow. Every assassination and attempted assassination has been by gun; and, if we could reduce that, we would at least gain something. Still, however, useful in making it harder for potential murderers to get guns, federal gun legislation deals with the symptoms and not with the causes of our trouble. We must go farther to account for the resurgence in recent years of our historical propensity toward violence.

The controlling idea, expressed in the series of questions posed in the first paragraph, explores the author's concern about the resurgence of violence in our society. The second and third paragraphs show the similarities and differences among several frontier and industrial societies, through homicides resulting from the use of guns. This organizational pattern helps persuade the reader that there is something more to account for the renewed violence of recent years in this country. The author expects the reader to be convinced of his point of view because of the comparisons and contrasts made in the development of this thesis.

Comparison and contrast also enables a writer to develop a general idea by means of details that are similar to and/or different from one another. The following selections are samples of the extended use of examples and comparison and contrast as organizational patterns. Each is examined according to "Questions for Determining Controlling Idea, Form, Purpose, and Response."

WHO SAID WILD WOMEN DON'T SING THE BLUES?

Margo Jefferson

The blues, with its 12-bar, 3-line structure, is as intimate and highly charged as a lyric poem, as spare and realistic as a newspaper story. The blues expresses and exorcises trials, tribulations, and survivals. A real folk music, it emerged from the work songs, shouts, chants, and spirituals of slavery. In a tradition that was African and from a necessity that was American, music, both for slaves and the closely watched free blacks, was a vital means of social, political, and personal expression.

The blues form is said to have appeard in the late 19th century, reflecting the psychic—and therefore the musical—changes that Emancipation had brought. There was a new individuality, solitude, and freedom. Work songs and spirituals are group expressions, whatever the singer's distinctiveness; blues are soliloquies, monologues, whatever the group's emotional participation. In its early rural form—sung in doorways, juke joints, alleys, on the roads and on back porches, with moans, slurs, falsetto notes, and rhythmic flexibility playing against simple structure—the blues was as close to speech as to singing. As it took up with other musical styles (vaudeville, Tin Pan Alley balladry, ragtime), it became smoother and more theatricalized, more calculated: formal rather than folk art. It invaded brothels, theaters, cabarets, dance halls, and the growing recording industry. And it was taken there by women.

Much has been made by blues collectors of the rough, itinerant lives of the male singers, as they moved from town to town, taking odd jobs, working, brawling, struggling, never far away from the long arm of the white man's law. But many women did escape from drudgery and domesticity through show business. Traveling circuses minstrel shows, and carnivals offered them adventure, excitement, and—if they were lucky—glamour and fame.

They began young. Gertrude "Ma" Rainey, born in 1886 and considered the link between the older folk style and the sleeker city one, was dancing and singing in minstrel shows by 1900, and performing the blues by 1902. She claimed to have first heard them from a young girl in Missouri who sang an odd, mournful lament about her man's desertion. Ma Rainey paid her tribute to this anonymous woman "composer" in the words of her "Last Minute Blues"': "If anybody asks you who wrote this lonesome song/Tell 'em you don't know the writer, but Ma Rainey put it on."

Blue songs are filled with melancholy portraits of young girls left by parents to make or break their lives as they can. Bessie Smith, born in 1894, and orphaned at the age of nine, sang for small change on the streets of Chattanooga, and joined Ma Rainey's minstrel shows in 1912. Ethel Waters, born in 1900, whose sweet sinuous voice eventually led her into musical theater, left her job as a $4.50-a-week chambermaid in 1917 to join a vaudeville troupe. And Alberta Hunter, the only veteran of the classic blues era still performing regularly, was born in 1895, ran away to Chicago at 11 or 12, began as a potato peeler in a boardinghouse, and within a few years became the "Idol of Dreamland." (Dreamland was the city's smartest black cabaret).

Blues women were flamboyant, commanding, and versatile: their repertoires ranged from "St. Louis Blues" to "Mammy's Little Coal Black Rose" to "A Good Man Is Hard To Find." At at time when popular music was apt to be arch and playful about sex and romance, blues dared to be erotic, frank, and cynical. And, if most popular song protagonists were lively, spanking-clean boys and girls, ladies and gents, blues protagonists were as apt to be prostitutes, drifters, and laundry workers as dashing belles and swells.

Like every blues voice, every blues song is personal, but there is a communal reserve of feelings, phrases, and emotional conventions that all singers drew upon again and again. In no other popular musical form do women chronicle and confront so directly the conditions of what used to be lightly called "the battle of the sexes." Or what is called, somewhat pompously, "existential loneliness"; or clinically, "depression"; or, quite simply, "the cost of living."

Listen to Memphis Minnie's "In My Girlish Days"*:

> I flagged a train,
> Didn't have a dime.
> Trying to run away from
> That home of mine.
> I didn't know no better
> In my girlish days.

Or Ida Cox's "Wild Women Don't Get the Blues"*:

> I've got a disposition
> and a way of my own.
> When my man starts kicking,
> I let him find another home.
> I get full of good liquor,
> walk the streets all night,
> Go home and put my man out,
> if he don't act right.
> 'Cause wild women don't
> worry—wild women don't have
> the blues.

Ma Rainey's ironic "Victim of the Blues"* is:

> Too mad to worry,
> Too mean to cry.
> Too slow to hurry,
> Too good to lie.
> That man he left me,
> Never said good-bye,
> Too old to stay here,
> Too sick to die. . . .

And Alberta Hunter's feisty heroine says "I've Got a Mind"†:

> It's snowing outside,
> my feet are on the ground,
> It's snowing outside
> and my feet are on the ground.
> If I ever want to be somebody,
> sure got to leave this town.
> I'd rather be in Mississippi
> floating like a log,

*publisher unknown
†"I've Got a Mind," ©1950, Alberta Hunter Music. Used by permission.

I'd rather be in the Mississippi
River floating like a log,
Than to be here in New York
Letting these men treat me like a
dog.

1. *Question:* Who or what is the subject of the work?
   Answer: The blues.

2. *Question:* What aspect(s) of the subject are discussed in the work?
   Answer: The form, origin, and development of the blues as a type of American music.

3. *Question:* What does the author want you to understand and remember in general, about the aspects of the subject discussed in the work?
   Answer: Women played an important role in the development of the blues as it became part of the American music. This controlling idea is expressed in the last two sentences of the second paragraph.

4. *Question:* How are the specific ideas presented?
   Answer: The specific ideas are presented by means of examples. The first example is offered in the fourth paragraph. Ma Rainey typifies the youthful female blues singer. The second set of examples in the fifth paragraph is related to the first because these examples are of other girls who, like Ma Rainey, began singing as youngsters. Each of these singers, Bessie Smith, Ethel Waters, and Alberta Hunter, is related by age and humble beginnings. Blues singers' flamboyance, command, and versatility are emphasized by their repertoires. Common themes of blues songs, which are both personal and communal, are exemplified by selected lyrics from four female blues singers' songs which conclude the selection.

   Although there are subtle comparisons made in the first paragraph between the structure of the blues and a lyric poem and the realism of blues and a newspaper and in the second paragraph between male and female blues singers, the predominant organizational pattern is examples.

5. *Question:* How do the examples develop the controlling idea?
   Answer: These examples provide evidence to support the author's claim that women were important to the development of the blues as an American musical art form.

6. *Question:* Does the work emphasize the author, the subject, or the audience?
   Answer: The selection emphasizes the subject and is, therefore, informative.

7. *Question:* What reaction does the author want to elicit?

Answer: The author seems to want the reader to learn more about
              women and the blues through the examples she provides.

Controlling Idea: Women played an important role in the development
of the blues as it became part of the American music.
Form (Organizational Pattern): Examples.
Purpose: To inform.
Reader Response: Learning.

INTELLECT AND INTELLIGENCE

Richard Hofstadter

Before attempting to estimate the qualities in our society that make
intellect unpopular, it seems necessary to say something about what
intellect is usually understood to be. When one hopes to understand
a common prejudice, common usage provides a good place to begin.
Anyone who scans popular American writing with this interest in mind
will be struck by the manifest difference between the idea of intellect
and the idea of intelligence. The first is frequently used as a kind of
epithet, the second never. No one questions the value of intelligence;
as an abstract quality it is universally esteemed, and individuals who
seem to have it in exceptional degree are highly regarded. The man
of intelligence is always praised; the man of intellect is sometimes
also praised, especially when it is believed that intellect involves intelligence, but he is also often looked upon with resentment or suspicion. It is he, and not the intelligent man, who may be called unreliable, superfluous, immoral, or subversive, sometimes he is even
said to be, for all his intellect, unintelligent.[1]

Although the difference between the qualities of intelligence and
intellect is more often assumed than defined, the context of popular
usage makes it possible to extract the nub of the distinction, which
seems to be almost universally understood: intelligence is an excellence of mind that is employed within a fairly narrow, immediate,
and predictable range; it is a manipulative, adjustive, unfailingly
practical quality—one of the most eminent and endearing of the animal virtues. Intelligence works within the framework of limited but
clearly stated goals, and may be quick to shear away questions of
thought that do not seem to help in reaching them. Finally, it is of
such universal use that it can daily be seen at work and admired
alike by simple or complex minds.

Intellect, on the other hand, is the critical, creative, and contemplative side of mind. Whereas intelligence seeks to grasp, manipulate,
reorder, adjust, intellect examines, ponders, wonders, theorizes, crit-

---

[1] I do not want to suggest that this distinction is made only in the United States,
since it seems to be common wherever there is a class that finds intellectuals a nuisance
and yet does not want to throw overboard its own claims to intelligence. Thus, in
France, after the intellectuals had emerged as a kind of social force, one finds Maurice
Barrès writing in 1902: "I'd rather be intelligent than an intellectual." Victor Brombert:
The Intellectual Hero: Studies in the French Novel. 1880–1955 (Philadelphia, 1961),
p. 25.

icizes, imagines. Intelligence will seize the immediate meaning in a situation and evaluate it. Intellect evaluates evaluations, and looks for the meanings of situations as a whole. Intelligence can be praised as a quality in animals; intellect, being a unique manifestation of human dignity, is both praised and assailed as quality in men. When the difference is so defined, it becomes easier to understand why we sometimes say that a mind of admittedly penetrating intelligence is relatively unintellectual; and why, by the same token, we see among minds that are unmistakably intellectual a considerable range of intelligence.

This distinction may seem excessively abstract, but it is frequently illustrated in American culture. In our education, for example, it has never been doubted that the selection and development of intelligence is a goal of central importance; but the extent to which education should foster intellect has been a matter of the most heated controversy, and the opponents of intellect in most spheres of public education have exercised preponderant power. But perhaps the most impressive illustration arises from a comparison of the American regard for inventive skill as opposed to skill in pure science. Our greatest inventive genius, Thomas A. Edison, was all but canonized by the American public, and a legend has been built around him. One cannot, I suppose, expect that achievements in pure science would receive the same public applause that came to inventions as spectacular and as directly influential on ordinary life as Edison's. But one might have expected that our greatest genius in pure science, Josiah Willard Gibbs, who laid the theoretical foundations for modern physical chemistry, would have been a figure of some comparable acclaim among the educated public. Yet Gibbs, whose work was celebrated in Europe, lived out his life in public and even professional obscurity at Yale, where he taught for thirty-two years. Yale, which led American universities in its scientific achievements during the nineteenth century, was unable in those thirty-two years to provide him with more than a half dozen or so graduate students who could understand his work, and never took the trouble to award him an honorary degree. . . .

1. *Question:* Who or what is the subject of the work?

   Answer: Intellect.

2. *Question:* What aspect of the subject is discussed in the work?

   Answer: The manifest difference between the idea of intellect and the idea of intelligence.

3. *Question:* What does the author want you to understand and remember, in general, about the aspect of the subject discussed in the work?

   Answer: That it is necessary to understand what is generally meant by the word *intellect* before attempting to consider the characteristics of our society that make intellect unpopular. This controlling idea is introduced in the first three sentences of the first paragraph.

4. *Question:* How are the specific ideas presented?

   Answer: The specific ideas are presented in a comparison-and-contrast pattern. Starting with the fourth sentence of the first paragraph, the author contrasts the words *intellect* and *intelligence* and then compares the praise each receives. In the second and third paragraph, the author defines each term and contrasts the two by comparing each definition with the other. In the fourth paragraph he gives concrete examples of two men, Thomas Edison and Josiah Willard Gibbs. By comparing the public's reactions to them, the author can compare and contrast inventive skill (intelligence) and skill in pure science (intellect) in a more tangible way. All of these examples are related. The examination of the two words in the first paragraph prepares the way for the definitions provided in the second and third paragraphs, and the definitions lead to the study of the two men as representative examples of each kind of thinker.

5. *Question:* How does the author develop the controlling idea?

   Answer: The author uses the similarity and dissimilarity between intellect and intelligence to explain and support his position that there are demonstrated differences between the two. These differences make intellect unpopular because our society seems to respect and reward intelligence much more often than it does intellect.

6. *Question:* Does the work emphasize the author, the subject, or the audience?

   Answer: The focus of the work is the subject; therefore, its purpose is informative.

7. *Question:* How does the author want the reader to respond to the work?

   Answer: The author seems to want the reader to learn about intellect by comparing and contrasting its qualities, characteristics, definitions, and examples with those of intelligence. This knowledge, in turn, will help explain the author's claim that intellect is unpopular.

Controlling Idea: It is necessary to understand what is generally meant by the word *intellect* before attempting to consider the characteristics of our society that make it unpopular.

Form (Organizational Pattern): Comparison and contrast.

Purpose: To inform.

Reader response: Learning.

Use these seven questions as you practice recognizing various organizational patterns in the materials you read. Their use will improve your comprehension of what you read and help you decide about what you write.

Exercises

1. Read each of the following selections, identify the pattern—example or comparison and contrast—and indicate the purpose—expressive, informative, persuasive.

a. WHY CAN'T COMPUTERS BE MORE LIKE US?

Lewis Thomas

Everyone must have had at least one personal experience with a computer error by this time. Bank balances are suddenly reported to have jumped from 379 dollars into the millions, appeals for charitable contributions are mailed over and over to people with crazy-sounding names at your address, utility companies write that they're turning everything off—that sort of thing. If you manage to get in touch with someone and complain, you then get instantaneously typed, guilty letters from the same computer, saying, "Our computer was in error, and an adjustment is being made in your account."

These are supposed to be the sheerest, blindest accidents. Mistakes are not believed to be part of the normal behavior of a good machine. If things go wrong, it must be a personal, human error, the result of fingering, tampering, a button getting stuck. The computer, at its normal best, is infallible.

I wonder whether this can be true. After all, the whole point of computers is that they represent an extension of the human brain, vastly improved upon but nontheless human, superhuman maybe. A good computer can think clearly and quickly enough to beat you at chess, and some of them have even been programmed to write obscure verse. They can do anything we can do, and more besides.

It is not yet known whether a computer has its own consciousness, it would be hard to find out about this. When you walk into one of those great halls now built for the huge machines, and stand listening, it is easy to imagine that the faint, distant noises are the sound of thinking, and the turning of the spools gives them the look of wild creatures rolling their eyes in the effort to concentrate, choking with information. But real thinking, and dreaming, are other matters.

On the other hand, the evidences for something like an *unconscious*, equivalent to ours, are all around, in every mail. As extensions of the human brain, they have been constructed with the same property of error, spontaneous,uncontrolled, and rich in possibilities.

Mistakes are at the very base of human thought, embedded there, feeding the structure like root nodules. If we were not provided with the knack of being wrong, we could never get anything useful done. We think our way along by choosing between right and wrong alternatives, and the wrong choices have to be made as frequently as the right ones. We get along in life this way. We are built to make mistakes, coded for error.

We learn, as we say, by "trial and error." Why do we always say that? Why not "trial and rightness," or "trial and triumph"? The old phrase puts it that way because that is, in real life, the way it is done.

A good laboratory, like a good bank, or a corporation or a government, has to run like a computer. Almost everything is done flawlessly, by the book, and all the numbers add up to the predicted sums. The days go by. And then, if it is a lucky day, and a lucky laboratory, somebody makes a mistake: the wrong buffer, something in one of the blanks, a decimal misplaced in reading counts, the warm room off by a degreee and half, a mouse out of his box, or just a misreading of the day's protocol. Whatever, when the results come in, something is obviously screwed up, and then the action can begin.

The misreading is not the important error; it opens the way. The next step is the crucial one. If the investigator can bring himself to say, "But even so, look at that!" the new finding, whatever it is, is ready for snatching. What is needed, for progress to be made, is the move based on the error.

Whenever new kinds of thinking are about to be accomplished, or new varieties of music, there has to be an argument beforehand. With two sides debating in the same mind, haranguing, there is an amiable understanding that one is right and the other wrong. Sooner or later the thing is settled, but there can be no action at all if there are not the two sides, and the argument. The hope is in the faculty of wrongness, the tendency toward error. The capacity to leap across mountains of information to land lightly on the wrong side represents the highest of human endowments.

We are at our human finest, dancing with our minds, when there are more choices than two. This process is called exploration and is based on human fallibility. If we had only a single center in our brains, capable of responding only when a correct decision was to be made, instead of the jumble of different, credulous, easily conned clusters of neurons that provide for being flung off into blind alleys, up wrong trees, down dead ends, out into blue sky, along wrong turnings, around bends, we could only stay the way we are today, stuck fast.

The lower animals do not have this splendid freedom. They are limited, most of them, to absolute infallibility. Fish are flawless in everything they do. Individual cells in a tissue are mindless machines, perfect in their performance, as absolutely inhuman as bees.

We should have this mind as we become dependent on more complex computers for the arrangement of our affairs. Give the computers their heads, I say; let them go their way. Your average good computer can make calculations in an instant that would take a lifetime of slide rules for any of us. Think of what we could gain from the near infinity of precise, machine-made miscomputation that is now so easily within grasp. We could begin the solving of some of our hardest problems. What we need for moving ahead is a set of wrong alternatives much longer and more interesting than the short list of mistaken courses that any of us can think up right now. We need, in fact, an infinite list, and when it is printed out we need the computer to turn on itself and select, at random, the next way to go. If it is a big enough mistake, we could find ourselves on a new level, out in the clear, ready to move again.

b. OF MARRIAGE AND SINGLE LIFE

Francis Bacon

He that hath wife and children hath given hostages to fortune; for they are impediments to great enterprises, either of virtue or mischief. Certainly the best works, and of greatest merit for the public, have proceeded from the unmarried or childless men, which both in affection and means have married and endowed the public. Yet it were great reason that those that have children should have greatest care of future times, unto which they know they must transmit their dearest pledges. Some there are who, though they lead a single life, yet their thoughts do end with themselves, and account future times impertinences. Nay, there are some other that account wife and children but as bills of charges. Nay more, there are some foolish rich covetous men that take a pride in having no children, because they may be thought so much the richer. For perhaps they have heard some talk, "Such an one is a great rich man," and another except to it, "Yea, but he hath a great charge for children"; as if it were an abatement to his riches. But the most ordinary cause of a single life is liberty, especially in certain self-pleasing and humorous minds, which are so sensible of every restraint, as they will go near to think their girdles and garters to be bonds and shackles. Unmarried men are best friends, best masters, best servants, but not always best subjects, for they are light to run away, and almost all fugitives are of that condition. A single life doth well with churchmen, for charity will hardly water the ground where it must first fill a pool. It is indifferent for judges and magistrates, for if they be facile and corrupt, you shall have a servant five times worse than a wife. For soldiers, I find the generals commonly in their hortatives put men in mind of their wives and children; and I think the despising of marriage amongst the Turks maketh the vulgar soldier more base. Certainly wife and children are a kind of discipline of humanity; and single men, though they be many times more charitable, because their means are less exhaust, yet, on the other side, they are more cruel and hard-hearted (good to make severe inquisitors), because their tenderness is not so oft called upon. Grave natures, led by custom, and therefore constant are commonly loving husbands, as was said of Ulysses, *Vetulam suam proetulit immortalitati*. Chaste women are often proud and forward, as presuming upon the merit of their chastity. It is one of the best bonds, both of chastity an obedience, in the wife if she think her husband wise, which she will never do if she find him jealous. Wives are young men's mistresses, companions for middle age, and old men's nurses, so as a man may have a quarrel to marry when he will. But yet he was reputed one of the wise men that made answer to the question when a man should marry: "A young man not yet, an elder man not at all." It is often seen that bad husbands have very good wives; whether it be that it raiseth the price of their husbands' kindness when it comes, or that the wives take a pride in their patience. But this never fails, if the bad husbands were of their own choosing, against their friends' consent; for then they will be sure to make good their own folly.

c. WINTER AND SUMMER

Henry Adams

Boys are wild animals, rich in the treasures of sense, but the New England boy had a wider range of emotions than boys of more equable climates. He felt his nature crudely, as it was meant. To the boy Henry Adams, summer was drunken. Among senses, smell was the strongest—smell of hot pine-woods and sweet-fern in the scorching summer noon; of new-mown hay; of ploughed earth; of box hedges, of peaches, lilacs, syringas; of stables, barns cow-yards; of salt water and low tide on the marshes; nothing came amiss. Next to smell came taste, and the children knew the taste of everything they saw or touched from pennyroyal and flagroot to the shell of pignut and the letters of a spelling book—the taste of A-B, AB, suddenly revived on the boy's tongue sixty years afterwards. Light, line, and color as sensual pleasures, came later and were as crude as the rest. The New England light is glare, and the atmosphere harshens color. The boy was a full man before he ever knew what was meant by atmosphere; his idea of pleasure in light was the blaze of a New England sun. His idea of color was a peony, with the dew of early morning on its petals. The intense blue of the sea, as he saw it a mile or two away, from the Quincy hills; the cumuli in a June afternoon sky; the strong reds and greens and purples of colored prints and children's picture-books, as the American colors then ran; these were ideals. The opposites or antipathies, were the cold grays of November evenings, and the thick, muddy thaws of Boston winter. With such standards, the Bostonian could not but develop a double nature. Life was a double thing. After a January blizzard, the boy who could look with pleasure into the violent snow-glare of the cold white sunshine, with its intense light and shade, scarcely knew what was meant by tone. He could reach it only by education.

Winter and summer, then, were two hostile lives, and bred two separate natures. Winter was always the effort to live; summer was tropical license. Whether the children rolled in the grass, or waded in the brook, or swam in the salt ocean, or sailed in the bay, or fished for smelts in the creeks, or netted minnows in the salt-marshes, or took to the pine-woods and the granite quarries, or chased muskrats and hunted snapping-turtles in the swamps, or mushrooms or nuts on the autumn hills, summer and country were always sensual living, while winter was always compulsory learning. Summer was the multiplicity of nature; winter was school.

The bearing of the two seasons on the education of Henry Adams was so fancy; it was the most decisive force he ever knew; it ran through life, and made the division between its perplexing, warring, irreconcilable problems, irreducible opposites, with growing emphasis to the last year of study. From earliest childhood the boy was accustomed to feel that, for him, life was double. Winter and summer, town and country, law and liberty, were hostile, and the man who pretended they were not, was in his eyes a schoolmaster—that is, a man employed to tell lies to little boys. Though Quincy was but two hours' walk from Beacon Hill, it belonged in a different world. For two hundred years, every Adams, from father to son, had lived within sight of State Street, and sometimes had lived in it, yet none had ever taken kindly to the town, or been taken kindly by it. The boy inherited his double nature. He knew as yet nothing about his great-grandfather, who had died a dozen years before his own birth: he took for granted that any great-grandfather of his must have always been good, and his enemies wicked, but he divined his grant-grandfather's character from his own. Never for a moment did he connect the two ideas of Boston and John Adams; they were separate and antagonistic; the idea of John Adams went with Quincy. He knew his grandfather John Quincy Adams only as an old man of seventy-five or eighty who was friendly and gentle with him, but except that he heard his grandfather always called "the President," and his grandmother, "the Madam," he had no reason to suppose that his Adams grandfather differed in character from his Brooks grandfather who was equally kind and benevolent. He liked the Adams side best, but for no other reason than that it reminded him of the country, the summer, and the absence of restraint. Yet he felt also that Quincy was in a way inferior to Boston, and that socially Boston looked down on Quincy. The reason was clear enough even to a five-year-old child. Quincy had no Boston style. Little enough style had either; a simpler manner of life and thought could hardly exist, short of cave-dwelling. The flint-and-steel with which his grandfather Adams used to light his own fires in the early morning was still on the mantelpiece of his study. The idea of a livery or even a dress for servants, or of an evening toilette, was next to blasphemy. Bathrooms, water-supplies, lighting, heating, and the whole array of domestic comforts, were unknown at Quincy. Boston had already a bathroom a water-supply, a furnace, and gas. The superiority of Boston was evident, but a child liked it no better for that.

The magnificence of his grandfather Brooks's house in Pearl Street or South Street has long ago disappeared, but perhaps his country house at Medford may still remain to show what impressed the mind of a boy in 1845 with the idea of city splendor. The President's place at Quincy was the larger and older and far the more interesting of the two; but a boy felt at once its inferiority in fashion.

It showed plainly enough its want of wealth. It smacked of colonial age, but not of Boston style or plush curtains. To the end of his life he never quite overcame the prejudice thus drawn in with his childish breath. He never could compel himself to care for nineteenth-century style. He was never able to adopt it, any more than his father or grandfather or great-grandfather had done. Not that he felt it as particularly hostile, for he reconciled himself to much that was worse; but because, for some remote reason, he was born an eighteenth-century child. The old house at Quincy was eighteenth century. What style it had was in its Queen Anne mahogany panels and its Louis Seize chairs and sofas. The panels belonged to an old colonial Vassall who built the house; the furniture had been brought back from Paris in 1789 or 1801 or 1817, along with porcelain and books and much else of old diplomatic remnants; and neither of the two eighteenth-century styles—neither English Queen Anne nor French Louis Seize—was comfortable for a boy, or for any else. The dark mahogany had been painted white to suit daily life in winter gloom. Nothing seemed to favor, for a child's objects, the older forms. On the contrary, most boys, as well as grown-up people, preferred the new, with good reason, and the child felt himself distinctly at a disadvantage for the taste.

Nor had personal preference any share in his bias. The Brooks grandfather was as amiable and as sympathetic as the Adams grandfather. Both were born in 1767, and both died in 1848. Both were kind to children, and both belonged rather to the eighteenth than to the nineteenth centuries. The child knew no difference between them except that one was associated with winter and the other with summer; one with Boston, the other with Quincy. Even with Medford, the association was hardly easier. Once as a very young boy he was taken to pass a few days with his grandfather Brooks under charge of his aunt, but became so violently homesick that within twenty-four hours he was brought back in disgrace. Yet he could not remember ever being seriously homesick again.

The attachment to Quincy was not altogether sentimental or wholly sympathetic. Quincy was not a bed of thornless roses. Even there the curse of Cain set its mark. There as elsewhere a cruel universe combined to crush a child. As though three or four vigorous brothers and sisters, with the best will, were not enough to crush any child, every one else conspired towards an education which he hated. From cradle to grave this problem of running order through chaos, direction through space, discipline through freedom, unity through multiplicity, has always been, and must always be, the task of education, as it is the moral of religion, philosophy, science, art, politics, and economy; but a boy's will is his life, and he dies when it is broken, as the colt dies in harness, taking a new nature in becoming tame. Rarely has the boy felt kindly towards his tamers. Between him and his master has always been war. Henry Adams never knew a boy of his generation to like a master, and the task of remaining on friendly terms with one's own family, in such a relation, was never easy.

All the more singular it seemed afterwards to him that his first serious contact with the President should have been a struggle of will, in which the old man almost necessarily defeated the boy, but instead of leaving, as usual in such defeats, a lifelong sting, left rather an impression of as fair treatment as could be expected from a natural enemy. The boy met seldom with such restraint. He could not have been much more than six years old at the time—seven at the utmost—and his mother had taken him to Quincy for a long stay with the President during the summer. What became of the rest of the family he quite forgot; but he distinctly remembered standing at the house door one summer morning in a passionate outburst of rebellion against going to school. Naturally his mother was the immediate victim of his rage; that is what mothers are for, and boys also; but in this case the boy had his mother at unfair disadvantage, for she was a guest, and had no means of enforcing obedience. Henry showed a certain tactical ability by refusing to start, and he met all efforts at compulsion by successful, though too vehement protest. He was in fair way to win, and was holding his own, with sufficient energy, at the bottom of the long staircase which led up to the door of the President's library, when the door opened, and the old man slowly came down. Putting on his hat, he took the boy's hand without a word, and walked with him, paralyzed by awe, up the road to the town. After the first moments of consternation at this interference in a domestic dispute, the boy reflected that an old gentleman close on eighty would never trouble himself to walk near a mile on a hot summer morning over a shadeless road to take a boy to school, and that it would be strange if a lad imbued with the passion of freedom could not find a corner to dodge around, somewhere before reaching the school door. Then and always, the boy insisted that this reasoning justified his apparent submission; but the old man did not stop, and the boy saw all his strategical points turned, one after another, until he found himself seated inside the school, and obviously the centre of curious if not malevolent criticism. Not till then did the President release his hand and depart.

The point was that this act, contrary to the inalienable rights of boys, and nullifying the social compact, ought to have made him dislike his grandfather for life. He could not recall that it had this effect even for a moment. With a certain maturity of mind, the child must have recognized that the President, though a tool of tyranny, had done his disreputable work with a certain intelligence. He had shown no temper, no irritation, no personal feeling, and had made no display of force. Above all, he had held his tongue. During their long walk he had said nothing; he had uttered no syllable of revolting cant about the duty of obedience and the wickedness of resistance to law; he had shown no concern in the matter; hardly even a consciousness of the boy's existence. Probably his mind at that moment was actually troubling itself little about his grandson's iniquities, and much about the iniquities of President Polk, but the boy could scarcely at that age feel the whole satisfaction of thinking that President Polk was to be the vicarious victim of his own sins, and he gave his grand-father credit for intelligent silence. For this forbearance he felt instinctive respect. He admitted force as a form of right; he admitted even temper, under protest; but the seeds of moral education would at that moment have fallen on the stoniest soil in Quincy, which is, as every one knows, the stoniest glacial and tidal drift known in any Puritan land.

chapter 9
Writing: Examples and Comparison and Contrast

In good writing, the structure should relate the points you make both to one another and to your controlling idea. The last chapter presented two standard organizational patterns—examples and comparison and contrast. But aside from exercises or paper assignments, you will rarely be asked to write in a specific pattern; moreover, you will not ordinarily sit down to compose a comparison-and-contrast essay. Rather, the decision to choose an organizational pattern depends on a variety of other decisions, including your choice of ideas, audience, and purpose. Nonetheless, in order to write well, you need to be able to control the various patterns available to you. You can learn this control by identifying these patterns when you read and by practicing them in writing exercises.

Discovering Form

Any organizational strategy for writing means establishing a relationship between a generalization and specific details that illustrate, expand, and refine that generalization, or controlling idea.

You should begin by thinking about your topic and then consider your audience and purpose. This should lead to the formation of a general or controlling idea. Individual ideas you discover early in the composing process provide the details you will need to develop your controlling idea. Your task at this point, is to shape these specifics into a pattern that will demonstrate their relationship to your controlling idea, your purpose, and your sense of audience.

You should also realize that writing is not a rigid step-by-step process; rather, the steps often overlap. In particular, you will continue to discover new ideas while you write. But once you have decided on a pattern, you can easily fit them into it.

We shall begin with the two patterns discussed in the last chapter and demonstrate how they can structure details, either as a series of examples or as a form of comparison and/or contrast.

Examples

The most obvious pattern for organizing details is a series of examples, each of which illustrates the controlling idea. Such an organization is flexible and permits the writer to include a variety of details, but that flexibility should not prevent the writer from somehow relating these examples to one another.

Suppose your topic concerns domestic pets. You could begin by asking yourself, What are domestic pets? The answer to that question might produce the following: Domestic pets are animals that can be kept in the home. Then ask, What kinds of animals are domestic pets? And answer with a list: dogs, cats, birds, fish, certain reptiles, certain rodents, and the like. This list should suggest the details for an essay on pets. A sense of purpose and audience will determine what you will do with this list, that is, which items you will include, exclude, or expand.

Let us suppose that you decide on an informative purpose for this essay and that you limit yourself to a discussion of dogs. You define your audience as those people who might be considering the purchase of a pet but who do not know much about dogs.

Because your purpose is informative, you will want to communicate information to your audience and because your audience can be assumed to be interested in but not knowledgeable about your topic, you will want to present ideas and facts to them. The purpose and audience together might shape a controlling idea such as the following: Different types of dogs will suit the different life-styles of prospective owners. This controlling idea will limit your approach to the topic, and so all of the details will relate directly to the proposition that the most suitable type of dog depends on the particular owner.

Suppose in your initial generation of ideas about dogs, you discover the following:

- Some dogs love to roam outdoors.
- Some dogs are happy in a small area.
- Large dogs often have quiet dispositions.
- Smaller dogs are sometimes feisty and combative.
- Some dogs, such as sheep dogs, require a lot of grooming.
- Dogs need to be exercised and given opportunities to relieve themselves.
- A dog's personality can complement or clash with its owner's.

Your controlling idea, however, demands another list, one that outlines the different life-styles of prospective owners:

- A person living alone often keeps irregular hours.
- Some people have inflexible schedules based on work, school, or domestic responsibilities.
- Some people are very concerned about appearances.
- Other people are less concerned about appearances and more interested in emotional qualities.
- Some prospective owners are lonely.
- Others are very outgoing.

Now you need to organize these details into a pattern that will support your controlling idea. If you combine the two lists, you can isolate certain characteristics that seem to complement one another:

- Type of environment.
- Flexibility of schedule.
- Temperament.

For each of these characteristics, the details from both lists can be fit into a pattern that develops the controlling idea:

1. Type of environment: matches types of dogs to the size and location of the owner's residence.
2. Flexibility of schedule: matches the owner's daily routine to the dog's needs.
3. Temperament: explores the disposition of the owners and the dogs that would be best suited to them.

For instance, the type of dwelling in which the owner lives is one variable that may determine what type of dog is chosen. You can divide type of dwelling into apartments, houses, urban, suburban, rural, and so on. In effect, you are breaking down each example into more detail so that you can arrive at a controlling idea for a paragraph. A controlling idea for a paragraph is called a *topic sentence*, and it governs the details in a paragraph. For this paragraph, a topic sentence could be: A dog should be comfortable in its environment. This topic sentence can help you discover additional details. In this way, as you write, you can integrate new ideas into an efficient and well-defined structure. Perhaps as you begin to write this paragraph, you may think of the following:

- Different-sized dogs require more or less room.
- Dog and owner must be able to share the same space comfortably.
- The dog's natural environment should be considered.

A paragraph that uses these ideas might be something like the following:

> Most dogs can adapt fairly well to their owner's environment, but certain considerations should be kept in mind. For example, very

large dogs, such as Saint Bernards, probably should not be cooped up in a tiny apartment. These dogs need to be able to stretch themselves every once in a while, and, if there is not enough space for them to maneuver comfortably, they might do serious damage to the furniture, guests, and the owner's nervous system. On the other hand, very small dogs, such as toy poodles or chihuahuas, might even be intimidated by too much space. Furthermore, although dogs can tolerate a wide range of environments, it might be unwise to place them in a situation that is extremely different from that in which they normally live. The heavy coat of a malamute, for example, might make it uncomfortable in a subtropical or desert climate. Less obviously, many breeds have been conditioned to retrieve game from rivers and lakes, and such dogs would probably feel better if they could occasionally splash around in some water. And seeing a dog enjoying itself, particularly in a spontaneous and natural way, is one of the joys of dog ownership.

This paragraph includes the ideas from the earlier list, along with others suggested by association and the need for illustrative detail discovered while writing. Each of these ideas demonstrates how dog and owner can share the same living space. The paragraph itself states the essay's controlling idea, namely, that the owner's life-style is a factor in choosing a particular type of dog as a pet. Here, the example focuses on the owner's residence as an important component of the life-style.

The second example discusses the owner's schedule, which requires more thought than does the size of a dog in relationship to the size of the owner's dwelling. For example, you could mention that different dogs are more or less dependent on their owner's presence, and therefore, the owner's schedule should be considered.

Topic Sentence: Different breeds of dogs require different amounts of affection from their owners.

Thinking about this topic sentence might generate the following ideas:

- Certain breeds seem to share personality traits.
- However, individual differences might be more significant.
- Dogs' personalities can often be ascertained by observing their parents.
- Owners should determine what kind of dog personality will be most complementary to their own scheduling needs.
- An owner with a settled routine has many options.
- But an owner with an unsettled routine should consider a dog with an independent nature.

A paragraph based on this topic sentence and these ideas might be something like the following:

Before buying a dog, the prospective owner should decide what kind of personality his or her pet should have, in order to blend in with the owner's schedule. Some dogs are more tied to their owners than are others, and such a dog would probably do better in a more settled routine. Other dogs are more independent and do not seem to mind as much being left alone. A dog's independence or dependence derives either from its breed or from characteristics inherited from its sire or dam, or perhaps a combination of both. Some experts believe that certain breeds, such as poodles, are more intelligent than are other breeds or that some are friendlier, such as hounds. Other experts, however, maintain that each dog has individual characteristics, shaped largely by the qualities of its parents. A middle ground between these positions can be found, though, as most dog owners agree that personality traits, whether or not common to the breed, are passed from the parents to the puppy. Therefore, buying a dog from a breeder is a good idea because the sire or dam would probably be available for inspection. In such a case, the buyer could see whether he or she would want to own the adult dog and whether it would fit his or her life-style and then be fairly sure that the puppy would be suitable. In particular, it would be possible to observe whether the adult dog has an even temperament or is nervous. It would be unwise for an owner whose schedule demands irregular hours to buy a puppy whose sire or dam appears nervous and high-strung, as such a puppy might require the security of a more stable environment.

This third example discusses the dog's temperament and how it relates to that of the prospective owner. In some ways, this focus is similar to that of the previous example, but it can easily be broadened so that it grows from the second instead of repeating it. For this part of the essay, you might generate the following ideas:

- People buy pets to fulfill some need, such as companionship or affection.
- Different people have different needs.
- Different dogs have different temperaments.
- Dogs will adjust, to an extent, to their owners, but certain character traits cannot be changed.
- A mismatch between owner personality and dog temperament will sour the experience for both parties.
- A match, on the other hand, will lead to a very comfortable life together.

These could produce the following topic sentence for a paragraph: It is important for the dog's temperament to blend with that of the owner.

In turn, this topic sentence could organize a paragraph such as the following:

Because people buy a pet to fulfill some need, such as companionship or affection, it is important for the dog's temperament to blend with that of the owner. A person who is outgoing and fun loving will want a dog of similar disposition, one that will match its owner's good spirits. On the other hand, a more reserved individual might be better off with a quiet and dignified pet. Imagine the sociable owner whose dog runs under the bed when company arrives or the dignified owner who has to tolerate the excessive friendliness of an overly affectionate pet. In either case, the dog and owner will conflict with each other, and neither will be happy. Whatever method of selection is employed, either judging by breed characteristics or inspecting a puppy along with its sire and dam, the prospective owner should make every effort to choose a dog whose temperament will match his or her own.

If we now look at the whole essay, with the introductory and concluding paragraphs added, we will see how each example develops and defines the controlling idea:

Each year thousands of people decide to buy a dog as a pet because dogs can be marvelous companions. However, buying a dog involves many responsibilities and choices for the owner. Chief among these choices is deciding what kind of dog will best suit a particular owner: more specifically, the owner's environment, schedule, and temperament should be considered before a dog is purchased.

Most dogs can adapt fairly well to their owners' environment, but certain considerations should be kept in mind. For example, very large dogs, such as Saint Bernards, probably should not be cooped up in a tiny apartment. These dogs need to be able to stretch themselves every once in a while, and if there is not enough space for them to maneuver comfortably, they might do serious damage to the furniture, guests, and the owner's nervous system. On the other hand, very small dogs, such as toy poodles or chihuahuas, might even be intimidated by too much space. Furthermore, although dogs can tolerate a wide range of environments, it might be unwise to place them in a situation that is extremely different from that in which they normally live. The heavy coat of a malamute, for example, might make it uncomfortable in a subtropical or desert climate. Less obviously, many breeds have been conditioned to retrieve game from rivers and lakes, and such dogs would probably feel better if they could occasionally splash around in some water. And seeing a dog enjoying itself, particularly in a spontaneous and natural way, is one of the joys of dog ownership.

Before buying a dog, a prospective owner should determine the kind of personality that his or her pet should have, in order to blend in with the owner's schedule. Some dogs are more tied to their owners than are others, and such a dog would probably do better in a more settled routine. Other dogs are more independent and do not seem to mind being left alone as much. A dog's independence or dependence derives either from its breed or from characteristics inherited from its sire or dam, or perhaps a combination of both. Some experts believe that certain breeds, such as poodles, are more intelligent than are other breeds or that some are friendlier, such as hounds. Other experts, however, maintain that each dog has individual characteristics, shaped largely by the qualities of its parents. A middle ground between these positions can be found, though, as most dog owners would agree that personality traits, whether or not common to the breed, are passed from dam and/or sire to puppy. Therefore, buying a dog from a breeder is a good idea because the sire or dam would probably be available for inspection. In such a case, the buyer could see whether he or she would want to own the adult dog and whether it would fit his or her life-style and then be fairly sure that the puppy will be suitable. In particular, it would be possible to observe whether the adult dog has an even temperament or is nervous. It would be unwise for an owner whose schedule demands irregular hours to buy a puppy whose father or mother appears nervous and high-strung. Such a puppy might require the security of a more stable environment.

Because people buy a pet to fulfill some need, such as companionship or affection, it is important for the dog's temperament to blend with that of the owner. A person who is outgoing and fun loving will want a dog of similar disposition, one that will match its owner's good spirits. On the other hand, a more reserved individual might be better off with a quiet and dignified pet. Imagine the sociable owner whose dog runs under the bed when company arrives or the dignified owner who has to tolerate the excessive friendliness of an overly affectionate pet. In either case, dog and owner will conflict with each other, and neither will be happy. Whatever method of selection is employed, either judging by breed characteristics or inspecting a puppy along with its sire and dam, the prospective owner should make every effort to choose a dog whose temperament will match his or her own.

If these factors are kept in mind, the owner will purchase a dog who will provide many years of happiness, and the dog will be living in a comfortable environment with an owner who appreciates the dog's disposition and character, and this match will ensure a good life together.

Comparison and Contrast

A more structured organizational strategy is to point out the similarities and differences between two things in the hope that by so doing each can be presented more clearly. Comparing and contrasting is, of course, a common human activity, governing choices that can range from deciding on one toothpaste instead of another to selecting a college or career. And, as with all writing, purpose and audience shape the final arrangement of details.

Suppose that instead of writing only about dogs, as in the previous section, you choose instead to compare and contrast dogs with cats. Further, you want to explore the qualities of each animal as a pet. It is natural in the comparison-and-contrast process to conclude that one of the things under discussion is superior in some or even most respects. Therefore, though both expressive and informative purposes are certainly available, you can profitably select the persuasive mode to develop this topic.

Begin with some ideas in response to the following questions:

How do dogs and cats compare; that is, how are they similar?
- Both are four-legged domestic animals.
- Both are reasonably intelligent.
- Both require the care of their owner.
- Both are generally permitted to roam around the house.

How do dogs and cats contrast; that is, how are they different?
- Dogs must be walked or let out regularly to relieve themselves.
- Cats can relieve themselves indoors in kitty litter boxes.
- Dogs generally are more affectionate and attached to their owners than cats are.
- Cats generally are more independent than dogs are.
- Dogs can be useful guardians of property.
- Cats are not often successful in this role.
- Dogs require grooming.
- Cats groom themselves.

Comparison-and-contrast essays usually are organized in either the block method or the alternating method. The block method describes the characteristics of one of the items being compared or contrasted and then presents the qualities of the other. In the alternating method, the qualities or characteristics of each item are matched, and then the details are applied to first one and then the other of the two items.

These patterns can be illustrated in the following outlines:

Block Method
  I. Item One
    A. Quality X
    B. Quality Y
    C. Quality Z
 II. Item Two
    A. Quality X
    B. Quality Y
    C. Quality Z

Alternating Method
  I. Quality X
    A. Item One
    B. Item Two

II. Quality Y
   A. Item One
   B. Item Two
III. Quality Z
   A. Item One
   B. Item Two

For the comparison-and-contrast essay on dogs and cats, it would be useful to concentrate on the points of contrast: because your purpose is persuasive, it will be these differences that will indicate why you prefer one pet to the other.

Let us suppose that you will try to persuade your audience that dogs make better pets than do cats. From your list of similarities, you can see that two qualities support this assertion: affection and protection. And with a little imagination, a dog's need to be walked can be seen as an advantage to owning a dog rather than a cat.

A full outline for this essay in block pattern could be the following:

Controlling Idea: Although dogs and cats are similar in many ways, dogs make better pets.

   I. Introduction
  II. Cats
      A. Cats are independent.
      B. Cats do not need to be walked.
      C. Cats do not provide much protection.
 III. Dogs
      A. Dogs are affectionate.
      B. Dogs provide an opportunity for exercise and sharing.
      C. Dogs protect their owners.
  IV. Conclusion

It is a good idea in a persuasive essay to discuss the least favorable item first so that your reader's last impression will be the more positive ideas associated with the item being endorsed.

An essay written according to this outline might be the following:

> Both dogs and cats are common domestic pets because both are intelligent and both can live comfortably in the owner's dwelling. Moreover, to a greater or lesser degree, both dogs and cats require care from the owner, and that requirement, because it gives the owner an opportunity to express affection for the pet, is one of the main reasons to own a pet. However, despite their similarities, dogs and cats differ in important respects.
>
> Cats are much more independent than are dogs. Although this may seem like a virtue, upon closer examination, it may be found to be a liability. If giving and receiving affection is a major reason for pet ownership, then cats are woefully deficient in this regard. It is not uncommon for a cat to scorn its owner's attention, and it is not

unusual for a cat to stroll away with an almost tangible look of contempt on its face at just the moment its owner decides to scratch its ears or rub its back. Further, cats delight in refusing to come on command, choosing instead to structure their interactions with their owners according to their own needs and feelings, and these center almost exclusively on their feeding time.

Cat lovers often point out that their pets do not require walking, that they can easily be trained to relieve themselves in a kitty litter box. However, this seeming advantage is not an unqualified blessing. First, the litter box must be placed somewhere in the house, the "litter" must be disposed of, and there is a reason that the manufacturers of kitty litter advertise how sanitary and odorless their products are.

Although cat advocates will argue for the advantages described above, no cat lover will seriously suggest that cats provide much protection for personal property. Cats do not bark at intruders and are not inclined to attack strangers in any meaningful way. A hiss or an arched back is not going to give many burglars pause or reason to reconsider entering a dwelling.

Though not nearly as independent as cats, dogs are far more affectionate. Most dogs find happiness in greeting their owners and in being near them when both human and animal are in the house at the same time. Dogs show affection much more openly than do cats. Give a dog a little attention, and you will be rewarded by a wagging tail, a lick of the tongue, and eyes filled with warmth.

This dependence on their owners includes their need to be walked to relieve themselves. However, walking a dog can be seen as a pleasurable experience during which both animal and owner get exercise. For the owner, the time spent walking a dog can be enjoyed as a period of reflection away from everyday pressures. For the dog, it is a time to be exclusively with its owner.

Because dogs are so closely attached to their owners, they will be much more likely than cats will to try to protect life and property. Not all dogs are watchdogs, but most feel some responsibility in this direction. Most will bark at an intruder, even without special training, and some will risk their lives to defend their owner's home or person. Law enforcement officials, though not willing to state that dogs prevent burglaries, do observe that a barking dog makes a house less attractive to a thief.

On balance, it can be seen that the supposed advantages of cats are personality traits that also produce negative characteristics such as stubborn independence and coolness of manner. Dogs, on the other hand, though they require a little more care, more than compensate for this extra effort, by being affectionate, loving, and protective.

This essay uses the characteristics of dogs and cats to argue that dogs make better pets. The same list of characteristics, however, can lead to a different conclusion, namely, that cats are better pets than dogs. Suppose that you want to persuade your audience that cats are superior pets and that you choose to do so by using a comparison-and-contrast format, organizing your details in the alternating method. An outline for such an essay could be the following:

   I. Introduction.
  II. Independence/dependence.
     A. Dogs
     B. Cats
 III. Hygiene.
     A. Dogs
     B. Cats
 IV. Protection.
     A. Dogs
     B. Cats
  V. Conclusion.

Just as dogs had the last word in the previous example, an essay supporting cats should discuss them after dogs. Because this essay is organized in the alternating pattern, each main section will begin with a description of dogs and then follow with a description of cats.

> If you are choosing between a dog or a cat as a household pet, you should examine the characteristics of both to see which will better suit your needs. Both animals offer many of the same advantages, but the differences between them are worth noting.
>
> Dog owners like to point out how affectionate their animals are, and it is true that dogs depend on their owners for emotional security. But how much of a virtue this affection and dependence are is open to question. Reflection should indicate that the affection of a dog is the unthinking dependence of an infant. Dogs are forever fixed at a level of emotional attachment to their owners that most parents are delighted to see their children leave. If you are thinking about owning a dog, consider whether you want to live with an eternal four-year-old.
>
> Cats, though not as outwardly demonstrative as dogs are, offer a more mature level of interaction with their owners. Cats' affections should not be treated lightly, as their respect must be earned. And when a cat chooses to demonstrate its feeling for its owner, the experience is much more meaningful because it comes from a more selective and independent mentality.
>
> Because dogs never mature beyond the level of a young child, they do not attain adequate control of their bodily functions. Owning a dog is like being the parent of a child who can never be adequately toilet trained. A dog owner is forever chained to his or her pet's digestive system. This liability is particularly disagreeable in the early morning of a cold winter's day or after dinner when it is raining heavily.
>
> Because cats achieve a higher degree of emotional development, they are better able to handle their bodily functions. Cats can be let out, or they can deposit their digestive by-products in an hygienic

receptacle. A kitty litter box is always available, no matter what the weather or time of day, and cats are responsible enough to use it when they need to.

As far as the valued quality of dogs as protectors of the owner and his or her property, most watchdogs can easily be subdued by even the most amateur burglar. It is rare, indeed, that a dog ever really serves this protective function. Most watchdogs do just that: they watch the intruder burglarize the house. Moreover, because dogs are rather simpleminded creatures, they are unable to distinguish between friend and foe. Therefore, dogs with watchdog aspirations are as likely to attack a neighbor or elderly relative as they are to harass a thief.

Cats, however, do not aspire to such unrealistic goals. They know that they can offer little resistance to a determined intruder, and therefore they do not expose themselves to unnecessary risk. This attitude is in keeping with their general level of sophistication. Furthermore, most law enforcement officials would not encourage a person to confront a thief; rather, the usual advice in such circumstances is not to give the intruder cause to panic or become violent. Cats know this commonsense wisdom without being instructed.

Owning a dog, therefore, is burdensome, and the rewards of dog ownership are far outweighed by their irritating dependence and lack of maturity. Cats, on the other hand, enable their owners to live freer lives and to relate to their pets on a more mature and meaningful level.

Exercises

1. Think of the quality that is most representative of your personality, and then write a controlling idea sentence that presents this quality in this form: "I am . . . ."

   Ask yourself questions about this quality in order to draw up a list of details that illustrate this controlling idea. Organize an essay, to be developed by examples, from this list, remembering to define your audience and purpose.

2. Pick two prominent elected officials whom you consider worthy of discussion. Make a list of details for each, including such things as political party and attitude, socioeconomic background, age, and public image.

   Write a comparison-and-contrast essay about these officials. Organize your lists so that you can see points of similarity and points of difference, remembering to define your audience and purpose. Outline a proposed essay, using either the block or the alternating method of presentation.

3. Choose one of the following topics for an essay to be developed through examples. Define your purpose and identify your audience:

   a. A memorable person.
   b. A good (or bad) job experience.

      c. An interesting book (or film).

      d. An old automobile.

      e. An ideal vacation.

4. Choose one of the following topics for an essay to be developed through comparison and contrast. Define your purpose and identify your audience. Select either the block or alternating method of development:

      a. Musical performers.

      b. Magazines.

      c. Fashionable clothing.

      d. Pets.

      e. Neighborhoods.

Questions for Revision

After you have written your essays for either Exercise 3 or 4, check your work for organization, purpose, and audience by asking the following questions:

Controlling Idea
1. Have I clearly identified the general subject about which I am writing?
2. Have I emphasized certain aspects of this subject?
3. Have I established a controlling idea by stressing those parts of the subject that I want the reader to understand and remember?

Form
4. How do I present details? Are they examples or illustrations, or are they in a comparison-and-contrast pattern? If they are in a comparison-and-contrast pattern, have I organized them according to the block or the alternating method?
5. How do each of the specific ideas relate to the controlling idea?

Purpose
6. Does my essay emphasize myself, the subject matter, or the audience?

Audience
7. What reaction or response to this essay do I want from my audience?

    Revise your work in light of your answers to these questions so that it demonstrates the relationship between its controlling idea and its details and establishes a good sense of audience and purpose.

chapter 10
Reading: Cause and Effect and Process

In addition to the examples and comparison-and-contrast organizational patterns, writers can arrange details into two patterns tied to chronology. *Cause-and-effect* patterns demonstrate how one event occurred after and because of a preceding event. *Process* patterns, on the other hand, predict the future sequence of events. The choice of organizational pattern should always be related to the writer's sense of purpose and audience.

Moreover, certain controlling ideas seem to suggest a particular organizational pattern. For example, the details of historical events often naturally fall into a cause-and-effect arrangement. On the other hand, a controlling idea that indicates how to do something, such as how to fix your car, usually requires a process organizational pattern.

Questions can be used to identify the controlling idea(s) and the relationship between the controlling idea(s) and details that serves a particular purpose and elicits a particular response:

Controlling Idea
1. Who or what is the subject of the work?
2. What aspect(s) of the subject is (are) discussed in the work?
3. What does the author want you to understand and remember, in general, about the aspect(s) of the subject discussed in the work?

Form
4. How are the details presented? Are they examples or illustrations, comparisons and/or contrasts, causes and/or effects, or a series of actions or events, classifications, or definitions (or qualities and characteristics of same)?
5. How do these details develop the controlling idea?

Purpose
6. Does the work emphasize the author (expressive mode), the subject (informative mode), or the audience (persuasive mode)?

Reader's response
7. What response does the author want to elicit: empathy, learning, or belief?

These questions will guide your analyses of reading materials in this chapter. Various selections are included to give you practice in identifying cause and effect and process as two of several organizational forms employed by writers to inform, persuade, or express their thoughts.

Cause and Effect

Presenting details in a cause-and-effect pattern explores the reasons that something took place: causes are the reasons, and effects are the results. The controlling idea for such a presentation establishes the relationship between what happened (the result or effect) and why it happened (the reasons or causes). These details can be introduced sequentially to suggest how several events led to a result or can be arranged in a cluster of cause-and-effect relations that explain a controlling idea.

The following paragraphs contain cause-and-effect statements that expand a controlling idea:

Everyone has heard people quarrelling. Sometimes it sounds funny and sometimes it sounds merely unpleasant; but however it sounds, I believe we can learn something very important from listening to the kinds of things they say. They say things like this: "How'd you like it if anyone did the same to you?"—"That's my seat, I was there first"—"Leave him alone, he isn't doing you any harm"—"Why should you shove in first?"—"Give me a bit of your orange, I gave you a bit of mine"—"Come on, you promised." People say things like that every day, educated people as well as uneducated, and children as well as grown-ups.

Now what interests me about all these remarks is that the man who makes them is not merely saying that the other man's behaviour does not happen to please him. He is appealing to some kind of standard of behaviour which he expects the other man to know about. And the other man very seldom replies: "To hell with your standard." Nearly always he tries to make out that what he has been doing does not really go against the standard, or that if it does there is some special excuse. He pretends there is some special reason in this particular case why the person who took the seat first should not keep it, or that things were quite different when he was given the bit of orange, or that something has turned up which lets him off keeping his promise. It looks, in fact, very much as if both parties had in mind some kind of Law or Rule of fair play or decent behaviour or morality or whatever you like to call it, about which they really agreed. And they have. If they had not, they might, of course, fight like animals, but they could not *quarrel* in the human sense of the world. Quarrelling means trying to show that the other man is in the wrong. And there would be no sense in trying to do that unless you and he had some sort of agreement as to what Right and Wrong are; just as there would be no sense in saying that a footballer had committed a foul unless there was some agreement about the rules of football. . . .

It seems, then, we are forced to believe in a real Right and Wrong. People may be sometimes mistaken about them, just as people sometimes get their sums wrong; but they are not a matter of mere taste and opinion any more than the multiplication table. Now if we are agreed about that, I go on to my next point, which is this. None of us are really keeping the Law of Nature. If there are any exceptions among you, I apologize to them. They had much better read some other work, for nothing I am going to say concerns them. And now, turning to the ordinary human beings who are left:

I hope you will not misunderstand what I am going to say. I am not preaching, and Heaven knows I do not pretend to be better than anyone else. I am only trying to call attention to a fact; the fact that this year, or this month, or, more likely, this very day, we have failed to practice ourselves the kind of behaviour we expect from other people. There may be all sorts of excuses for us. That time you were so unfair to the children was when you were very tired. That slightly shady business about the money—the one you have almost forgotten—came when you were very hard up. And what you promised to do for old So-and-so and have never done—well, you never would have promised if you had known how frightfully busy you were going to be. And as for your behaviour to your wife (or husband) or sister (or brother) if I knew how irritating they could be, I would not wonder at it—and who the dickens am I, anyway? I am just the same. That is to say, I do not succeed in keeping the Law of Nature very well, and the moment anyone tells me I am not keeping it, there starts up in my mind a string of excuses as long as your arm. The question at the moment is not whether they are good excuses. The point is that they are one more proof of how deeply, whether we like it or not, we believe in the Law of Nature. If we do not believe in decent behaviour, why should we be so anxious to make excuses for not having behaved decently? The truth is, we believe in decency so much—we feel the Rule of Law pressing on us so—that we cannot bear to face the fact that we are breaking it, and consequently we try to shift the responsibility. For you notice that it is only for our bad behaviour that we find all these explanations. It is only our bad temper that we put down to being tired or worried or hungry; we put our good temper down to ourselves.

These, then, are the two points I wanted to make. First, that human beings, all over the earth, have this curious idea that they ought to behave in a certain way, and cannot really get rid of it. Secondly, that they do not in fact behave in that way. They know the Law of Nature; they break it. These two facts are the foundation of all clear thinking about ourselves and the universe we live in.

The author's controlling idea is that what people say when quarreling implies a standard of right and wrong that they interpret according to their needs and that helps them make excuses. To develop this idea, the author cites examples of the things people say when they quarrel.

The first two paragraphs contain the controlling idea and the first set of causes and effects. A second cause and effect is discussed in the third paragraph, "[People] . . . believe in a real Right and Wrong." (cause); "[they] . . . may be sometimes mistaken about them . . ." (effect). The instances presented in the fourth paragraph are more effects of that cause, including those pertaining to the author. The final paragraph clarifies and restates the cause (his first point) and the effect (his second point). The relationship between these causes and effects is that each expands or builds upon the last. Taken together, they supply "proof" of the author's theory of excuse making. The emphasis is on the subject of quarreling and excuses, and the mode is, therefore, informative. The writer hopes to show the reader the basis for ". . . all clear thinking about ourselves and the universe we live in" (last paragraph).

Another author uses the cause-and-effect organizational pattern in these paragraphs:

Anyone who claims it is impossible to get rid of the random violence of today's mean streets may be telling the truth, but is also missing the point. Street crime may be normal in the U.S., but it is not inevitable at such advanced levels, and the fact is that there are specific reasons for the nation's incapacity to keep its street crime down. Almost all these reasons can be traced to the American criminal justice system. It is not that there are no mechanisms in place to deal with American crime, merely that the existing ones are impractical, inefficient, anachronistic, uncooperative, and often lead to as much civic destruction as they are meant to curtail.

Why does the system fail? For one thing, the majority of criminals go untouched by it. The police learn about one-quarter of the thefts committed each year, and about less than half the robberies, burglaries and rapes. Either victims are afraid or ashamed to report crimes, or they may conclude gloomily that nothing will be done if they do. Murder is the crime the police do hear about, but only 73% of the nation's murders lead to arrest. The arrest rates for lesser crimes are astonishingly low—59% for aggravated assault in 1979, 48% for rape, 25% for robbery, 15% for burglary.

Even when a suspect is apprehended, the chances of his getting punished are mighty slim. In New York State each year there are some 130,000 felony arrests; approximately 8,000 people go to prison. There are 94,000 felony arrests in New York City; 5,000 to 6,000 serve time. A 1974 study of the District of Columbia came up with a similar picture. Of those arrested for armed robbery, less than one-quarter went to prison. More than 6,000 aggravated assaults were reported; 116 people were put away. A 1977 study of such cities as Detroit, Indianapolis and New Orleans produced slightly better numbers, but nothing to counteract the exasperation of New York Police Commissioner Robert McGuire: "The criminal justice system almost creates incentives for street criminals."

It is hard to pinpoint any one stage of the system that is more culpable than any other. Start with the relationship between police and prosecutors. Logic would suggest that these groups work together like the gears of a watch since, theoretically, they have the same priorities: to arrest and convict. But prosecutors have enormous caseloads, and too often they simply focus on lightening them. Or they work too fast and lose a case; or they plea bargain and diminish justice. The police also work too fast too often, are concerned with "clearing" arrests, for which they get credit. They receive no credit for convictions. Their work gets sloppy—misinformation recorded, witnesses lost, no follow-up. That 1974 study of the District of Columbia indicated that fully one-third of the police making arrests failed to process a single conviction. A study released this week of 2,418 police in seven cities showed that 15% were credited with half the convictions; 31% had no convictions whatever.

The criminal justice system is also debased by plea bargaining. At present nine out of ten convictions occur because of a guilty plea arrived at through a deal between the state and defendant, in which the defendant foregoes his right to trial. Of course, plea bargaining keeps the courts less crowded and doubtless sends to jail, albeit for a shorter stretch, some felons who might have got off if judged by their peers. And many feel that a bargain results in a truer level of justice, since prosecutors tend to hike up the charge in the first place in anticipation of the defendant's copping a plea. Still, there are tricks like "swallowing the gun"—reducing the charge of armed robbery to unarmed robbery—that are performed for expediency, not for justice. . . .

Detroit Deputy Police Chief James Bannon believes that trial delays work against the victim. "The judge doesn't see the hysterical, distraught victim. He sees a person who comes into court after several months or years who is totally different. He sees a defendant that bears no relationship to what he appeared to be at the time of the crime. He sits there in a nice three-piece suit and keeps his mouth shut. And the judge doesn't see the shouting, raging animal the victim saw when she was being raped, for example. Both the defendant and victim have lawyers, and that's what the court hears: law. It doesn't hear the guts of the crime."

Here the author's controlling idea is that the justice system fails to keep street crime low, which is stated in the first paragraph. Each successive paragraph provides a cause in a topic sentence. The effects of each cause ("the majority of criminals go untouched by it," "when a suspect is apprehended, the chances of his getting punished are . . . slim," "the relationship between police and prosecutors," "plea bargaining," "trial delays work against the victim") are stated as details of each paragraph. Although dissimilar in style to the previous example about excuse making, this example also uses a cause-and-effect pattern. The causes and effects all relate to the author's controlling idea and to one another because they pertain to various aspects of the court system. They serve the author's informative purpose by focusing on the subject and by providing statistical and factual material in each paragraph. Finally, the author's use of cause and effect enables him to explain to the reader why the justice system has failed.

A third example of the cause-and-effect pattern appears in the following four paragraphs:

> Our inventive, up-to-the-minute, wealthy democracy makes new tests of the human spirit. Our very instruments of education, of information and of "progress" make it harder every day for us to keep our bearings in the larger universe, in the stream of history and in the whole world of peoples who feel strong ties to their past. A new price of our American standard of living is our imprisonment in the present.
>
> That imprisonment tempts us to a morbid preoccupation with ourselves, and so induces hypochondria. That, the dictionary tells us, is "an abnormal condition characterized by a depressed emotional state and imaginary ill health; excessive worry or talk about one's health." We think we are the beginning and the end of the world. And as a result we get our nation and our lives, our strengths and our ailments, quite out of focus.
>
> We will not be on the way to curing our national hypochondria unless we first see ourselves in history. This requires us to accept the unfashionable possibility that many of our national ills are imaginary and that others may not be as serious as we imagine. Unless we begin to believe that we won't be dead before morning, we may not be up to the daily tasks of a healthy life. By recalling some of the premature obituaries pronounced on other nations, we may listen more skeptically to the moralists and smart alecks who pretend to have in their pocket a life-expectancy chart for nations.
>
> Overwhelmed by the instant moment—headlined in this morning's newspaper and flashed on this hour's newscast—we don't see the whole real world around us. We don't see the actual condition of our long-lived body national.

In this passage, the author states his controlling idea, "Our inventive, up-to-the-minute, wealthy democracy makes new tests of the human spirit," in the first sentence of the first paragraph and restates it in the last sentence of the same paragraph. The idea, in both sentences, is stated in cause-and-effect terms: our democracy (cause) tests the human spirit (effect); our American standard of living (restated cause) and our imprisonment in the present (restated effect). The second paragraph shows how the effect—imprisonment in the present—causes a second effect—hypochondria. The third paragraph suggests what the author feels we must do (cause) to cure ourselves (effect). We must heed history (cause) before we can cure this hypochondria (effect). The final paragraph notes concrete causes of our imprisonment ("this morning's newspaper," "this hour's newscast") for our myopic view of the world or, in the author's words, "we don't see the whole real world around us." Here a cause-and-effect pattern combines both general and specific ideas. In turn, each specific idea relates to another by expanding the controlling idea through concrete instances or behaviors: "Our very instruments of education . . . make it harder every day for us to keep our bearings in the larger universe . . ."; because of "our imprisonment in the present . . . we get our nation and our lives, our strengths and our ailments, quite out of focus"; if we recall "some of the premature obituaries pronounced on other nations, we may listen more skeptically to the moralists and smart alecks who pretend to have in their pocket a life-expectancy chart for nations." A persuasive purpose is served by the writer's insistence that we have to "begin to believe that we won't be dead before morning," and that we still have life as a nation.

Process

A process pattern establishes how something is made or done or how something happens or works. It explains this in a series of sequential steps, actions, or events. It can, and often is, combined with cause and effect because reasons and results can be in the form of a series of steps, actions, or events (causes) that lead to predetermined outcomes (effects). Remember, however, that process predicts what will happen, whereas cause and effect explains what has already happened. When used alone, process is rather easy to spot as an organizational pattern because relationships are usually formed on the basis of how one thing leads to the next, either chronologically or sequentially. The controlling idea is usually a statement that introduces a certain process as necessary for something to occur or be achieved.

Notice how the process pattern in the following paragraphs organizes specific ideas:

> The common yo-yo is crudely made, with a thick shank between two widely spaced wooden disks. The string is knotted or stapled to the shank. With such an instrument nothing can be done except the simple up-down movement. My yo-yo, on the other hand, was a perfectly balanced construction of hard wood, slightly weighted, flat, with only a sixteenth of an inch between the halves. The string was not attached to the shank, but looped over it in such a way as to allow the wooden part to spin freely on its own axis. The gyroscopic effect thus created kept the yo-yo stable in all attitudes.
>
> I started at the beginning of the book and quickly mastered the novice, intermediate, and advanced stages, practicing all day every day in the woods across the street from my house. Hour after hour of practice, never moving to the next trick until the one at hand was mastered.
>
> The string was tied to my middle finger, just behind the nail. As I threw—with your palm up, make a fist; throw down your hand, fingers unfolding, as if you were casting grain—a short bit of string would tighten across the sensitive pad of flesh at the tip of my finger. That was the critical area. After a number of weeks I could interpret the condition of the string, the presence of any imperfections on the shank, but most importantly the exact amount of spin or inertial energy left in the yo-yo at any given moment—all from that bit of string on my fingertip. As the throwing motion became more and more natural I found I could make the yo-yo "sleep" for an astonishing length of

time—fourteen or fifteen seconds—and still have enough spin left to bring it back to my hand. Gradually the basic moves became reflexes. Sleeping, twirling, swinging, and precise aim. Without thinking, without even looking, I could run through trick after trick involving various combinations of the elemental skills, switching from one to the other in a smooth continuous flow. On particularly good days I would hum a tune under my breath and do it all in time to the music.

After using several sentences in the first and second paragraphs to state his controlling idea (a well-made yo-yo and hour-by-hour practice led to his mastery of basic moves), the author explains in the third paragraph the process that made his mastery possible. He arranges sequentially the series of actions that led to his yo-yo skill (interpreting the string's condition and throwing the yo-yo, making the yo-yo sleep, and making it return to his hand). Each skill's mastery relates to the next through an implied hierarchy of difficulty. The author suggests that his mastery was chronological, and therefore the details form a brief process analysis that explains how the author learned to master the yo-yo and how you could do the same if you followed the same steps. Because the emphasis is primarily on the process, or subject matter, the purpose of this piece is informative.

The next example shows a different kind of process analysis, in which the writer explains how to do something that requires special expertise:

In the autumn of 1973 a woman in her early fifties noticed, upon closing one eye while reading, that she was unable to see clearly. Her eyesight grew slowly worse. Changing her eyeglasses did not help. She saw an ophthalmologist, who found that her vision was seriously impaired in both eyes. She then saw a neurologist, who confirmed the finding and obtained X-rays of the skull and an EMI scan—a photograph of the patient's head. The latter revealed a tumor growing between the optic nerves at the base of the brain. The woman was admitted to the hospital by a neurosurgeon.

Further diagnosis, based on angiography, a detailed X-ray study of the circulatory system, showed the tumor to be about two inches in diameter and supplied by many small blood vessels. It rested beneath the brain, just above the pituitary gland, stretching the optic nerves to either side and intimately close to the major blood vessels supplying the brain. Removing it would pose many technical problems. Probably benign and slow-growing, it may have been present for several years. If left alone it would continue to grow and produce blindness and might become impossible to remove completely. Removing it, however, might not improve the patient's vision and could make it worse. A major blood vessel could be damaged, causing a stroke. Damage to the undersurface of the brain could cause impairment of memory and changes in mood and personality. The hypothalamus, a most important structure of the brain, could be injured, causing coma, high fever, bleeding from the stomach, and death.

The neurosurgeon met with the patient and her husband and discussed the various possibilities. The common decision was to operate.

The patient's hair was shampooed for two nights before surgery. She was given a cortisonelike drug to reduce the risk of damage to the brain during surgery. Five units of blood were cross-matched, as a contingency against hemorrhage. At 1:00 P.M. the operation began. After the patient was anesthetized her hair was completely clipped and shaved from the scalp. Her head was prepped with an organic iodine solution for ten minutes. Drapes were placed over her, leaving exposed only the forehead and crown of the skull. All the routine instruments were brought up—the electrocautery used to coagulate areas of bleeding, bipolar coagulation forceps to arrest bleeding from individual blood vessels without damaging adjacent tissues, and small suction tubes to remove blood and cerebrospinal fluid from the head, thus giving the surgeon a better view of the tumor and surrounding areas.

A curved incision was made behind the hairline so it would be concealed when the hair grew back. It extended almost from ear to ear. Plastic clips were applied to the cut edges of the scalp to arrest bleeding. The scalp was folded back to the level of the eyebrows. Incisions were made in the muscle of the right temple, and three sets of holes were drilled near the temple and the top of the head because the tumor had to be approached from directly in front. The drill, powered by nitrogen, was replaced with a fluted steel blade, and the holes were connected. The incised piece of skull was pried loose and held out of the way by a large sponge.

Beneath the bone is a yellowish leatherlike membrane, the dura, that surrounds the brain. Down the middle of the head the dura carries a large vein, but in the area near the nose the vein is small. At that point the vein and dura were cut, and clips made of tantalum, a hard metal, were applied to arrest and prevent bleeding. Sutures were put into the dura and tied to the scalp to keep the dura open and retracted. A malleable silver retractor, resembling the blade of a butter knife, was inserted between the brain and skull. The anesthesiologist began to administer a drug to relax the brain by removing some of its water, making it easier for the surgeon to manipulate the retractor, hold the brain back, and see the tumor. The nerve tracts for smell were cut on both sides to provide additional room. The tumor was seen approximately two-and-one-half inches behind the base of the nose. It was pink in color. On touching it, it proved to be very fibrous and tough. A special retractor was attached to the skull, enabling the other retractor blades to be held automatically and freeing the surgeon's hands. With further displacement of the frontal lobes of the brain, the tumor could be seen better, but no normal structures—the carotid arteries, their branches, and the optic nerves—were visible. The tumor obscured them.

A surgical microscope was placed above the wound. The surgeon had selected the lenses and focal length prior to the operation. Looking through the microscope, he could see some of the small vessels supplying the tumor and he coagulated them. He incised the tumor to attempt to remove its core and thus collapse it, but the substance of the tumor was too firm to be removed in this fashion. He then began to slowly dissect the tumor from the adjacent brain tissue and from where he believed the normal structures to be.

Using small squares of cotton, he began to separate the tumor from very loose fibrous bands connecting it to the brain and to the right side of the part of the skull where the pituitary gland lies. The right optic nerve and carotid artery came into view, both displaced considerably to the right. The optic nerve had a normal appearance. He protected these structures with cotton compresses placed between them and the tumor. He began to raise the tumor from the skull and slowly to reach the point of its origin and attachment—just in front of the pituitary gland and medial to the left optic nerve, which still could not be seen. The small blood vessels entering the tumor were cauterized. The upper portion of the tumor was gradually separated from the brain, and the branches of the carotid arteries and the branches to the tumor were coagulated. The tumor was slowly and gently lifted from its bed, and for the first time the left carotid artery and optic nerve could be seen. Part of the tumor adhered to this nerve. The bulk of the tumor was amputated, leaving a small bit attached to the nerve. Very slowly and carefully the tumor fragment was resected.

The tumor now removed, a most impressive sight came into view—the pituitary gland and its stalk of attachment to the hypothalamus, the hypothalamus itself, and the brainstem, which conveys nerve impulses between the body and the brain. As far as could be determined, no damage had been done to these structures or other vital centers, but the left optic nerve, from chronic pressure of the tumor, appeared gray and thin. Probably it would not completely recover its function.

After making certain there was no bleeding, the surgeon closed the wounds and placed wire mesh over the holes in the skull to prevent dimpling of the scalp over the points that had been drilled. A gauze dressing was applied to the patient's head. She was awakened and sent to the recovery room.

Even with the microscope, damage might still have occurred to the cerebral cortex and hypothalamus. It would require at least a day to be reasonably certain there was none, and about seventy-two hours to monitor for the major postoperative dangers—swelling of the brain and blood clots forming over the surface of the brain. The surgeon explained this to the patient's husband, and both of them waited anxiously. The operation had required seven hours. A glass of orange juice had given the surgeon some additional energy during the closure of the wound. Though exhausted, he could not fall asleep until after two in the morning, momentarily expecting a call from the nurse in the intensive care unit announcing deterioration of the patient's condition.

At 8:00 A.M. the surgeon saw the patient in the intensive care unit. She was alert, oriented, and showed no sign of additional damage to the optic nerves or the brain. She appeared to be in better shape than the surgeon or her husband.

Roy Selby's description of the steps of one patient's brain surgery is an excellent example of a process analysis that organizes the presentation of information. He takes time to include the reason(s) that each step in the process was necessary (paragraphs 2, 4, 5, and 11). Every paragraph explains a step, first by stating it in a topic sentence and then by elaborating upon it with specific sentences that graphically detail the procedures and, sometimes, the reasons for that step. The process outlined covers chronologically those events that occurred before (paragraphs 1, 2, and 3), during (paragraphs 4 through 10), and after (paragraphs 11 and 12) the operation. Its purpose is informative—to teach the reader something about brain surgery. Notice, however, that this analysis differs from the yo-yo example: anyone can attempt to master that toy, but only trained specialists can perform brain surgery. Both predict that certain steps will lead to a particular conclusion.

Next, read a selection with a different purpose:

You know you have to read "between the lines" to get the most out of anything. I want to persuade you to do something equally important in the course of your reading. I want to persuade you to "write between the lines." Unless you do, you are not likely to do the most efficient kind of reading.

I contend, quite bluntly, that marking up a book is not an act of mutilation but of love. . . .

Even if you wrote on a scratch pad, and threw the paper away when you had finished writing, your grasp of the book would be surer. But you don't have to throw the paper away. The margins (top and bottom, as well as side), the end-papers, the very space between the lines, are all available. They aren't sacred. And, best of all, your marks and notes become an integral part of the book and stay there forever. You can pick up the book the following week or year, and there are all your points of agreement, disagreement, doubt, and inquiry. It's like resuming an interrupted conversation with the advantage of being able to pick up where you left off.

And that is exactly what reading a book should be: a conversation between you and the author. Presumably he knows more about the subject than you do; naturally, you'll have the proper humility as you approach him. But don't let anybody tell you that a reader is supposed to be solely on the receiving end. Understanding is a two-way operation; learning doesn't consist in being an empty receptacle. The learner has to question himself and question the teacher. He even has to argue with the teacher, once he understands what the teacher is saying. And marking a book is literally an expression of your differences, or agreements of opinion, with the author.

There are all kinds of devices for marking a book intelligently and fruitfully. Here's the way I do it:

1. Underlining: Of major points, of important or forceful statements.
2. Vertical lines at the margin: To emphasize a statement already underlined.
3. Star, asterisk, or other doo-dad at the margin: To be used sparingly, to emphasize the ten or twenty most important statements in the book. (You may want to fold the bottom corner of each page on which you use such marks. It won't hurt the sturdy paper on which most modern books are printed, and you will be able to take the book off the shelf at any time and, by opening it at the folded-corner page, refresh your recollection of the book.)
4. Numbers in the margin: To indicate the sequence of points the author makes in developing a single argument.
5. Numbers of other pages in the margin: To indicate where else in the book the author made points relevant to the point marked; to tie up the ideas in a book, which, though they may be separated by many pages, belong together.
6. Circling of key words or phrases.
7. Writing in the margin, or at the top or bottom of the page, for the sake of: Recording questions (and perhaps answers) which a passage raised in your mind; reducing a complicated discussion to a simple statement; recording the sequence of major points right through the book. I use the end-papers at the back of the book to make a personal index of the author's points in the order of their appearance.

The front end-papers are, to me, the most important. Some people reserve them for a fancy bookplate. I reserve them for fancy thinking. After I have finished reading the book and making my personal index on the back end-papers, I turn to the front and try to outline the book, not page by page, or point by point (I've already done that at the back), but as an integrated structure, with a basic unity and an order of parts. This outline is, to me, the measure of my understanding of the work.

If you're a die-hard and anti-book-marker, you may object that the margins, the space between the lines, and the end-papers don't give you room enough. All right. How about using a scratch pad slightly smaller than the page-size of the book—so that the edges of the sheets won't protrude? Make your index, outlines, and even your notes on the pad, and then insert these sheets permanently inside the front and back covers of the book.

Or, you may say that this business of marking books is going to slow up your reading. It probably will. That's one of the reasons for doing it. Most people have been taken in by the notion that speed of reading is a measure of our intelligence. There is no such thing as the right speed for intelligent reading. Some things should be read quickly and effortlessly, and some should be read slowly and even laboriously. The sign of intelligence in reading is the ability to read different things differently according to their worth. In the case of good books, the point is not to see how many of them you can get through, : ut rather how many can get through you—how many you can make your own. A few friends are better than a thousand acquaintances. If this be your aim, as it should be, you will not be impatient if it takes more time and effort to read a great book than it does a newspaper.

You may have one final objection to marking books. You can't lend them to your friends because nobody else can read them without being distracted by your notes. Furthermore, you won't want to lend them because a marked copy is a kind of intellectual diary, and lending it is almost like giving your mind away.

If your friend wishes to read your Plutarch's Lives, "Shakespeare," or *The Federalist Papers* tell him gently but firmly, to buy a copy. You will lend him your car or your coat—but your books are as much a part of you as your head or your heart.

In the first paragraph's second sentence, this author's purpose is clear: he wants to persuade you to write in books and to convince you that marking up a book is "an art of love." He uses process analysis by listing seven ways to mark a book (paragraphs 6 through 12). Their only connection is that they are devices; they do not constitute an overall sequential pattern, but they do serve as a process. These devices and the sentences that describe them are directly related to the first part of the author's controlling idea: how to mark up a book in order to read it most efficiently. If his ideas are convincing, the reader will be induced to follow his suggestions for "writing between the lines."

To give you additional practice with cause-and-effect and process organizational patterns, we offer two more articles. Find in each the controlling idea, form, purpose, and response.

HOW TO CHANGE YOUR POINT OF VIEW

Caroline Seebohm

The famous Dr. Edward Jenner was busy trying to solve the problem of smallpox. After studying case after case, he still found no possible cure. *He had reached an impasse in his thinking.* At this point, he changed his tactics. Instead of focusing on people who had smallpox, he switched his attention to people who did *not* have smallpox. It turned out that dairymaids apparently never got the disease. From the discovery that harmless cowpox gave protection against deadly smallpox came vaccination and the end of smallpox as a scourge in the Western world.

We often reach an impasse in our thinking. We are looking at a problem and trying to solve it and it seems there is a dead-end, an "aporia" (the technical term in logic meaning "no opening"). It is on these occasions that we become tense, we feel pressured, overwhelmed, in a state of stress. We struggle vainly, fighting to solve the problem.

Dr. Jenner, however, did something about this situation. He stopped fighting the problem and simply changed his point of view—from patients to dairymaids. Picture the process going something like this: Suppose the brain is a computer. This computer has absorbed into its memory bank all your history, your experiences, your training, your information received through life, and it is programmed according to all this data. To change your point of view, you must reprogram your computer, thus freeing yourself to take in new ideas and develop new ways of looking at things. Dr. Jenner, in effect, by reprogramming his computer, erased the old way of looking at his smallpox problem and was free to receive new alternatives.

That's all very well, you may say, but how do we actually *do* that?

Doctor and philosopher Edward de Bono has come up with a technique for changing our point of view, and he calls it Lateral Thinking.

The normal Western approach to a problem is to *fight* it. The saying, "When the going gets tough, the tough get going," epitomizes this aggressive, combat-ready attitude toward problem-solving. No matter what the problem is, or the techniques available for solving it, the framework produced by our Western way of thinking is *fight*. Dr. de Bono calls this *vertical* thinking: the traditional, sequential, Aristotelian thinking of logic, moving firmly from one step to the next, like toy blocks being built one on top of the other. The flaw is, of course, that if at any point one of the steps is not reached, or one of the toy blocks is incorrectly placed, then the whole structure collapses. Impasse is reached, and frustration, tension, feelings of *fight* take over.

Lateral thinking, Dr. de Bono says, is a new technique of thinking about things—a technique that avoids this fight altogether, and solves the problem in an entirely unexpected fashion.

In one of Sherlock Holmes's cases, his assistant, Dr. Watson, pointed out that a certain dog was of no importance to the case because it did not appear to have done anything. Sherlock Holmes took the opposite point of view and maintained that the fact the dog had done nothing was of the utmost significance, for it should have been expected to do something, and on this basis he solved the case. . . .

Lateral thinking sounds simple. And it is. Once you have solved a problem laterally, you wonder how you could ever have been hung up on it. The knack is making that vital shift in emphasis, that sidestepping of the problem, instead of grappling with it head-on. It could even be as simple as going to a special part of the house, which is quiet and restful; buying a special chair, an "escape" chair, where we can lose our day-to-day preoccupations and allow our computers to reprogram themselves and become free to take in new ideas, see things in a different light.

Dr. A. A. Bridger, psychiatrist at Columbia University and in private practice in New York, explains how lateral thinking works with his patients. "Many people come to me wanting to stop smoking, for instance," he says. "Most people fail when they are trying to stop smoking because they wind up telling themselves, 'No, I will not smoke; no, I shall not smoke; no, I will not; no, I cannot . . .' It's a fight—and fighting makes as much sense as telling yourself over and over again not to think of what you want—what happens is you end up smoking more.

"So instead of looking at the problem from the old way of *no,* and fighting it, I show them how to reinforce a position of *yes.* I give them a whole new point of view—that you are your body's keeper, and your body is a physical plant through which you experience life. If you stop to think about it, there's really something helpless about your body. It can do nothing for itself. It has no choice, it is like a baby's body. You begin then a whole new way of looking at it—'I am now going to take care of myself, and give myself some respect and protection, by not smoking.' So that *not* giving yourself respect and protection becomes a deprivation.

"There is a Japanese parable about a jackass tied to a pole by a rope. The rope rubs tight against his neck. The more the jackass fights and pulls on the rope, the tighter and tighter it gets round his throat—until he winds up dead as a doornail. On the other hand, as soon as he stops fighting, he finds that the rope gets slack, he can walk around, maybe find some grass to eat. . . . That's the same principle: The more you fight something, the more anxious you become—the more you're involved in a bad pattern, the more difficult it is to escape pain.

"Lateral thinking," Dr. Bridger goes on, "is simply approaching a problem with what I would call an Eastern flanking maneuver. You know, when a zen archer wants to hit the target with a bow and arrow, he doesn't concentrate on the target, he concentrates rather on what he has in his hands, so when he lets the arrow go, his focus is on the end-result of the arrow, rather than the target. This is what an Eastern flanking maneuver implies—instead of approaching the target directly, you approach it from a sideways point of view—or laterally instead of vertically."

Dr. Bridger has made a shift away from traditional thinking in his practice. "We are finally beginning to realize that many long-term problems can be resolved in short-term ways. People for years have always felt that problems that have been around for a long time will take a very long time to solve. That just does not happen to be so. For instance, when a patient is anxious, fighting a problem, often he can be taught, in one hypnotic session, how to relax and lower his psychic tension. This creates a much more workable feeling-tone for problem solving. While medicines can also lower tension, all medicines, after all, are poisons. Other forms of relaxation, such as transcendental meditation, take a very long period of time to get going. Hypnosis, by contrast, is a safe, quick lateral technique of lowering psychic tension and shifting gears. This increases receptivity for looking at a problem in a new way."

Reminding ourselves we are in a period called an *Intermediate Impossible* is another useful technique. That is, looking at our current situation in life as only an intermediate step toward something else, so that we don't get bogged down and can go on to the next step. The medical student, for instance, unless he accepted his training as an intermediate impossible, would never get through it. Another familiar example is the harassed mother raising young children— going through the "Terrible Twos." She sees her life as a nightmare, "God, this is going to be the way it is until they are grown up . . ." as opposed to seeing the "Terrible Twos" as an intermediate impossible. If only she could remind herself that the current situation is intermediate, only a phase, she might relax—if only she could look at her situation laterally, instead of fighting it.

Lateral thinking, in short, is most valuable in those problem situations where vertical thinking has been unable to provide a solution. When you reach that impasse, and feel the *fight* upon you, quickly reprogram your thinking.

1. Is there any other way the problem can be expressed?
2. What random ideas come to mind when you relax and think about it?
3. Can you turn the problem upside down?
4. Can you invent another problem to take its place?
5. Can you shift the emphasis from one part of the problem to another?

These are difficult questions, and it takes imagination to ask and to answer them. But that is how we change our point of view—by being imaginative enough to think up new ideas, find new ways of looking at our problems, invent new methods for dealing with old patterns. Think laterally instead of vertically. Take the *fight* out of our lives. Move Eastward in our attitudes.

"I think the answer lies in that direction," affirms Dr. Bridger. "Take the situation where someone is in a crisis. The Chinese word for crisis is divided into two characters, one meaning *danger* and the other meaning *opportunity*. We in the Western world focus only upon the danger aspect of crisis. Crisis in Western civilization has come to mean danger, period. And yet the word can also mean opportunity. Let us now suggest to the person in crisis that he cease concentrating so upon the dangers involved and the difficulties, and concentrate instead upon the opportunity—for there is always opportunity in crisis. Looking at a crisis from an opportunity point of view is a lateral thought.

"It's about time we stopped fighting in order to find a solution. Let us float along with the problem so that we can look at it from lateral points of view. Then we can be receptive to new ideas, renew and restimulate our senses, find a new way of living."

1. **Question:** What is the subject of the work?
   Answer: Lateral thinking.
2. **Question:** What aspect of the subject is discussed in the work?

        Answer: That it is a new technique for thinking about things.

3. **Question:**   What does the author want you to understand and remember, in general, about the aspect of the subject discussed in the work?

        Answer: That lateral thinking is a new technique for thinking about things that allows people to avoid feelings of "fight" and thus to solve a problem in an unexpected manner. This controlling idea is stated in paragraph 7.

4. **Question:**   How are the specific ideas presented?

        Answer: Although Seebohm uses examples, cause and effect, definition, and comparison and contrast to explain lateral thinking, the predominant organizational pattern is process, as shown in paragraphs 3, 10, 11, and 16. In the third paragraph, Dr. Jenner's hypothetical use of lateral thinking uses process, and in paragraphs 10 and 11, Dr. Bridger's explanation of how he helps patients stop smoking uses process by indicating the steps he takes to change the patients' thinking. Paragraph 16 summarizes the value of lateral thinking over vertical thinking and asks five questions that can help change vertical thinking to lateral. These questions also demonstrate the process of reprogramming the mind for lateral thinking.

5. **Question:**   How do these questions develop the controlling idea?

        Answer: They develop the controlling idea by indicating the steps (which Drs. Jenner and Bridger use) or series of actions (the five questions the author asks to change one's thinking from vertical to lateral) needed for this reasoning technique. The specifics identified as steps are related because of sequence; the five questions are related not by sequence but by what they accomplish: a change in approach to problem solving.

6. **Question:**   Does the work emphasize the author, the subject, or the audience?

        Answer: The article's overall emphasis is on the subject; however, paragraphs 17, 18, and 19 show the author's attempt to influence behavior by providing reasons that we should adopt lateral thinking as a new means of problem solving ("Take the fight out of our lives," "cease concentrating upon the dangers involved . . . and concentrate instead upon the opportunity," "float along with the problem so that we can look at it from lateral points of view," "we can be receptive to new ideas, renew and restimulate our senses, find a new way of living"). Clearly, her intent is also to persuade.

7. **Question:**   What response does the author want to elicit: empathy, learning or belief?

        Answer: Both learning and belief seem to be the desired responses, because of the emphasis on the subject (paragraphs 1 through 16) and the audience (paragraphs 17 through 19).

Controlling idea: Lateral thinking is a new technique for thinking about things and allows one to avoid feelings of "fight" and thus to solve a problem in an unexpected manner.

Form: Predominantly process.

*Purpose:*To inform and to persuade.

Reader Response: Learning and believing as the author does.

HOW TO OBTAIN POWER

Michael Korda

My friend and I are sitting at the Central Park Zoo, on the terrace of the cafeteria, one of those hot summer afternoons when the park is so crowded with people that the animals seem more human than oneself. To our right are the towers of commercial New York, a high, brutal cliff of great buildings, rising through the layers of haze like the dreaded tower of Barad-Dûr in Tolkien's *The Lord of the Rings.* I can understand how one can become a powerful person in simpler societies and cultures; it may be a long, hard initiation, but the distractions are fewer. The sheer size of the city distorts the ego. We are either reduced to the impotence of a meaningless daily routine— sleep, eat, work—made even more painful by the knowledge that we have no power over our lives; or worse, we destroy ourselves by trying to become bigger, more famous, more powerful than the city itself. Can one have power here, I want to know, in a life full of compromises, decisions, worries, pressures, in a place where even the mayor seldom seems able to control anything at all? I can understand the meaning of power in the desert, the significance of the rites of power, the sudden illuminations of self-awareness that come when one is alone with Nature—all that makes sense. But in an office on the thirty-eighth floor of a huge building in which thousands of people work? How does one seek power there?

My friend smiles. There are rules, they are the same for everybody, this terrace is not so very different from a jungle clearing. The rules of power do not change because one is on the subway, or in Central Park, or in an office without windows, where everything is made of plastic. "The first rule," he says, "is simple. Act impeccably! Perform every act as if it were the only thing in the world that mattered."

I can understand that all right. It's an old Zen principle—you put your whole soul and being and life into the act you're performing. In Zen archery your entire being wills the arrow into the bull's-eye with an invisible force. It's not a question of winning, or even caring, it's making the everyday acts we all perform important to ourselves. No matter how small the task, we have to teach ourselves that it *matters.* If we are going to intervene in a meeting, we must do so at the right moment, prepare for what we want to say, speak up at the crucial point when our intervention will be heard and listened to, make sure that attention is paid. Otherwise, it's best to remain silent. It is better to do nothing than to do something badly.

"Second rule: never reveal all of yourself to other people, hold something back in reserve so that people are never quite sure if they really know you."

I can see that too. It's not that anybody seeking power should be secretive—secrecy isn't the trick at all. It's more a question of remaining slightly mysterious, as if one were always capable of doing something surprising and unexpected. Most people are so predictable and reveal so much of themselves that a person who isn't and who doesn't automatically acquires a kind of power. For this reason, it is important to give up the self-indulgent habit of talking about oneself. The power person listens instead, and when he *does* talk about himself, it is in order to change the subject of conversation. Good players can always tell when someone is about to ask them to do something they don't want to do, and they effortlessly but firmly move the conversation onto a personal level. One of the best players I know can talk about himself for hours at the slightest sign of opposition or a demand about to be made on him. Even so, he reveals nothing. Sometimes he gives the impression that he has two children, sometimes three, occasionally none, and he has at various times given people to understand that he was graduated from Yale, Harvard, Stanford, and Ol' Miss. Some confusion exists as to whether or not he is Jewish or Protestant, since he has claimed to be both, and also crosses himself when he passes St. Patrick's Cathedral. Nobody really knows the truth about him, and he is therefore respected. Once we know everything about a person, we have squeezed him dry like a juiced orange, he is no longer of any use or interest to us, we can throw him away.

"Third rule: Learn to use time, think of it as a friend, not an enemy. Don't waste it in going after things you don't want."

Using time! Of course, but how seldom we do! Time uses us, we are merely its servants. We fight it as if it were the enemy, trying to force two hours' work into forty-five minutes if we're ambitious, or to stretch forty-five minutes' work into two hours if we're not. Powerful people devote exactly as much time to what they're doing as they need to or want to. They do not try to answer two telephones at once, or begin a meeting and then end it before a conclusion has been reached because "time has run out," or interrupt one conversation to begin another. They are willing to be late, to miss telephone calls, and to postpone today's work to tomorrow if they have to. Events do not control them—they control events.

"Fourth rule: learn to accept your mistakes. Don't be a perfectionist about everything."

True enough. Half the people we know are rendered powerless by their need to be perfect, as if making one mistake would destroy them. Powerful people accept the necessity of taking risks and of being wrong. They don't waste time justifying their mistakes, either, or trying to transform them into correct decisions. Nothing makes one seem more foolish or impotent than the inability to admit a mistake.

"Last rule: don't make waves, move smoothly without disturbing things."

That makes sense too, even in our world. Half the art of power lies in arranging for things to happen the way we want them to, just as a good hunter stays in one place and draws the game toward him, instead of wearing himself out pursuing it. The skills of the hunter are not out of place in our world; they must merely be applied differently.

My friend smiles again. "What more can I say?" he asks, waving to the buildings south of the park. "It's your world. You picked it—telephones, Telex machines, credit cards and all. Myself, I wouldn't care to live in it all the time. I'm not interested in negotiating contracts, or buying a new car, or running a corporation—we don't have the same ambitions and desires. But I could live here as easily as I can anywhere else. You only need power. And since *you* live in it, you have to examine this world of yours coldly and clearly, as if your life depended on it. Because it *does*."

1. **Question:** What is the subject of the work?

   Answer: Power.

2. **Question:** What aspect of the subject is discussed in the work?

   Answer: Obtaining power.

3. **Question:** What does the author want you to understand and remember, in general, about the aspect of the subject discussed in the work?

   Answer: That there are rules to follow in order to obtain power that are the same for everybody. Korda's two questions in the first paragraph ("Can one have power here . . . ?" "How does one seek power there?") and his friend's answer ("There are rules . . .") provide us with the controlling idea.

4. **Question:** How are the specific ideas presented?

   Answer: Korda uses process combined with cause and effect to present his ideas. Process is easily identified by his friend's enumeration of five rules (paragraphs 2, 4, 6, 8, and 10). These rules are a series of actions that suggest the process by which power may be obtained. Korda incorporates cause and effect into each rule; each indicates either the reason for the rule and/or how a certain result will occur if it is followed. ("Act impeccably! Perform every act as if it were the only thing in the world that mattered"; "never reveal all of yourself to other people, hold something back in reserve so that people are never quite sure if they really know you"; "Learn to use time, think of it as a friend, not an enemy. Don't waste it . . ."; "Learn to accept your mistakes. Don't be a perfectionist about everything"; "don't make waves, move smoothly without disturbing things"). In addition, Korda's response to each rule includes cause and effect (paragraphs 3, 5, 7, 9, and 11). In short, the even-numbered paragraphs (all but the last) present the rules and therefore show the process by which power is attained; the odd-numbered par-

agraphs present the author's reactions to the rules and organize those reactions into a cause-and-effect fashion.

5. **Question:** How does the author develop the controlling idea?

   Answer: He develops the controlling idea by indicating the series of
   actions to take to obtain power and the causes and/or effects
   of following those rules. Furthermore, Korda's response to
   each rule comes in the form of agreement and is substan-
   tiated by his own illustrations or explanations, which provide reasons and outcomes. The rules are a related series
   of actions, and the causes and effects in each of the odd-
   numbered paragraphs are related to each rule they expand.

6. **Question:** Does the work emphasize the author, the subject, or the
   audience?

   Answer: The article emphasizes the subject and is therefore informative. Although there is a hint of expression in the last paragraph, it comes from the friend and not the author.

7. **Question:** What response does the author want to elicit: empathy,
   learning or belief?

   Answer: The desired response seems to be learning.

Controlling idea: There are rules to follow in order to obtain power that
are the same for everybody.
Form: Process and cause and effect.
Purpose: To inform.
Reader response: Learning.

Cause and effect and process are two of several organizational techniques
discussed in this section. Learn to recognize them when you read and to
use them when you write.

Exercises _____

1. Read each of the following articles and decide whether cause and effect,
   process, or both are the organizing pattern.

   ## a. THAT FLASH OF AWE

   ### Bill Russell

   During my junior year in high school, in 1950, I had a mystical
   revelation. One day while I was walking down the hall from one class
   to another, by myself as usual, it suddenly dawned on me that it was
   all right to be who I was. The thought just came to me: "Hey, you're
   all right. Everything is all right." The idea was hardly earthshaking,
   but I was a different person by the time I reached the end of the hall.
   Had I been methodical I would have immediately written down my

thoughts. Over and over again I received the idea that everything was all right about me—so vividly that the thought seemed to have colors on it. I remember looking around in class to make sure the other kids didn't think I was acting strange.

Those moments in the hall are the closest I've come to a religious experience. For all I know, it may have actually been one. A warm feeling fell on me out of nowhere. I wondered why the idea hadn't occurred to me before; everything seemed to fall into place, the way it does for a kid when he first understands simple multiplication.

Everybody remembers the "Aha!" sensation when a good idea hits you. I remember sitting in a logic class at the University of San Francisco, puzzling over something the priest had been explaining to us for the previous few days. Then it came to me. Bells went off; the mental pleasure was so great that I jumped as if someone had pinched me and yelled "Hey!"

The priest said, "Congratulations, Mr. Russell. You have just had your first real and complete thought. How does it feel?" He was patronizing me, but I didn't care because he had just given me a new way of seeing things.

What I saw in the hallway at high school that day was more than just an idea; it was a way out of self-rejection. In the four years since my mother had died, everybody I encountered felt that there was something wrong with me. Worse, I *agreed* with them. I was clumsy at everything. When I opened a soup can, it felt as if I was trying to take apart a watch with a sledgehammer. I was insulted at the time. At my first and only football practice the coach lined up players to run over me all afternoon, and then complained to the team that he'd gotten the "bum of the family" instead of my brother, who was a star football player at a rival high school. I dropped football, swallowed my pride and went out for the cheerleading team. I didn't even make that. I was the classic ninety-pound weakling—except that nobody would have dreamed of using my picture in an advertisement.

The white cops in Oakland stopped me on the streets all the time, grilled me and routinely called me "nigger." Whenever they said it, it put me in such a state that I would shrivel up inside and think, "Oh, God. They're right." I gave everybody the benefit of the doubt—friends who ignored me, strangers who were mean—because I thought they were probably justified.

All this changed after that trip down the hall. I finished classes that day and went home feeling as if some golden bird had landed on my shoulder. Every time I checked to see if it was still there, I had expected it to be gone. Maybe it would leave just as mysteriously as it had come, and then I'd turn back into my old self. I remember going to bed that night thinking that sleep would be the real test. If I still had the warm feeling the next morning, I told myself, I'd accept that change as permanent; otherwise it would be just another of life's mysteries. I was so eager to find out whether I could keep this new gift that it took me hours to doze off.

I woke up the next morning and checked my mind to see what

thoughts were in it. "Hey, you're all right," my mind told me, and I realized the feeling was still there. I jumped out of bed so happy that I embarrassed myself; you could have made moonbeams out of my smile. I decided I was a man.

From that day on, whenever I've felt hostility from someone, I've assumed that it was their problem rather than mine. It was just the opposite from the way I had been before. The teachers at Mc-Clymonds High School seemed different to me, for example. I knew that nearly all the teachers did not like their students, and since I had always looked up to these teachers as adults and authority figures, I'd assumed they must be right; there must be something wrong with all of us. But after my revelation I decided that there was nothing wrong with me, or with most of the other kids, so it must be the teachers.

There *was* something wrong with them. They were stuck in a ghetto school at low pay, trapped there just as firmly as their pupils. None of the kids really expected to go to college, and very few of the faculty expected to go anywhere either. It was not a school that inspired high hopes for anybody, and most of the teachers were bitter about it. They ran kids through "job-training" classes that consisted mainly of personal errands. They prepared kids for the harsh realities of the ouside world by deflating their dreams with cynical comments. Once I almost told a teacher that I wanted to be an architect, but I stopped myself; I knew what she would say.

Hostility and failure were still all around me, but I no longer accepted responsibility for them. Now people had a hard time making me feel guilty, and those who called me "nigger" saw me raise my hackles instead of tucking in my tail. I kept telling myself that it was all right to be who I was, and if I was all right, then anybody who insulted me when I was minding my own business deserved to be pushed back into his own territory. That's what I tried to do. I had a lot of fights in my late teens, and I was big enough to win most of them. My cowering look turned into a glowering one. The adults in my neighborhood, who seemed to notice every inch I grew as I pushed up past them, said I was growing up.

The process of growing up was anything but routine. In fact, I don't think I even *would* have if it hadn't been for that revelation which shook me out of self-hatred. It gave me a sense of confidence. At that time, no reasonable person could have looked at me or the circumstances of my life and predicted that I would accomplish anything. I was trapped and basically untalented; I had a way of gnawing on my failures as if they were leftovers from yesterday's lunch; and even after that day in the hall, I had no great sense of purpose. There were no thoughts of being a president or a star. I was still aimless, but one crucial factor had changed: whatever happened to me, I realized, I would still know that I was not fundamentally flawed. And if *I* knew that, what other people thought didn't matter. Most of them were probably attacking me because of some failing that they saw in themselves. I was basically sound, everything looked brighter to me, and I had a new sense of wonder. It was like waking up.

I knew at the time that this was a significant event in my life, but I didn't realize just how important it was. I was only sixteen, after all, and so every little change would look big. I kept waiting for something to come along and top the experience, something just as startling but more mature that I couldn't even imagine. But many experiences have come and gone in the decades since, and I'm still waiting for something to have a greater impact on me. Kids think that their really important life will begin when they're an adult, but many adults realize later that the important things in their lives happened when they were kids.

Magic interested me a lot in those days. I wondered if there was magic in the universe. If not, how could I explain my revelation? As far as I could tell, it came for no reason. Magic had preoccupied me for a long time, going back to the days of the haints in Louisiana and to my mother's stories about how I was charmed, but it was not something I thought about seriously until high school. I could see both sides. On magic's behalf I could easily accept the idea, for instance, that the earth could lie as barren as the moon for thirty-five thousand years after a nuclear holocaust, without a single weed growing, and that then, suddenly everything could start growing again. Poof, like magic. I still believe that most of what people really care about comes from the realm of magic—sex, religion, art, the spark in someone's personality.

But I also see so much logic in nature that I'm inclined to believe the scientists' theory that there is a logical explanation for everything, including how the universe got there. We just don't know enough yet. Scientists are fascinated by magic, probably more so than astrologers or mystics, but they want to evaporate all magical happenings with the heat of their intelligence. That can be very boring.

I have gone around and around in my internal debate about magic. To deny it completely would be to set myself against the special moments I've experienced. Of course I could relate to them by denying the very quality that made them special—their magic. I could claim that the magic I have known was a product of ignorance on my part, that it was only an unsolved problem. But I can't do that. I have to allow a place in my world for magic. Still, how big a place? Everything I've seen in my travels tells me that if you let magic get its foot in the door, pretty soon that foot will be on your neck. Once you allow for magic's existence, you'll soon be explaining all sorts of unknowns and taboos with rules and formulas based on magic— and from there it's a short jump to superstition and bigotry. My guess is that racism, most wars, and all religious dogmas originated as innocent bits of magic. Somewhere back in dim history, somebody saw something go poof, and he felt warm and awed. His experience itself was a mystery, and magic was the answer. Everybody who heard about the experience got the same feeling, and they all wanted answers. Eventually the magic would become the source of power, interpretations, rules, punishments and heartache.

The compromise I've worked out for myself is designed to keep magic in its place. I believe in magic's first seed, that first marvelous moment of awe when the feeling seems to glow like a lightning bug. It's the kind of rush you get when you discover how amazing nature is while climbing around in the Rocky Mountains or chugging down the Congo River. That flash of awe is the heart of religion; it's more of a question than an answer. Or maybe it's just an intense appreciation for feeling able to ask such big questions. Whatever it is, it's very pesonal. I don't try to communicate my thoughts on the sources or implications of magic because I think the very process of explaining ruins it. Ask me a thousand different questions about religion and I'll say only that I believe there's something going on out there that fills me with joy and wonder.

It's one thing to have your vision in some romantic place like the peak of Mount Kilimanjaro; it's quite another to have it at McClymonds High School in West Oakland. It was so unexpected that I didn't know what to do with it. But though there was no outlet for the new optimism, I didn't really care at the time. Then I gradually woke up to basketball, which was well suited to my new confidence. In fact, I developed more assurance in just about everything except women. Over the years I've decided that the magic of women comes from an entirely different department in the store.

b. ECONOMY

Henry David Thoreau

Near the end of March, 1845, I borrowed an axe and went down to the woods by Walden Pond, nearest to where I intended to build my house, and began to cut down some tall arrowy white pines, still in their youth, for timber. It is difficult to begin without borrowing, but perhaps it is the most generous course thus to permit your fellow-men to have an interest in your enterprise. The owner of the axe, as he released his hold on it, said that it was the apple of his eye; but I returned it sharper than I received it. It was a pleasant hillside where I worked, covered with pine woods, through which I looked out on the pond, and a small open field in the woods where pines and hickories were springing up. The ice in the pond was not yet dissolved, though there were some open spaces, and it was all dark colored and saturated with water. There were some slight flurries of snow during the days that I worked there; but for the most part when I came out onto the railroad, on my way home, its yellow sand heap stretched away gleaming in the hazy atmosphere, and the rails shone in the spring sun, and I heard the lark and pewee and other birds already come to commence another year with us. They were pleasant spring days, in which the winter of man's discontent was thawing as well as the earth, and the life that had lain torpid began to stretch itself. One day, when my axe had come off and I had cut a green hickory for a wedge, driving it with a stone, and had placed the whole to soak in a pond hole in order to swell the wood, I saw a striped snake run into the water, and he lay on the bottom, apparently without inconvenience, as long as I stayed there, or more than a quarter of an hour; perhaps because he had not yet fairly come out of the torpid state. It appeared to me that for a like reason men remain in their present low and primitive condition; but if they should feel the influence of the spring of springs arousing them, they would of necessity rise to a higher and more ethereal life. I had previously seen the snakes in frosty mornings in my path with portions of their bodies still numb and inflexible, waiting for the sun to thaw them. On the 1st of April it rained and melted the ice, and in the early part of the day, which was very foggy, I heard a stray goose groping about over the pond and cackling as if lost, or like the spirit of the fog.

So I went on for some days cutting and hewing timber, and also studs and rafters, all with my narrow axe, not having many communicable or scholar-like thoughts, singing to myself.

> Men say they know many things;
> But lo! they have taken wings—
> The arts and sciences,
> And a thousand appliances;
> The wind that blows
> Is all that anybody knows.

I hewed the main timber six inches square, most of the studs on two sides only, and the rafters and floor timbers on one side, leaving the rest of the bark on, so that they were just as straight and much stronger than sawed ones. Each stick was carefully mortised or tenoned by its stump, for I had borrowed other tools by this time. My days in the woods were not very long ones; yet I usually carried my dinner of bread and butter, and read the newspaper in which it was wrapped, at noon, sitting amid the green pine boughs which I had cut off, and to my bread was imparted some of their fragrance, for my hands were covered with a thick coat of pitch. Before I had done I was more the friend than the foe of the pine tree, though I had cut down some of them, having become better acquainted with it. Sometimes a rambler in the wood was attracted by the sound of my axe, and we chatted pleasantly over the chips which I had made.

By the middle of April, for I made no haste in my work, but rather made the most of it, my house was framed and ready for the raising. I had already bought the shanty of James Collins, an Irishman who worked on the Fitchburg Railroad, for boards. James Collins' shanty was considered an uncommonly fine one. When I called to see it he was not at home. I walked about the ouside, at first unobserved from within, the window was so deep and high. It was of small dimensions, with a peaked cottage roof, and not much else to be seen, the dirt being raised five feet all around as if it were a compost heap. The roof was the soundest part, though a good deal warped and made brittle by the sun. Doorsill there was none, but a perennial passage for the hens under the door board. Mrs. C. came to the door and asked me to view it from the inside. The hens were driven in by my approach. It was dark, and had a dirt floor for the most part, dank, clammy, and aguish, only here a board and there a board which would not bear removal. She lighted a lamp to show me the inside of the roof and the walls, and also that the board floor extended under the bed, warning me not to step into the cellar, a sort of dust hole two feet deep. In her own words, they were "good boards overhead, good boards all around, and a good window"—of two whole squares originally, only the cat had passed out that way lately. There was a stove, a bed, and a place to sit, an infant in the house where it was born, a silk parasol, gilt-framed looking-glass, and a patent new coffee-mill nailed to an oak sapling, all told. The bargain was soon concluded, for James had in the meanwhile returned. I to pay four dollars and twenty-five cents tonight, he to vacate at five tomorrow morning, selling to nobody else meanwhile: I to take possession at six. It were well, he said, to be there early, and anticipate certain indistinct but wholly unjust claims on the score of ground rent and fuel. This he assured me was the only encumbrance. At six I passed him and his family on the road. One large bundle held their all—bed, coffee-mill, looking-glass, hens—all but the cat; she took to the woods and became a wild cat and, as I learned afterward, trod in a trap set for woodchucks, and so became a dead cat at last.

I took down this dwelling the same morning, drawing the nails, and removed it to the pond side by small cartloads, spreading the boards on the grass there to bleach and warp back again in the sun. One early thrush gave me a note or two as I drove along the woodland path. I was informed treacherously by a young Patrick that neighbor Seeley, an Irishman, in the intervals of the carting, transferred to still tolerable, straight, and drivable nails, staples, and spikes to his pocket, and then stood when I came back to pass the time of day, and look freshly up, unconcerned, with spring thoughts, at the devastation; there being a dearth of work, as he said. He was there to represent spectatordom, and help make this seemingly insignificant event one with the removal of the gods of Troy.

I dug my cellar in the side of a hill sloping to the south, where a woodchuck had formerly dug his burrow, down through sumach and blackberry roots, and the lowest stain of vegetation, six feet square by seven deep, to a fine sand where potatoes would not freeze in any winter. The sides were left shelving, and not stoned; but the sun having never shone on them, the sand still keeps its place. It was but two hours' work. I took particular pleasure in this breaking of ground, for in almost all latitudes men dig into the earth for an equable temperature. Under the most splendid house in the city is still to be found the cellar where they store their roots as of old, and long after the superstructure had disappeared posterity remark its dent in the earth. The house is still but a sort of porch at the entrance of a burrow.

At length, in the beginning of May, with the help of some of my acquaintances, rather to improve so good an occasion for neighborliness than from any necessity, I set up the frame of my house.

No man was ever more honored in the character of his raisers than I. They are destined, I trust, to assist at the raising of loftier structures one day. I began to occupy my house on the 4th of July, as soon as it was boarded and roofed, for the boards were carefully feather-edged and lapped, so that it was perfectly impervious to rain, but before boarding I laid the foundation of a chimney at one end, bringing two cartloads of stones up the hill from the pond in my arms. I built the chimney after my hoeing in the fall, before a fire became necessary for warmth, doing my cooking in the meanwhile out of doors on the ground, early in the morning: which mode I still think is in some respects more convenient and agreeable than the usual one. When it stormed before my bread was baked, I fixed a few boards over the fire, and sat under them to watch my loaf, and passed some pleasant hours in that way. In those days, when my hands were much employed, I read but little, but the least scraps of paper which lay on the ground, my holder, or tablecloth, afforded me as much entertainment, in fact answered the same purpose as the Iliad.

2. Use the seven "Questions for Determining Controlling Idea, Form, Purpose, and Response" to analyze the following article. Summarize your findings by indicating the controlling idea, form, purpose, and response.

a. PACKAGED SENTIMENT

Richard Rhodes

Christmas is come, the holiday season, and with it our annual deluge of cards, whose successful dispersal across the land the Postal Service heralds to justify failing us for the rest of the year. "By God, we moved the Christmas cards!" Well, half of all the personal mail moved annually in the United States is greeting cards. Cards for Christmas but also cards for New Year's, Valentine's Day, Easter, Mother's Day, Father's Day, Independence Day and Thanksgiving and Halloween, the official holidays of the American year. And for the occasions greeting-card people call "Everyday," though they are not, births and birthdays, graduations, weddings, anniversaries, showers, vacations, friendship, promotion, hello, love, thanks, good-bye, illness and bereavement, and even to have Thought O'You and for a Secret Pal. We are a nation not of letter writers but of card signers. If the personal letter is long dead, maimed by the penny post and murdered by the telephone, the mass-produced card thrives, picturing what we haven't skill to picture, saying what we haven't words to say. Cards knot the ties that bind in a land where a fourth of us change residence with every change of calendar and where grown children no longer live at home. They show us at our best, if in borrowed finery. You may buy a card made of pansies and doggerel or you may buy a card made of da Vinci and the Sermon on the

Mount. Whoever receives it will understand what you meant, and that you meant well.

The Christmas card was an English invention, but the greeting card an American one. One hundred twenty-eight years ago this season, an Englishman distracted by business matters failed to get his Christmas cards written. Boldly he turned an embarrassment into an opportunity, commissioned a paper tableau of Pickwickians, their glasses raised in toast, and inside each engraved and colored folio he printed a verse. His friends' reactions were not recorded. No doubt some found the idea distastefully impersonal and lamented the decline of manners in a declining age. Others, alert for new twists, thought it charming. The sensible saw its efficiency. It met the first requirement of all mechanical inventions: it saved time.

We have taken the idea and made it ours. The English send few cards today, and Europeans fewer still. We send cards for everything, mechanizing and standardizing the complex relationships we maintain with one another, to give us time to breathe. We needn't be ashamed of our custom. Elegant mechanizing is what we do best. It is the form our national character has taken. Look at our office buildings raised on narrow pillars ten feet off the ground as if someone had dared us to float a fifty-story building in the air. Compare our white and graceful moon rockets to the Soviet Union's drab boiler plate. Look at our cards, little shuttles of sentiment weaving across the land.

Some of the old cards, the nineteenth-century cards that borrowed the Englishman's invention, were masterpieces of reproduction, printed in as many as twelve colors with verses selected in national contests with cash prizes, verses no better than they should be for all the fanfare. The Victorian Age produced German cards that opened up into three-dimensional sleighing scenes of marvelous intricacy, cards with moving parts, cards fringed like a love-seat pillow with gaudy silks, cards as ornate as any gingerbread house. Cards, one presumes, for the wealthy, because the rest of us hadn't begun sending them in today's incredible numbers, today's fifteen or twenty *billion* cards a year. Now that we do, the special effects that delicate handwork once supplied have had to be scaled down, though the cards we send today carry their weight of handwork too, and with it their weight of amusing stories, cautionary tales of American ingenuity gone berserk. I remember a humorous card that required for its gag a small plastic sack of what it called "belly-button fuzz" stapled below its punch line. No supplier could thumb out enough of the authentic material to meet the demand, so the manufacturer turned to the clothes dryers of a nearby college town, bought up the lint franchise, sterilized the lint to meet health regulations, and bagged it and stapled it on, by hand, and got the effect it was seeking and probably, college towns being college towns, got some belly-button fuzz too. "Attachments," such devices are called—plastic tears, toy scissors, miniature boxes of crayons, feathers, spring-and-paper jumping jacks, pencils, beans, the detritus of industrial civilization shrunk to card size. An attachment will sell a humorous card all by itself if it isn't stolen first, a problem for greeting-card manufacturers as surely as it is a problem for the sellers of screws and beads and hair ribbons in dime stores. Like children we lust to get our hands on little things, finding magic in tiny representations of the lumbering world.

The business of greeting cards began in the ambitions of hungry men, and they improvised as they went. There are schools of nursing and schools of nuclear physics, but there are no schools for the makers of greeting cards, only apprenticeships. When Joyce Hall of country Nebraska began his enterprise in Kansas City, Missouri, more than sixty years ago, there weren't even many kinds of cards. Christmas, Easter, birthdays, and weddings were about the only occasions we announced. Hall, Fred Rust of Rust Craft, and a few people like them had to teach us to send cards by making cards we wanted to send. In that work, Hall's career strikingly parallels the career of another Midwesterner, Walt Disney, for both men learned to parse our emotions and recast them in visual and verbal form. Disney, for example, took some shadowy figures from a fairy tale, clothed them in universals, and gave us the Seven Dwarfs. Hall and his people took our need to signal our degrees of social familiarity and our various notions of good taste and gave us a choice among greeting cards.

For any given social occasion, depending on how well you know someone and what you want him to think of you, you may select a card for him that is Formal, Traditional, Humorous, Floral, Cute, Contemporary, or some other among Hallmark's many categories of mood. Two cards for a friend who is hospitalized give the flavor. One, an embossed vase of flowers, says, "Glad your Operation's Over" on the cover, and inside:

That this card comes to tell you,
And then let you know
How much you are wished
A recovery that's quick—
For someone like you
Is too nice to be sick!

The other card, a photograph of a cotton bunny in a flower-bedecked four-poster, opens with, "Hope you'll soon be out of that *blooming bed!*" and carries the flower pun through:

Sure like to see you back in the *pink,*
So just take it easy, 'cause then
You'll soon be in *clover,*
Feeling just *rosy,*
And fresh as a *daisy* again!

Moods and tones and levels, you see. You are not likely to send a Contemporary card to your maiden aunt nor a Formal card to your spouse. The greeting-card people give you a range of choices. It may be a narrower range than you would prefer, but if you are a sender of cards at all, the choices will not be so narrow that you turn away in disgust and write a letter. You may choose frank sentiment;

humor ranging from the modestly ethnic (hillbillies, Indians, Dead End Kids—blacks, Italians, and Eastern Europeans are out today, though they used to be a staple) to the heavily punned to the backward compliment to the gentle slap; simple statement, favored for Christmas and sympathy cards, both occasions being to some people matters serious enough for prose; and a number of alternatives between. Visually, you may choose flowers, cartoons, arabesque gilding, photographs, even reproductions of fine art, though few enough of those because few people buy them. Or stylized little children with ink-drop eyes, or encrustations of plastic jewels, or velvet flocking, or metallic glitter. Variations in texture and surface are legion—and the pride of the older generation of greeting-card men, who believed in making a quality product, who learned what would sell by selling, and who relied for their judgment in such matters on what Joyce Hall once called "the vapors of past experience."

Even if you have never given thought to such matters as categories of emotion and levels of taste, greeting-card people know you operate by them, and know how many cards to make to meet your needs. Such is the variety, of cards and of needs, that the largest of the manufacturers, Hallmark Cards, would have collapsed a decade ago if the computer hadn't come along to speed their sorting. The company claims 12,000 products, counting each separate design a product, and the figure is certainly conservative. Twelve thousand different products in quantities of six to perhaps 20,000 different stores: you can do the multiplication yourself, but count in the envelopes; count in as many as ten or twenty different manufacturing operations on every card; count in all the designs being prepared for future publication, designs that pass through hundreds of hands at drawing boards and typewriters and approval committees and lithographic cameras and printing plants; count in all these different bits of information and many more besides, and you arrive at a total that demands the kind of machines that track astronauts to the moon.

And count in one thing more: every display in every store is a modest computer of its own, each of its pockets filled with designs that favor the social and cultural biases of the neighborhood around the store, and among those favored designs the best sellers of the day. "Tailoring," Hallmark calls it—loading the display to favor the preferences of the young or old or black or white or Catholic or Jewish or rich or poor who regularly shop there. The salesman sets up the display with the help of the owner; after that the computer in Kansas City keeps track. The point, of course, is to give you a maximum range of choice among the choices available. Tucked away in the stock drawer below the display, quietly humming, an IBM card meters every design.

Despite appearances, then, greeting-card manufacture is no work of hand coloring performed by elderly ladies in lace. The Hallmark plant in Kansas City occupies two city blocks, and the company doesn't even do its own printing. Times Square would fit nicely inside the new distribution center Hallmark is building on a railroad spur outside of town. More than one printing firm in the United States owes its giant color presses to Hallmark orders, which is why the company gets the kind of quality it is known for—because it has the heft to stop the presses and pull a proof. It claims 400 artists in residence, the largest art department in the world, and if you include the girls who separate out the colors of a design by hand, a procedure that still costs less for certain designs than separating the colors by machine, the claim is fair.

So many different operations go into the production of greeting cards that even a glimpse of them boggles the mind, serene and simple as the cards look when they finally reach the store. Hallmark buys paper by the boxcar, paper of every imaginable texture and weight, parchment, deckle, bond, pebble-grained, leather-grained, cloth-grained, board, brown wrapping, hard-finished, soft-finished, smooth. Special committees earnestly debate the future popularity of roses or ragamuffins. An artist conceives a group of cards that feature cartoon mice, and the cards sell and the artist is rewarded with a trip to San Francisco. Down in the bowels of the building, behind a secret door, a master photographer labors as he has labored for most of a decade to perfect flat three-dimensional photography using a camera on which Hallmark owns the license, a camera that rolls around in a semicircle on model railroad tracks, its prisms awhirr. In California a contract artist makes dolls of old socks and ships them to Kansas City to be photographed for children's cards. Market-research girls carry cards mounted on black panels to meetings of women's clubs, where the ladies, at a charitable fifty cents a head, choose among different designs with the same verses, or different verses with the same design, helping Hallmark determine the very best that you might care to send. An engineer, a stack of handmade designs before him on his desk, struggles to arrange them on a lithography sheet to get the maximum number of designs per sheet so that they can be printed all at once with minimum waste of paper— "nesting," the process is called. Artists roam the streets of major cities at Christmastime, studying shop windows and the offerings of art galleries to discover new trends in visual design. A deputation of sales managers retreats to an Ozark resort for a multimedia presentation of next year's line. A mechanical genius grown old in the service of the firm remembers the tricks he has taught mere paper cards to do: walking, talking, sticking out their tongues, growling, snoring, squeaking, issuing forth perfume at the scratch of a fingernail across microscopic beads. An engineer sits down at a handwork table and conducts a motion study and designs a system and lines and lines of young girls in gray smocks follow the system to assemble a complicated card by hand, their hands making the memorized motions while they dream of boyfriends or listen to the rhythm of the gluing machines interweaving fugally along the line. A master engraver puts the finishing touches on a die that will punch a dotted line around a paper puppet on a get-well card. A committee of executives meets and decides that the pink of a card isn't cheerful enough and the cartoon figure on another card not sufficiently neuter to appeal both to men and to women. A shipment of paper for a line of children's books is frozen into a harbor in Finland when it should be steaming its way to a printing plant in Singapore. A baby leopard runs loose in the photography department while an editor upstairs sorts through another shipment of amateur verse mailed in by the card lovers of America. He has not found a writer worth encouraging in three years. Greeting cards aren't simply manufactured, like soap or breakfast cereal. They are rescued from the confusing crosscurrents of American life, every one of them a difficult recovery. John Donne found the King's likeness on a coin: greeting-card manufacturers must discover Everyman's likeness and somehow fix it on paper with all its idiosyncrasies smoothed away.

Hallmark employs far fewer writers than artists, about fifteen or twenty. Unlike designs, verses enjoy a long half-life if they are adjusted for minor changes in the language along the way. These days they are often selected—selected entire, not written—by computer from a stock of the most popular verses of the past. The writers try to think up new words, and from time to time they do. Greeting-card verse has come in for its share of ridicule, which perhaps it deserves, but before it is ridiculed its distinction ought to be explained. Most song lyrics look equally ridiculous when printed bald, because the rhetoric of a song lyric, the source of its emotional impact, is the music that accompanies it. The rhetoric of greeting-card verse is the card, the physical and visual accompaniment to the verse. A few greeting-card makers have caught on to the similarity between song lyrics and greeting-card verse and have begun to borrow effects they can use, as in this verse from one of American Greetings' new "Soft Touch" cards, cards for young people that feature soft-focus photography:

> untold the times i've kissed you
> in the moments i have missed you
> and our love goes on forever . . .
> with you softly on my mind

If that doesn't quite make sense, well, neither do most lyrics away from their music, or greeting-card verses away from their cards. A poem, a real poem, the thing itself, works no better on a greeting card or in a song, because it contains its own orchestration and goes dissonant when larded with the scrapings of Mantovani strings.

Modern young people don't like eight-line rhymed verses, preferring song words or evocative sentences. One card on my desk is captioned merely "Peace," which makes it appropriate to almost every occasion except Halloween. Finding the right words for a card is harder today than it used to be because a generation trained on the film expects the words and images to subtly interlock. Getting new words approved by management is harder still. Like most American corporations of healthy middle age, Hallmark has discovered the benefits of redundant personnel and of a certain resistance to fad.

Good ideas don't come along every morning, and they must always be weighed against the success of the old: there are only so many pockets in a greeting-card display. Joyce Hall, a tall, spare man with a W. C. Fields nose and a lifetime of practical experience, used to approve every card Hallmark made, words, music, and all; and his son, Donald Hall, who is now president of the firm, still approves every Contemporary card that gets past his secretary, or did when I worked there. A friend of mine who free-lanced for Hallmark once earned that secretary's enmity with a design she thought in questionable taste. "It's nice, Bill," she told him, "but it's not Hallmark." You cannot be too careful, and who is to say she wasn't right?

If the process of selection was once a matter of subjective judgment, it is today at least outwardly scientific. For reasons that only statisticians understand, Kansas City is a superb test market. If products sell in Kansas City, they will sell to the nation, a fact that city sophisticates might soberly consider the next time they buy a card. The formula doesn't always work—the East Coast prefers the word "Pop" to the word "Dad" on its Father cards, for example—but it works often enough to keep Hallmark researchers close to home. Yet market research is often discounted at Hallmark. The vapors of past experience still blow through the halls, and men whose only business experience has been with greeting cards still ignore the information of market tests if it conflicts with the information of the gut.

Daring subjectivity was Joyce Hall's genius, and remains a legacy of sorts in the hands of less remarkable men now that he has reluctantly relinquished command. Like every successful self-made man he has found retirement difficult. He is a man of quirks and crotchets and always was, but the enterprise he began out of a suitcase stashed under his bed at the Kansas City YMCA now ranks high on *Fortune* magazine's list of the 500 leading privately owned American corporations. The Hall family still owns the place lock, stock, and barrel. It is one of the few privately owned companies of any size left in Kansas City, where wealthy sons of fathers who sweated their way up from poverty tend to sell out to national conglomerations and pass their time at Martha's Vineyard or Harbor Point or Cannes. "You can teach your children everything but poverty," Hall once said, but he taught his son to care about the family firm; and today Hallmark thrives, branching out into gift books, stationery, party goods, calendars and albums, puzzles, candy, pens, urban redevelopment, retail stores on the Neiman-Marcus model, and whatever other enterprises it can find that fit its broad conception of its business, which it calls, modestly enough, "social expression."

I could complain against greeting cards. It isn't difficult to do in a world where more people feel pain than feel pleasure. There is even the risk that if I don't complain you will take me for a patsy. The greeting card's contribution to literacy will not be decisive, but I don't believe it does us that much harm. By definition, popular art can only be defended numerically, and to those who equate numbers with mediocrity, to the antipopulists, a numerical defense amounts to a certain conviction. Television is mediocre because it caters to popular taste, and greeting cards too. No. If either of them has a glaring weakness, it is that among their plethora of choices they do not give us all the choices we might want, or need. That is the effect of the marketplace, lopping off the ends of the bell curve, but the marketplace pays our bills. And if you would like to consider an opposing view, consider Joyce Hall's, who remembers this nation when it was largely rural and uneducated, and who believed that one of Hallmark's responsibilities was the elevation of American taste, a view that might seem didactic of him, but I was a country boy too, and the first play I ever saw, chills running down my back, was *Macbeth,* on television's *Hallmark Hall of Fame.*

Hallmark established its considerable reputation with thought and care, spending far less on advertising than most companies that make consumer products do. It sponsors television specials and between the acts simply shows its cards. Can you remember a year when the *Hall of Fame* didn't come in for at least one Emmy? Do you know how many Americans traipsed through art galleries they had never visited before to see the collection of paintings by Winston Churchill that Hallmark shipped around the land? No breath of public scandal has ever blown through the organization. It does not make napalm and until very recently was old-fashioned enough to pay its bills in cash. One of its best men, now retired, a German Jew named Hans Archenhold whose printing plant was seized by the Nazis, came to Kansas City in its gangster years and found the printing industry there a sty of kickbacks and corruption. With the leverage of Hallmark printing orders he helped to clean it up. Hall himself switched his employees from coffee to milk breaks during the Depression, reasoning, in memory of his own hungry years, that they probably ate no breakfast and might not be sure of lunch, and I doubt that many complained of paternalism. By all means rail against the size and impersonality of American corporations—your arguments will be well taken—but remember also that most are little Swedens now, dispensing profits and medical care and life insurance and retirement funds with a cheerful hand.

Today Hallmark's brand identity, an elusive commodity in a competitive society, approaches 100 per cent. Schoolchildren, asked to make cards in class, often draw a crown on the back of their productions or attempt the famous slogan, "When you care enough to send the very best," in sturdy Big Chief print. There are other greeting-card companies, American, Buzza-Cardozo, Rust Craft, and Hallmark's own poor cousin, Ambassador Cards, to name only the biggest, but the one giant has come to stand for them all.

Strangely, 80 per cent of the buyers of greeting cards are women. That is why cards are tested at women's clubs. Even cards for men are designed with a woman buyer in mind, featuring scenes so romantically masculine that only the coldest feminine heart would not be touched: pipes and slippers, a red-capped hunter knocking down a brace of ducks, a fleet of galleons in harbor unaccountably full-sailed, knightly shields and lordly crests, racy automobiles, workshop tools, or smiling Dad (Pop) himself. Why do women buy most of the cards? The answer may be simpler than it seems. Men think themselves too busy running the nation to find time for the smaller amenities, but they rationalize. The truth is that they are locked into an office or on a production line all day. Running an office, doing a job, no more takes all day than housework—few of us have brains that run so uniformly by the clock—but when the housework is done the woman who does it is free to go visiting or wander through the shops, while the man must shuffle papers and watch the clock. The woman may feel uncomfortable with her freedom, may feel she buys it at too high a price. It is hers nonetheless, and she uses it, among other good works, to buy cards. The new cards, by the way, the cards for young people, don't draw such sharp distinctions between masculine and feminine roles. They are androgynous. We all are, underneath: the kids have found us out.

I suspect we send each other cards partly from guilt, believing we haven't kept our friendships in good repair. If we are gregarious, we are also shy, uneasy as only a people raised in a society straining toward egalitarianism can be. Most of us were never rich and never desperately poor. We never learned our place: we started this country so we wouldn't have to, but our mobility leaves us unsure of where our elbows belong. We are known for our humor, but not for our wit; for our ability, but not for our style; for our strength, but not for our grace. We find ourselves harried and we fumble, or think we do.

Our guilt is misplaced. Thoreau's three chairs for company and two for friendship nicely defines our human limits. They are no longer limits to which we can comfortably adhere. We would hurt too many feelings if we did, the feelings of the people we work with, of our relatives and our neighbors and the neighbors we left behind. Anyone who has moved recently knows how much sheer matter we accumulate in our houses, but imagine also the long list of acquaintances we have accumulated, back to our earliest years. If we are fond of people at all, we have met thousands in our lives. Perhaps that is why so few of us read. Perhaps our culture is really oral, despite the science fiction of our media, satellites above and wires and presses below and the air itself in fervent vibration. One recalls the theory that ghetto children have difficulty in school not because of deprivation but because of excess, of overstimulation by the teeming world in which they live. It is true to some degree of us all. With China and the Soviet Union, and for much of the same reasons of origin and purpose, we are a national people far more than we are local. Our traditions and our associations extend from ocean to ocean, and our burden of communication too. The Communist nations, not having finished their first industrial revolution, turn to party meetings and rallies to stay in touch; with a more ritualized social structure, we send cards.

Making greeting cards to suit us isn't easy. Try to imagine a card that would please both your grandmother and your revolutionary son—and yet your Christmas card probably did. For reasons no one knows, green cards don't sell. Writers of greeting cards must search their verses for unintentional double entendres, and because of that danger, the word "it" used as a direct object is taboo. "Today's your day to get *it!*" It won't do. St. Patrick's Day cards that kid Irish drinking habits elicit indignant letters from Hibernian Societies, a sign that the Irish are ready to melt the rest of the way into the pot. A card is two years in the making: what if hemlines change? Superman cards reached the stores the day the Superman fad collapsed. And what do you say, in a card, in mere words, to a widow whose world has emptied of the life she loved? (You say, in rhymed verse, that words can't express your sympathy.)

When I worked at Hallmark I sometimes thought of cards as pretty packages with nothing inside, but I am a year older now and I wonder. Perhaps, ephemeral though they are, they carry a greater weight of emotion to a greater number of people than we can bear to carry ourselves. They are tactful, discreet; they strike the right tone. Their designers sweat blood, believe me, to make them so. Even when they fail we forgive the sender and blame the card, as we forgive a caller a bad connection on the phone. Greeting cards have inertia. Like Santa's bag they hang a little behind. They are innately conservative because the occasions of our lives are too important for fads, of style or of spirit. Hallmark has discovered that the young people who buy its breezily pessimistic Contemporary cards return to more traditional forms when they acquire families and careers. Pessimism becomes a luxury they can no longer afford.

We grow older; the cards for our stops along the way await us in the store. They are not dangerous or subversive or mean; they espouse no causes except the old mute causes of life itself, birth and marriage and begetting and death, and these gently. I celebrate them as E. M. Forster celebrated democracy, with a hearty two cheers. Merry Christmas.

chapter 11
Writing: Cause and Effect and Process

One of the most useful and interesting thought processes is placing events in chronological order. History is the study of social, political, and economic changes, and therefore it relies on just such an approach to detail: historical studies place individual events into a meaningful context organized by time. These studies attempt to explain not only what happened but also why these events happened or, more to the immediate point, if one event or series of events *caused* another. From this point of view, history is largely concerned with cause-and-effect analysis.

Physical scientists, on the other hand, are often interested in a different emphasis. A *process* is a series of events that leads to a predictable conclusion. Although in some respects, an analysis of process is similar to studying cause and effect, the difference is that process analyses are much more narrowly and concretely defined. The physicists who designed the first nuclear chain reaction had figured out a process that would produce, if they were correct, the tremendous energy of nuclear fission. They were certainly dealing with cause and effect, but in a significantly limited way. As complicated as nuclear fission is, its variables are considerably fewer than those involved in identifying the causes of a war, for example, or the reasons for the decline of feudalism. Process, then, is a focused and clearly defined cause-and-effect analysis. And, as pointed out in the previous chapter, process predicts what will happen, whereas cause and effect explains what has happened.

Cause and Effect

Ascribing causes to effects is ordinary and widespread, but it is also difficult and quite frequently done in questionable ways. The difficulty arises because of the conflict between our need to understand why events occur and the complexity of factors, some much more important than others, that influences them.

To illustrate, consider the following simple example:

> A salesman arrives late for a meeting. As he enters the room, he stumbles and falls. His head strikes the corner of the conference table, and a large bump begins to form on his forehead.

What caused the bump?

The effect in this example is the bump on the salesman's head. The question asks about the cause that produced that effect.

One way to explain cause and effect is to determine what most immediately preceded the effect in time. Because cause-and-effect relationships occur in a definite time period, identifying the event that comes right before the effect is a good place to begin an analysis.

In this case, the bump on the salesman's forehead was immediately preceded by the rupturing of small blood vessels beneath the skin. Therefore, in terms of time, the damage to those blood vessels is the cause that came right before the effect.

Because causes come before effects in time, it makes sense to list the sequence of cause and effects leading to the bump in the order in which they occurred:

Cause 1: Salesman stumbling and falling.

Effect 1: Contact of the salesman's head with the conference table.

Cause 2: Contact of the salesman's head with the conference table.

Effect 2: Rupture of blood vessels.

Cause 3: Rupture of blood vessels.

Effect 3: Bump on salesman's head.

Notice that each effect becomes a cause that produces another effect, and so the series of actions is a sequence of cause-and-effect relationships.

If you examine this sequence, you will see that Causes 2 and 3, the two that most immediately precede the last effect, are the most obvious and clear. If the salesman's head had not hit the conference table and if that impact had not ruptured the blood vessels, he would not have a bump on his head.

However, you would probably be more interested in knowing why he stumbled and fell in the first place; that is, you would want to identify a cause for this action:

Cause: ?

Effect: Salesman stumbling and falling.

But you would not have enough information to answer this question, because all you know is that the salesman arrived late for the meeting. It is possible that his lateness caused him to rush into the room, and because he was rushing, he tripped. But it is also possible that his lateness had nothing whatever to do with his stumbling. Perhaps his shoelace was untied, or there was a wet spot on the floor. Maybe he was nervous because he had to make an important presentation at the meeting, and so forth. Any one of the above could have caused him to fall, or possibly several of these circumstances worked together:

Effect: Salesman stumbling and falling.

Possible Causes: Rushing? Shoelace? Wet spot? Nervousness?

Without additional information, it would be impossible to identify the precise cause. Moreover, that information might be difficult to obtain, particularly if the physical causes such as the shoelace or the wet spot on the floor were eliminated. We would then be left with the circumstances that pertain to the salesman's state of mind when he entered the room, and so it would be hard to pin down exactly what factor, alone or in combination with another, produced his stumble.

Nonetheless, identifying causes offers the most challenging and rewarding cause-and-effect analyses. We are not usually that interested in knowing how someone raised a bump on his or her head; rather, we want to know the answers to more significant questions.

Writing Cause-and-Effect Essays

Suppose your topic is the growing popularity of video games. Begin by phrasing your effect: Video games have become increasingly popular. This statement is a generalization based on observation, namely, that over the past couple of years, more and more such games have become available, both in homes and in commercial establishments. To explain their popularity, however, will require a careful cause-and-effect analysis, because in all probability it will be impossible to identify the precise cause, and even the possible causes will be elusive.

You can begin by seeking a chronological pattern: What has happened recently that can help explain the increased popularity of video games? Perhaps a recent event can be related to the effect as a cause. There are two possible responses to this question:

1. National literacy has declined over the past decade, as evidenced by such standardized measures as the College Board Examinations.
2. The technology necessary for video games has become increasingly sophisticated and inexpensive.

Both of these are correct; that is, they can be verified as having occurred at about the same time, or before, the increased popularity of video games. The first could be suggested as a cause, but to do so would be speculative and difficult to prove. Just because one circumstance precedes another in time does not automatically make the first a cause for the second. Though there might be a relationship between declining literacy and the increasing popularity of video games, that connection has not been proved. And, in fact, it is possible to argue the point in reverse order, that because teenagers spend so much time playing video games, they are less involved in their studies, and therefore they are not as well educated. A carefully formulated and statistically sound analysis of the relationship between literacy and video games might reveal a cause-and-effect pattern, but again it might not.

The second response is more attractive because the relationship is clearer. If video games were prohibitively expensive to manufacture, they would not be as readily available: they would remain the toys of the well-to-do who would be able to afford them. However, because technology has advanced to the point that such games can be moderately priced, this improved technology can be said to have made the games accessible to a wider audience.

The improved technology used to manufacture video games can be listed as a cause for their increased popularity. But this should be considered only one cause, because it influences but does not determine the effect. If people did not want to play video games, it would not matter how inexpensive or accessible they were; they still would not be popular. Your next step in this cause-and-effect analysis is to determine why the games are popular.

Try to list the characteristics of video games that might make them appealing to a variety of people:

1. They are exciting.
2. They are competitive.
3. They are challenging.
4. They offer a sensuous experience.

The underlying premise for all of these possible causes is that each offers something people want: excitement, competition, challenge, and sensuousness. If that premise is correct, then each of these four factors are possible causes of the increased popularity of video games. Each, however, demands further investigation, in order to compile the details necessary for a full treatment of the subject.

They are exciting.

Question:	What makes them exciting?
Answer:	They are fast moving.
Question:	Why does this make them exciting?
Answer:	Fast-moving entertainments hold interest.
Question:	What else makes them exciting?
Answer:	They involve an element of imagined danger.
Question:	What makes danger exciting?
Answer:	We all enjoy danger, particularly if it is not real.
Question:	What else makes them exciting?
Answer:	They also include a suggestion of violence.
Question:	Is violence exciting?
Answer:	Yes, whether or not we would like to admit it.

The underlined responses can become the details that can expand and explain the first suggested cause for the increased popularity of video games.

They are competitive.

Question:	Is competition something that draws people's interest?
Answer:	Yes, witness all the professional sports based on competition.
Question:	What makes these games competitive?
Answer:	Most of them have a scoring system.
Question:	But don't people play them alone?
Answer:	Yes, but the score still provides competition.
Question:	How so?
Answer:	The person playing alone can compete against his or her best score, or even against some standard of high performance for a particular game.

Now go to the third suggested cause.

They are challenging.

Question:	Is challenge a component of popularity?
Answer:	Yes, people like to be stretched toward some goal.
Question:	What is the challenge of these games?
Answer:	Besides the competition, which is a kind of challenge, these games are designed to become increasingly difficult.
Question:	In what way?
Answer:	Generally, they speed up the action, becoming progressively faster as the player advances to higher levels of proficiency.

Finally, consider the fourth suggested cause:

They provide a sensuous experience.

Question:	What exactly does that mean?
Answer:	That is an experience that appeals to the senses.
Question:	How are the games sensuous?
Answer:	They involve moving characters that are colorful and that are sometimes accompanied by sound effects.
Question:	That makes them sensuous, but are they attractive?
Answer:	The sounds and colors are either pleasing and/or stimulating to the senses, and therefore attractive.

You now have enough information to begin thinking about writing a cause-and-effect discussion of the increased popularity of video games. The exact approach you choose depends on your purpose and your sense of audience.

For example, you might want to write persuasively and argue that video games are detrimental to the mental well-being of the population. You could base such an approach on the ideas generated from the preceding questioning. You might state that the excitement they offer is shallow and superficial, that the competition they foster is unhealthy, that their challenge is a distraction from more worthwhile efforts, and that the sensuousness is a mindless diversion when compared with the appreciation of fine art or music.

Or you could decide to compose an informative essay on the topic, in which you would discuss each of these causes as contributing to the popularity of the games, without attempting to evaluate whether this popularity is good or bad. Using such an approach, you might suggest that the needs for excitement, competition, challenge, and sensuous experience are components of the human personality and that because these games offer the means to satisfy these needs, they are popular.

Let us suppose, however, that you select an expressive purpose. You want to share your enthusiasm for these games and explain why you have become addicted to playing them. Your intended audience would be people who are not similarly attracted to the games and who, therefore, do not understand why you are. Your controlling idea would be: I am addicted to playing video games because I find that playing them makes me feel better.

Your outline, in broad terms, would look like this:

   I. Introduction.
  II. The excitement of video games.
 III. The competition of video games.
 IV. The challenge of video games.
  V. The sensuous experience of video games.
 VI. Conclusion.

The development of these topics would draw on the details suggested in the questioning process, supplemented by others that occur to you as you write. Your style would be subjective because you are writing expressively, and your intention would be to have your audience share your enthusiasm.

> I have discovered a readily available cure for depression and a lack of enthusiasm for life. I do not need prescription medicine or expensive psychological counseling. Whenever I am feeling blue, all I need to do is find my way to the local pizza parlor, shopping mall, or some other commercial establishment that houses video games. There, for a modest quarter a pop, I can exercise my mind and stimulate my heart to pump faster, just as if I were doing a more traditional form of exercise, and at the same time vent my nervous energies or even my hostilities.
>
> Although I have particular favorites among the games, such as Pac Man and Space Invaders, I do not need to limit myself to just those, as most of the popular games offer the same sort of satisfaction. To begin with, these games are exciting.

Imagine a typical blue Monday with all that means: getting up late for work or class, sitting bored at lunchtime with a whole week of dreariness staring you in the face, and then think about a game that will chase away the blues. I sometimes skimp on my lunch break just so I can hit the game machines. I'll gulp down a slice or two of pizza and then start popping quarters instead of pills. I put my first quarter in the slot, and the machine lights up, immediately followed by a gleam in my eyes. Instantly, I am immersed in a fantasy world of moving colors and sounds over which I exercise some measure of control. Things begin to happen fast. Pac Man rounds a corner and then heads through a side exit, only to emerge on the other side, safe and sound ready to gobble up those inviting dots. I make Pac Man move, and that is exciting; as Pac Man I pursue and am pursued, and that's double excitement. The dreary spell of the day is broken.

This excitement alone, however, does not explain my fascination. I would become bored with these games if there were not other elements, and of course there are. Playing these games also satisfies my need to compete, either against myself or against a friend. Because I so often squeeze in my playing time among other activities, I find that I usually play alone. But actually I am playing against the machine, trying each time to reach a higher score and to make the machine reward me with a kaleidoscopic display of congratulatory lights and sounds. Just as the old-fashioned pinball machines gave a good player an extra game for a high score, these electronic games reward proficiency, but with a much more interesting display made possible by the more sophisticated technology of these machines. Moreover, I have one or two friends who share my addiction, and we like nothing better than to match our wits against the machine and one another, reaching for the highest score. These matches are as rewarding as a good game of tennis or racquetball, but much less strenuous. I've never pulled a hamstring muscle playing a video game.

The competition is increased because of the challenge offered by these machines. They are programmed to become more difficult as you become better as a player. If you survive the first round of electronic adventures, the machine will offer you a second or a third, and each demands greater concentration and greater coordination. The action is speeded up, more variables are introduced, and I find myself stretching myself both physically and mentally to keep up with the accelerated pace of the action. And because these games involve computer programs, the patterns can be varied. Pac Man will not always pursue and be pursued through the maze in the same fashion. You may learn to stay out of dangerous corners, but the pursuit does not always come at you in the same way, and you might wind up trapped anyway. Each time I'm caught, I immediately reach for another quarter, for such is the compelling challenge of the games.

Sometimes, though, I am not moved by the excitement, the competition, or even the challenge. I just want to immerse myself in the sensuous experience of the game which is something like a controlled light show. Depending on the game, the colors are mellow or vibrant and stimulating, but they are always pleasing to the eye. As I play the game, I am as much interested in creating new patterns of exploding color as I am in winning or outwitting the program. I bathe my tired mind in the cool blues, or I wake up my tired spirits with the bright reds and oranges. When the game is over, I am refreshed. At these times, whether or not I play well is irrelevant.

I sometimes feel that I should be doing something more productive with my time than playing video games, but then I realize that my guilt comes from somebody else's values, and I remember that these games provide me with more than just amusement: they have become essential to my well-being.

Because this sample essay is expressive, it personalizes the controlling idea developed for the topic. Instead of trying to explain the effect—the increased popularity of video games—in terms of causes that might offer widespread application, it seeks only to present an individual effect—one person's addiction to the games—in terms of that person's particular causes. The expected response is empathy, as the writer reveals feelings that he or she expects the audience to share and understand.

Process

Process analysis is similar to cause and effect in that it involves a series of actions that lead to a conclusion. But a process analysis is usually much more limited and well defined, as it is concerned not so much in identifying causes that lead to an effect but, rather, in outlining steps that produce a predictable and repeatable conclusion. For this reason, process analysis often takes the form of instructions on how to do something; that is, if you follow certain steps, you will inevitably produce the desired result. The other common form of process analysis explains how something is done, not to emulate, but to understand. The first type of process analysis might instruct you how to bake a cake or change the oil in your car, and the second would show you how a nuclear power plant produces energy or how a cancerous tumor might be removed. You could attempt to do the first type of activity, but certainly not the second.

Both forms of process analysis, the *instructional* in which you tell your audience how to do something and the *demonstrative* in which you describe to your audience how something works, require sufficient expertise to present the particular process clearly and in detail. In choosing to write a process analysis, therefore, you should select a topic with which you are familiar.

Writing Process Analysis Essays

For a process analysis essay, you can assume that your audience does not know your topic as well as you do and that it will be interested in what you write. Though process essays can be expressive or persuasive, they usually are informative, as a process analysis nearly always emphasizes the subject matter, in order to instruct the reader.

You can begin by asking yourself, "What process do I know fully and completely?" Suppose you answer, "I know how to start growing a good lawn." Ask yourself, "What are the necessary steps in growing a good lawn?" Answer:

Fertilization.

Planting.

Water.

Soil preparation.

Good seed.

In process analysis, it is absolutely necessary to think through the process from the first step to the last. Usually, you will assume that your audience knows very little about the process that you are describing, and so you will have to be clear, detailed, and logical.

Place the components of the process listed above in a logical, chronologically correct order:

Seed selection.

Ground preparation.

Planting.

Fertilizing.

Watering.

Cutting.

Provide details for each:

Seed selection:
    Cheap versus expensive.
    Soil condition.
    Exposure.
    Wear.
Ground preparation:
    Clearing.
    Raking.
    Consistency.
    Grooving.
Planting:
    Coverage.
    Timing.
    Spreading.
    Covering.
Fertilizing:
    Nutritional needs.
    Amount.
    Type.
Watering:
    Frequency.
    Amount.

Develop a controlling idea: Starting a good lawn from scratch depends on proper planning and carrying out each step of the process.

Each step in the process will become one section of the essay, perhaps one or two paragraphs, depending on the complexity of the particular activity. A completed essay, conforming to this outline, might be something like the following:

A lush, richly green lawn does not result from magic, and it does not require special skill or a great deal of money. Such a lawn can be grown by anyone who takes the time to plan carefully and execute that plan step by step.

The first step is to study the area where you intend to grow your lawn. Check to see how much sun it will receive, and take note of any trees that will shade parts of the lawn. Examine the soil for its consistency to see if it is sandy or mostly clay. If it is sandy, it will not retain moisture well, and soil that is too hard might make it difficult for the seed to take root. Choose your seed with all of these factors in mind. Seed manufacturers specify the type of soil and sun requirements of the particular seed.

You will also have to decide whether to plant an expensive or an inexpensive seed. The expensive varieties of seed, such as pure blue grass, usually take longer to germinate and longer to become established and fill out the lawn area. They may also be more vulnerable to disease and may not wear as well. However, such a lawn offers unparalleled beauty and is well worth the extra initial cost. Less expensive seeds, such as perennial rye, will germinate and spread faster but will also be coarser and more uneven. Whatever grass seed you choose, do not buy a type that includes a significant quantity of weed or crop matter: these pests will be very difficult to remove once they root in your lawn. You will spend more money on weed killer to remove them than you would have spent buying a somewhat more expensive seed.

As with many other things, the proper initial preparation is well worth the investment in time and energy in starting a lawn. The ground, therefore, should be cleared of all debris. If it is particularly rocky, it should be raked thoroughly so that the surface is clear. If it is extremely sandy or clayey, you might want to consider buying some topsoil to provide a better bed for the grass seed. When it is smooth, it should be raked lightly to provide grooves for the seeds to nestle in.

The proper coverage for any seed is specified on the package, often as so many pounds per so many thousands of square feet. Sowing too much seed is just wasteful, and too little will start you off with an unnecessarily sparse lawn. Use the proper amount and sow evenly. You can sow the seed by sprinkling it from your hand. That procedure has the advantage of putting you in touch with nature, but the disadvantage of being difficult to control. You might be better off using a spreader that will distribute the seed evenly and at the proper rate. For the best possible germination, seed should be sowed at a time when the nights are relatively long and the days are cool, as grass is a cool-weather plant. It is very difficult to start a lawn during hot, dry weather.

After the seed is planted, you might want to cover it with a thin layer of soil. You can do this by raking lightly or by using a roller that can be rented from a landscaping or general rental store.

Newly seeded lawns require proper fertilization to ensure good initial growth. Many fertilizer companies now sell special products designed for new lawns, and these products are rich in the nitrogen that is necessary for sprouting grass plants. Again, as with the seeding, each manufacturer recommends a certain rate of application, and this specification should be carefully observed. Too much fertilizer will burn the tender grass shoots, and too little will not provide sufficient nutrition. Evenness of application is also very important to ensure complete coverage. For this purpose, a rotary spreader that tosses the fertilizer in a circular pattern is accurate and efficient. A drop spreader will also be accurate, but it demands a more careful application. Because it drops the product straight down, the operator must carefully guide it in straight rows to ensure even coverage. If you use a drop spreader, you might want to cut the suggested application rate in half and walk the spreader over your lawn area twice, once in either direction.

Grass demands regular watering for good growth. An established lawn might be able to tolerate a drought period, but germinating seed cannot. The germination of specific grass seed is listed on the product's package, and during this period it is essential to keep the ground moist. Again, too much or too little water will be detrimental. Too much water will probably wash your seed into the street, or at least cause pools to form in which the majority of your seed will gather so that when it sprouts you will have scattered clumps of thick green separated by expanses of brown dirt. Too little water, on the other hand, will not provide enough moisture to support the germinating seed. If at all possible, a germinating lawn should be watered twice a day with light applications each time. The best times are late morning and late afternoon to provide moisture during the heat of the day. The cool evenings and morning dews should take care of the rest.

These steps may seem a little time-consuming, but they are well worth following precisely. The few shortcuts available will not save much time or energy, but they will seriously endanger your prospects for success. Take your time so that you will be able to relax on a comfortable lawn chair, surrounded by the lush green results of your planning and your labor.

As with the other model essays in this and previous sections, most of the details were generated in the initial discovery stage of the writing process. Others were added as they came to mind.

This sample process essay is clear and logical, providing step-by-step instructions to teach the reader how to do something. A process analysis that demonstrates how something works, as opposed to how an activity is performed, would be developed and organized in the same manner: Its focus would be on clarity, precision, and logical presentation in a carefully delineated chronological organization.

The possibilities for expressive and persuasive purposes might well include other organizational patterns. For example, a persuasive purpose might be served by comparing and contrasting two processes, that is, two ways to do something, so that the reader will be convinced that one way is better than another. An expressive purpose would demand making the process subjective, that is, particularly meaningful to the writer, and might be an essay that shares the writer's experience in doing something important, such as how the writer gave up smoking, lost weight, or learned to advance in his or her career, and so on. These would still be process analyses because they would present steps or stages over a period of time leading to a definite conclusion, one that could be emulated by other people, but they would be expressive because they would concentrate on the writer's feelings and attitudes.

Exercises

1. Choose one of the following ordinary occurrences:
   a. A car refusing to start in cold weather.
   b. A television show being taken off the air.
   c. Long lines at the registrar's office at the beginning of a semester.
   d. A sale at a department store.
   e. The success of a best-selling novel.
   For the occurrence you choose, establish a chain of causes.
2. Cause-and-effect reasoning can explain both why individuals make certain decisions and why larger, social situations occur.
   Choose a personal decision, such as a career choice, preference for living in a particular neighborhood, or purchase of a substantial consumer item. Analyze the causes that led to your decision.
   Define an audience and purpose for an essay that will discuss your choice. Generate ideas for the essay, refine your sense of audience and purpose, and establish a controlling idea. Write the essay.
3. Examine the processes below. Which would lend themselves to an instructional and which a demonstrative treatment. Why?
   a. The workings of an internal combustion engine.
   b. Instructions accompanying prescription medicine.
   c. A successful job interview.
   d. Studying for a test.
   e. Training a dog.
   f. Satellite communications.
4. Most of us know how to do at least one thing well, and that thing is a process. Using that process as a subject for an essay, define an audience and purpose, generate ideas, develop a controlling idea, and write the essay.

5. Discover how something works, such as the plumbing in your house, the billing system of a charge account, or the merchandising of goods in a local store. Write an instructional process essay, following the composition steps of audience and purpose definition, idea generation, and development of a controlling idea.

Questions for Revision

After you have written your essays for either Exercise 3 or 4, check your work for organization, purpose, and audience by asking the following questions:

Controlling Idea
1. Have I clearly identified the general subject about which I am writing?
2. Have I emphasized certain aspects of this subject matter?
3. Have I established a clear controlling idea by stressing those parts of the subject that I want the reader to understand and remember?

Form
4. Does my controlling idea establish a cause-and-effect relationship? If so, can each cause be logically linked to the effect I have identified?
5. Does my controlling idea show how to do something or how something works? If so, have I observed a proper time sequence and included all necessary steps in the process?

Purpose
6. Does my essay emphasize me, the subject matter, or the audience?

Audience
7. What response do I want my audience to have to this essay?

Revise your work in light of your answers to these questions so that it demonstrates a clear relationship between its controlling idea and its specific details and establishes a good sense of audience and purpose.

chapter 12
Reading: Classification and Definition

Every day of your life you react to hundreds of stimuli. Considered in this way, the world is chaotic until you impose some order on it. For example, observe all of the things that are occurring when you wake up in the morning: there is traffic moving along on the street outside your window; somebody is walking a dog or calling after a child; your brother or sister is in the bathroom; somebody else is having coffee at the breakfast table; your cat is looking at you from his perch on your dresser; your neighbor has just retrieved the morning newspaper; your mouth is dry; and your stomach is empty. The list could be extended indefinitely, and no one person can deal with so many stimuli without some mental sorting.

One of the ways we sort through things is to classify them. When you go to a supermarket, you can see that the different goods are separated into certain sections: fresh produce, frozen foods, meats, canned goods, and so on. If supermarkets did not organize their products in such a way, it would be all but impossible to find the particular products you wished to purchase. This method of organization found in every supermarket or department store is classification.

Classification

Classification is organizing content by dividing broad topics into small parts. Because it is a basic way of organizing thoughts and perceptions, it is a common organizational pattern for writers. Because classification is an attempt to improve your understanding of a complex topic, it is generally easy to identify in the materials you read. Quite often, the writer of a classification essay will announce the basis for the categories in a controlling idea statement.

The sample passages below all use a classification organizational pattern:

Having proposed to myself to treat of the kind of government established at Rome, and of the events that led to its perfection, I must
at the beginning observe that some of the writers on politics distinguished three kinds of government, vis. the monarchical, the aristocratic, and the democratic; and maintain that the legislators of a
people must choose from these three the one that seems to them
most suitable. Other authors, wiser according to the opinion of many,
count six kinds of governments, three of which are very bad, and
three good in themselves, but so liable to be corrupted that they
become absolutely bad. The three good ones are those which we
have just named; the three bad ones result from the degradation of
the other three, and each of them resembles its corresponding original, so that the transition from the one to the other is very easy.
Thus monarchy becomes tyranny; aristocracy degenerates into oligarchy; and the popular government lapses readily into licentious-
ness. So that a legislator who gives to a state which he founds either
of these three forms of government, constitutes it but for a brief time;
for no precautions can prevent either one of the three that are reputed
good from degenerating into its opposite kind; so great are in these
the attractions and resemblances between the good and the evil.

Chance has given birth to these different kinds of governments
amongst men; for at the beginning of the world the inhabitants were
few in number and lived for a time dispersed, like beasts. As the
human race increased, the necessity for uniting themselves for defence made itself felt; the better to attain this object they chose the
strongest and most courageous from amongst themselves and placed
him at their head promising to obey him. Thence they began to know
the good and the honest, and to distinguish them from the bad and
vicious; for seeing a man injure his benefactor aroused at once two
sentiments in every heart, hatred against the ingrate and love for the
benefactor. They blamed the first, and on the contrary honoured those
the more who showed themselves grateful, for each felt that he in
turn might be subject to a like wrong; and to prevent similar evils,
they set to work to make laws, and to institute punishments for those
who contravened them. Such was the origin of justice. This caused
them, when they had afterwards to choose a prince, neither to look
to the strongest nor bravest, but to the wisest and most just. But
when they began to make sovereignty hereditary and non-elective,
the children quickly degenerated from their fathers; and, so far from
trying to equal their virtues, they considered that a prince had nothing
else to do than to excel all the rest in luxury, indulgence, and every
other variety of pleasure. The prince consequently soon drew upon
himself the general hatred. An object of hatred, he naturally felt fear;
fear in turn dictated to him precautions and wrongs, and thus tyranny
quickly developed itself. Such were the beginning and causes of dis-

orders, conspiracies, and plots against the sovereigns, set on foot, not by the feeble and timid, but by those citizens who, surpassing the others in grandeur of soul, in wealth, and in courage, could not submit to the outrages and excesses of their princes.

Under such powerful leaders the masses armed themselves against the tyrant, and after having rid themselves of him, submitted to these chiefs as their liberators. These, abhorring the very name of prince, constituted themselves a new government; and at first bearing in mind the past tyranny, they governed in strict accordance with the laws which they had established themselves; preferring public interests to their own, and to administer and protect with greatest care both public and private affairs. The children succeeded their fathers, and ignorant of the changes of fortune, having never experienced its reverses, and indisposed to remain content with this civil equality, they in turn gave themselves up to cupidity, ambition, libertinage, and violence, and soon caused the aristocratic government to degenerate into an oligarchic tyranny, regardless of all civil rights. They soon, however, experienced the same fate as the first tyrant; the people, disgusted with their government, placed themselves at the command of whoever was willing to attack them, and this disposition soon produced an avenger, who was sufficiently well seconded to destroy them. The memory of the prince and the wrongs committed by him being still fresh in their minds, and having overthrown the oligarchy, the people were not willing to return to the government of a prince. A popular government was therefore resolved upon, and it was so organized that the authority would not again fall into the hands of a prince or a small number of nobles. And as all governments are at first looked up to with some degree of reverence, the popular state also maintained itself for a time, but which was never of long duration, and lasted generally only about as long as the generation that had established it; for it soon ran into that kind of licence which inflicts injury upon public as well as private interests. Each individual only consulted his own passions, and a thousand acts of injustice were daily committed, so that, constrained by necessity, or directed by the counsels of some good man, or for the purpose of escaping from this anarchy, they returned anew to the government of a prince, and from this they generally lapsed again into anarchy, step-by-step, in the same manner and from the same causes as we have indicated.

Such is the circle which all republics are destined to run through. Seldom, however, do they come back to the original form of government, which results from the fact that their duration is not sufficiently long to be able to undergo these repeated changes and preserve their existence. But it may well happen that a republic lacking strength and good counsel in its difficulties becomes subject after a while to some neighbouring state, that is better organized than itself; and if such is not the case, then they will be apt to revolve indefinitely in the circle of revolutions. I say, then, that all kinds of government are defective; those three which we have qualified as good because they are too short-lived, and the three bad ones because of their inherent viciousness. Thus sagacious legislators, knowing the vices of each of these systems of government by themselves, have chosen one that should partake of all of them, judging that to be the most stable and solid. In fact, when there is combined under the same constitution a prince, a nobility, and the power of the people, then these three powers will watch and keep each other reciprocally in check.

This passage's stated controlling idea establishes, in the first paragraph, three kinds of government, each of which has a good and a bad form. The second paragraph explains how monarchy, the first form of government, is established in the name of justice but later degenerates into tyranny. The third paragraph explains how tyranny's influence sets the stage for the second form of government, the aristocratic. It too, like the first, degenerates and is then followed by democracy which in turn becomes anarchy and finally returns to monarchy, thus showing the cycle of governments. In the fourth paragraph, the writer offers a compromise of combination to resolve the problem of choosing one lasting, ideal government. Classifying the governments as part of the controlling idea and then discussing each as a separate but related form is the basis for the body of the work. The author wishes to educate the reader and therefore concentrates on his subject.

A second example of the use of classification follows next:

It is altogether curious, your first contact with poverty. You have thought so much about poverty—it is the thing you have feared all your life, the thing you knew would happen to you sooner or later; and it is all so utterly and prosaically different. You thought it would be quite simple; it is extraordinarily complicated. You thought it would be terrible; it is merely squalid and boring. It is the peculiar *lowness* of poverty that you discover first; the shifts that it puts you to, the complicated meanness, the crust-wiping.

You discover, for instance, the secrecy attaching to poverty. At a sudden stroke you have been reduced to an income of six francs a day. But of course you dare not admit it—you have got to pretend that you are living quite as usual. From the start it tangles you in a net of lies, and even with the lies you can hardly manage it. You stop sending clothes to the laundry, and the laundress catches you in the street and asks you why; you mumble something, and she, thinking you are sending the clothes elsewhere, is your enemy for life. The tobacconist keeps asking why you have cut down your smoking. There are letters you want to answer, and cannot, because stamps are too expensive. And then there are your meals—meals are the worst difficulty of all. Every day at meal-times you go out, ostensibly to a restaurant, and loaf an hour in the Luxembourg Gardens, watching the pigeons. Afterwards you smuggle your food home in your pockets. Your food is bread and margarine, or bread and wine, and even the nature of the food is governed by lies. You have to buy rye bread instead of household bread, because the rye loaves, though dearer, are round and can be smuggled in your pockets. This wastes you a franc a day. Sometimes, to keep up appearances, you have to spend sixty centimes on a drink, and go correspondingly short of food. Your linen gets filthy, and you run out of soap and razor-blades. Your hair wants cutting, and you try to cut it yourself, with such fearful results that you have to go to the barber after all, and spend the equivalent of a day's food. All day you are telling lies, and expensive lies.

You discover the extreme precariousness of your six francs a day. Mean disasters happen and rob you of food. You have spent your last eighty centimes on half a litre of milk, and are boiling it over the spirit lamp. While it boils a bug runs down your forearm; you give the bug a flick with your nail, and it falls, plop! straight into the milk. There is nothing for it but to throw the milk away and go foodless.

You go to the baker's to buy a pound of bread, and you wait while the girl cuts a pound for another customer. She is clumsy, and cuts more than a pound. *"Pardon, monsieur,"* she says, "I suppose you don't mind paying two sous extra?" Bread is a franc a pound, and you have exactly a franc. When you think that you too might be asked to pay two sous extra, and would have to confess that you could not, you bolt in panic. It is hours before you dare venture into a baker's shop again.

You go to the greengrocer's to spend a franc on a kilogram of potatoes. But one of the pieces that make up the franc is a Belgium piece, and the shopman refuses it. You slink out of the shop, and can never go there again.

You have strayed into a respectable quarter, and you see a prosperous friend coming. To avoid him you dodge into the nearest café. Once in the café you must buy something, so you spend your last fifty centimes on a glass of black coffee with a dead fly in it. One could multiply these disasters by the hundred. They are part of the process of being hard up.

You discover what it is like to be hungry. With bread and margarine in your belly, you go out and look into the shop windows. Everywhere there is food insulting you in huge, wasteful piles; whole dead pigs, baskets of hot loaves, great yellow blocks of butter, strings of sausages, mountains of potatoes, vast Gruyère cheeses like grindstones. A snivelling self-pity comes over you at the sight of so much food. You plan to grab a loaf and run, swallowing it before they catch you; and you refrain, from pure funk.

You discover the *boredom* which is inseparable from poverty; the times when you have nothing to do and, being underfed, can interest yourself in nothing. For half a day at a time you lie on your bed, feeling like the *jeune squelette* in Baudelaire's poem. Only food could rouse you. You discover that a man who has gone even a week on bread and margarine is not a man any longer, only a belly with a few accessory organs.

This—one could describe it further, but it is all in the same style— is life on six francs a day. Thousands of people in Paris live it— struggling artists and students, prostitutes when their luck is out, out-of-work people of all kinds. It is the suburbs, as it were, of poverty.

The author of these paragraphs begins with the beliefs that he assumes the reader holds regarding poverty. The reality of poverty is his topic and is the basis for the five discoveries that are the categories of his subject's development. The discoveries are secrecy attached to poverty, the risks of having little money, the nature of hunger, the boredom of poverty, and the emasculating effects of poverty, which are discussed in paragraphs 2, 3, 7, and 8. The concluding paragraph presents Paris as a city in which thousands of people live in poverty. The author has broken down the broad subject of poverty, focusing on its lowness, and then subdivided that perception into categories discovered by the poor person. The reality of poverty and the discoveries one makes when it occurs are seen in relationship to one another. Again, the author's purpose is to inform an audience.

Now read the next selection.

We all listen to music according to our separate capacities. But, for the sake of analysis, the whole listening process may become clearer if we break it up into its component parts, so to speak. In a certain sense we all listen to music on three separate planes. For lack of a better terminology, one might name these: (1) the sensuous plane, (2) the expressive plane, (3) the sheerly musical plane. The only advantage to be gained from mechanically splitting up the listening process into these hypothetical planes is the clearer view to be had of the way in which we listen.

The simplest way of listening to music is to listen for the sheer pleasure of the musical sound itself. That is the sensuous plane. It is the plane on which we hear music without thinking, without considering it in any way. One turns on the radio while doing something else and absent-mindedly bathes in the sound. A kind of brainless but attractive state of mind is engendered by the mere sound appeal of the music.

You may be sitting in a room reading this book. Imagine one note struck on the piano. Immediately that one note is enough to change the atmosphere of the room—proving that the sound element in music is a powerful and mysterious agent, which it would be foolish to deride or belittle.

The surprising thing is that many people who consider themselves qualified music lovers abuse that plane in listening. They go to concerts in order to lose themselves. They use music as a consolation or an escape. They enter an ideal world where one doesn't have to think of the realities of everyday life. Of course they aren't thinking about the music either. Music allows them to leave it, and they go off to a place to dream, dreaming because of and apropos of the music yet never quite listening to it.

The second plane on which music exists is what I have called the expressive one. Here, immediately, we tread on controversial ground. Composers have a way of shying away from any discussion of music's expressive side. Did not Stravinsky himself proclaim that his music was an "object," a "thing," with a life of its own, and with no other meaning than its own purely musical existence? This intransigent attitude of Stravinsky's may be due to the fact that so many people have tried to read different meanings into so many pieces. Heaven knows it is difficult enough to say precisely what it is that a piece of music means, to say it definitely, to say it finally so that everyone is satisfied with your explanation. But that should not lead one to the other extreme of denying the music the right to be "expressive."

My own belief is that all music has an expressive power, some more and some less, but that all music has a certain meaning behind the notes and that that meaning behind the notes constitutes, after all, what the piece is saying, what the piece is about. This whole problem can be stated quite simply by asking, "Is there a meaning to music?" My answer to that would be, "Yes." And "Can you state in so many words what the meaning is?" My answer to that would be, "No." Therein lies the difficulty.

Simple-minded souls will never be satisfied with the answer to the second of these questions. They always want music to have a meaning, and the more concrete it is the better they like it. The more the music reminds them of a train, a storm, a funeral, or any other familiar conception the more expressive it appears to be to them. This popular idea of music's meaning—stimulated and abetted by the usual run of musical commentator—should be discouraged wherever and whenever it is met. One timid lady once confessed to me that she suspected something seriously lacking in her appreciation of music because of her inability to connect it with anything definite. That is getting the whole thing backward, of course.

Still, the question remains, How close should the intelligent music lover wish to come to pinning a definite meaning to any particular work? No closer than a general concept, I should say. Music expresses, at different moments, serenity or exuberance, regret or triumph, fury or delight. It expresses each of these moods, and many others, in a numberless variety of subtle shadings and differences. It may even express a state of meaning for which there exists no adequate word in any language. In that case, musicians often like to say that it has only a purely musical meaning. They sometimes go further and say that *all* music has only a purely musical meaning. What they really mean is that no appropriate word can be found to express the music's meaning and that, even if it could, they do not feel the need of finding it.

But whatever the professional musician may hold, most musical novices still search for specific words with which to pin down their musical reactions. That is why they always find Tschaikovsky easier to "understand" than Beethoven. In the first place, it is easier to pin a meaning-word on a Tschaikovsky piece than on a Beethoven one. Much easier. Moreover, with the Russian composer, every time you come back to a piece of his it almost always says the same thing to you, whereas with Beethoven it is often quite difficult to put your finger right on what he is saying. And any musician will tell you that that is why Beethoven is the greater composer. Because music which always says the same thing to you will necessarily soon become dull music, but music whose meaning is slightly different with each hearing has a great chance of remaining alive.

Listen, if you can, to the forty-eight fugue themes of Bach's *Well Tempered Clavichord.* Listen to each theme, one after another. You will soon realize that each theme mirrors a different world of feeling. You will also soon realize that the more beautiful a theme seems to you the harder it is to find any word that will describe it to your complete satisfaction. Yes, you will certainly know whether it is a gay theme or a sad one. You will be able, in other words, in your own mind, to draw a frame of emotional feeling around your theme. Now study the sad one a little closer. Try to pin down the exact quality of its sadness. Is it pessimistically sad or resignedly sad; is it fatefully sad or smilingly sad?

Let us suppose that you are fortunate and can describe to your own satisfaction in so many words the exact meaning of your chosen theme. There is still no guarantee that anyone else will be satisfied. Nor need they be. The important thing is that each one feel for himself the specific expressive quality of a theme or, similarly, an entire piece of music. And if it is a great work of art, don't expect it to mean exactly the same thing to you each time you return to it.

Themes or pieces need not express only one emotion, of course. Take such a theme as the first main one of the *Ninth Symphony,* for example. It is clearly made up of different elements. It does not say only one thing. Yet anyone hearing it immediately gets a feeling of strength, a feeling of power. It isn't a power that comes simply because the theme is played loudly. It is a power inherent in the theme itself. The extraordinary strength and vigor of the theme results in the listener's receiving an impression that a forceful statement has been made. But one should never try to boil it down to "the fateful hammer of life," etc. That is where the trouble begins. The musician, in his exasperation, says it means nothing but the notes themselves, whereas the nonprofessional is only too anxious to hang on to any explanation that gives him the illusion of getting closer to the music's meaning.

Now, perhaps, the reader will know better what I mean when I say that music does have an expressive meaning but that we cannot say in so many words what that meaning is.

The third plane on which music exists is the sheerly musical plane. Besides the pleasurable sound of music and the expressive feeling that it gives off, music does exist in terms of the notes themselves and of their manipulation. . . .

Professional musicians, on the other hand, are, if anything, too conscious of the mere notes themselves. They often fall into the error of becoming so engrossed with their arpeggios and staccatos that they forget the deeper aspects of the music they are performing. But from the layman's standpoint, it is not so much a matter of getting over bad habits on the sheerly musical plane as of increasing one's awareness of what is going on, in so far as the notes are concerned.

When the man in the street listens to the "notes themselves" with any degree of concentration, he is most likely to make some mention of the melody. Either he hears a pretty melody or he does not, and he generally lets it go at that. Rhythm is likely to gain his attention next, particularly if it seems exciting. But harmony and tone color are generally taken for granted, if they are thought of consciously at all. As for music's having a definite form of some kind, that idea seems never to have occurred to him.

It is very important for all of us to become more alive to music on its sheerly musical plane. After all, an actual musical material is being used. The intelligent listener must be prepared to increase his awareness of the musical material and what happens to it. He must hear the melodies, the rhythms, the harmonies, the tone colors in a more conscious fashion. But above all he must, in order to follow the line of the composer's thought, know something of the principles of musical form. Listening to all of these elements is listening on the sheerly musical plane.

Let me repeat that I have split up mechanically the three separate planes on which we listen merely for the sake of greater clarity. Actually, we never listen on one or the other of these planes. What we do is to correlate them—listening in all three ways at the same time. It takes no mental effort, for we do it instinctively.

The component parts of the listening process provide the controlling idea for this passage. The author states his classification system: listening to music can be divided into three "planes." Each plane (sensuous, expressive, and musical) is thoroughly discussed. Paragraphs 2, 3, and 4 explain the sensuous plane. Paragraphs 5 through 13 describe the expressive or second plane, and paragraphs 14 through 17 clarify the musical plane. The typographical cues in the first paragraph signal the reader to look for three components and further establish the relationship of these planes to the listening process. We learn about the listening process from these divisions, the author's purpose for and focus of the work.

Classification develops an idea by permitting the author to break down a broad or complex topic into parts. Learn to recognize it in reading materials that explore large subjects so that you will better understand the writer's ideas. Use this form of development for the broad and/or complicated subjects you write about.

Definition

Both classification and definition sort out specific details. Classification serves this end by breaking down a broad subject into meaningful categories. Definition, on the other hand, seeks to clarify the place of *one* thing in relationship to other things.

Writers who use definition as an organizational method explain a thing, a term, or an idea so that we will understand what the writer believes to be the most important characteristics of that one item. By so doing, the writer will show us how this item might be similar to others in some ways and different in others. A definition essay, then, will ask you to accept the writer's understanding of what makes something what it is, that is, why we should call this thing X and not Y.

The definition of a physical thing is generally straightforward. Nobody would challenge the definition of a dog as "a four-legged, domesticated canine," but many people might reject a definition of success as "the affluence that permits you to feed your dog fresh filet mignon every night for dinner." When writers define an abstract idea or a feeling, they face a formidable challenge, one that you as a reader must share.

The passages below all are examples of definition as a method of development. The explanations that follow each include identification of the controlling idea, form, purpose, and responses.

> Three, four, sometimes five times a month, I spend the day in bed with a migraine headache, insensible to the world around me. Almost every day of every month, between these attacks, I feel the sudden irrational irritation and the flush of blood into the cerebral arteries which tell me that migraine is on its way, and I take certain drugs to avert its arrival. If I did not take the drugs, I would be able to function perhaps one day in four. The physiological error called migraine is, in brief, central to the given of my life. When I was 15, 16, even 25, I used to think that I could rid myself of this error by simply denying it, character over chemistry. "Do you have headaches *sometimes? frequently? never?*" the application forms would demand. "Check one." Wary of the trap, wanting whatever it was that the successful circumnavigation of that particular form could bring (a job, a scholarship, the respect of mankind and the grace of God), I would check one. *"Sometimes,"* I would lie. That in fact I spent one or two days a week almost unconscious with pain seemed a shameful secret, evidence not merely of some chemical inferiority but of all my bad attitudes, unpleasant tempers, wrongthink.
>
> For I had no brain tumor, no eyestrain, no high blood pressure, nothing wrong with me at all: I simply had migraine headaches, and migraine headaches were, as everyone who did not have them knew, imaginary. I fought migraine then, ignored the warnings it sent, went to school and later to work in spite of it, sat through lectures in Middle English and presentations to advertisers with involuntary tears running down the right side of my face, threw up in washrooms, stumbled home by instinct, emptied ice trays onto my bed and tried to freeze the pain in my right temple, wished only for a neurosurgeon who would do a lobotomy on house call, and cursed my imagination.
>
> It was a long time before I began thinking mechanistically enough to accept migraine for what it was: something with which I would be living, the way some people lived with diabetes. Migraine is something more than the fancy of a neurotic imagination. It is an essentially hereditary complex of symptoms, the most frequently noted but by no means the most unpleasant of which is a vascular headache of blinding severity, suffered by a surprising number of women, a fair number of men (Thomas Jefferson had migraine, and so did Ulysses

S. Grant, the day he accepted Lee's surrender), and by some unfortunate children as young as two years old. (I had my first when I was eight. It came on during a fire drill at the Columbia School in Colorado Springs, Colorado. I was taken first home and then to the infirmary at Peterson Field, where my father was stationed. The Air Corps doctor prescribed an enema.) Almost anything can trigger a specific attack of migraine: stress, allergy, fatigue, an abrupt change in barometric pressure, a contretemps over a parking ticket. A flashing light. A fire drill. One inherits, of course, only the predisposition. In other words I spent yesterday in bed with a headache not merely because of my bad attitudes, unpleasant tempers and wrongthink but because both my grandmothers had migraine, my father has migraine and my mother has migraine.

No one knows precisely what it is that is inherited. The chemistry of migraine, however, seems to have some connection with the nerve hormone named serotonin, which is naturally present in the brain. The amount of serotonin in the blood falls sharply at the onset of migraine, and one migraine drug, methysergide, or Sansert, seems to have some effect on serotonin. Methysergide is a derivative of lysergic acid (in fact Sandoz Pharmaceuticals first synthesized LSD-25 while looking for a migraine cure), and its use is hemmed about with so many contraindications and side effects that most doctors prescribe it only in the most incapacitating cases. Methysergide, when it is prescribed, is taken daily, as a preventive; another preventive which works for some people is old-fashioned ergotamine tartrate, which helps to constrict the swelling blood vessels during the "aura," the period which in most cases precedes the actual headache.

Once an attack is under way, however, no drug touches it. Migraine gives some people mild hallucinations, temporarily blinds others, shows up not only as a headache but as a gastrointestinal disturbance, a painful sensitivity to all sensory stimuli, an abrupt overpowering fatigue, a strokelike aphasia, and a crippling inability to make even the most routine connections. When I am in a migraine aura (for some people the aura lasts fifteen minutes, for others several hours), I will drive through red lights, lose the house keys, spill whatever I am holding, lose the ability to focus my eyes or frame coherent sentences, and generally give the appearance of being on drugs, or drunk. The actual headache, when it comes, brings with it chills, sweating, nausea, a debility that seems to stretch the very limits of endurance. That no one dies of migraine seems, to someone deep into an attack, an ambiguous blessing.

My husband also has migraine, which is unfortunate for him but fortunate for me: perhaps nothing so tends to prolong an attack as the accusing eye of someone who has never had a headache. "Why not take a couple of aspirin," the unafflicted will say from the doorway, or "I'd have a headache, too, spending a beautiful day like this inside with all the shades drawn." All of us who have migraine suffer not only from the attacks themselves but from this common conviction that we are perversely refusing to cure ourselves by taking a couple of aspirins, that we are making ourselves sick, that we "bring it on ourselves." And in the most immediate sense, the sense of why we have a headache this Tuesday and not last Thursday, of course we often do. There certainly is what doctors call a "migraine personality," and that personality tends to be ambitious, inward, intolerant of error, rather rigidly organized, perfectionist. "You don't look like a migraine personality," a doctor once said to me. "Your hair's messy. But I suppose you're a compulsive housekeeper." Actually my house is kept even more negligently than my hair, but the doctor was right nonetheless: perfectionism can also take the form of spending most of a week writing and rewriting and not writing a single paragraph.

But not all perfectionists have migraine, and not all migrainous people have migraine personalities. We do not escape heredity. I have tried in most of the available ways to escape my own migrainous heredity (at one point I learned to give myself two daily injections of histamine with a hypodermic needle, even though the needle so frightened me that I had to close my eyes when I did it), but I still have migraine. And I have learned how to live with it, learned when to expect it, and how to outwit it, even how to regard it, when it does come, as more friend than lodger. We have reached a certain understanding, my migraine and I. It never comes when I am in real trouble. Tell me that my house is burned down, my husband has left me, that there is gunfighting in the streets and panic in the banks, and I will not respond by getting a headache. It comes instead when I am fighting not an open but a guerrilla war with my own life, during weeks of small household confusions, lost laundry, unhappy help, canceled appointments, on days when the telephone rings too much and I get no work done and the wind is coming up. On days like that my friend comes uninvited.

And once it comes, now that I am wise in its ways, I no longer fight it. I lie down and let it happen. At first every small apprehension is magnified, every anxiety a pounding terror. Then the pain comes, and I concentrate only on that. Right there is the usefulness of migraine, there in that imposed yoga, the concentration on the pain. For when the pain recedes, ten or twelve hours later, everything goes with it, all the hidden resentments, all the vain anxieties. The migraine has acted as a circuit breaker, and the fuses have emerged intact. There is a pleasant convalescent euphoria. I open the windows and feel the air, eat gratefully, sleep well. I notice the particular nature of a flower in a glass on the stair landing. I count my blessings.

In this essay, the writer defines a migraine headache. Her sense of audience tells her that most people do not understand what a migraine is, thinking that it is either only a very bad headache or perhaps that it is psychosomatic. Because she is defining an experience—what it is like to suffer a migraine attack—she presents details that are familiar to the reader. The definition has two main parts: a scientific characterization of the condition and the writer's personal experiences with it. Doctors define migraine as "an essentially hereditary complex of symptoms, the most frequently noted but by no means the most unpleasant of which is a vascular headache of blinding severity . . ." (paragraph 3). The author also explains what might cause a particular attack of these symptoms and indicates which drugs may alleviate the symptoms. Her definition also includes her personal attempts to deal with migraine, including her early efforts to deny it by exercising "character over chemistry" (paragraph 1). Both the scientific and the personal approaches to this definition show that although migraine is similar to other headaches, it is very much a separate thing. The author's implied controlling idea seems to be that migraine headaches are a part of her life, something with which she must cope. Because she emphasizes her feelings and experiences, the essay's purpose is expressive, and she expects her readers to empathize with her predicament.

Another author uses definition to organize a short passage about being a "good ole boy."

> It is Friday night at any of ten thousand watering holes of the small towns and crossroads hamlets of the South. The room is a cacophony of the pingpong-dingdingding of the pinball machine, the pop-fizz of another round of Pabst, the refrain of *Red Necks, White Socks and Blue Ribbon Beer* on the juke box, the insolent roar of a souped-up engine outside and, above it all, the sound of easy laughter. The good ole boys have gathered for their fraternal ritual—the aimless diversion that they have elevated into a life-style.
>
> Being a good ole boy is not a consequence of birth or breeding; it cuts across economic and social lines; it is a frame of mind based on the premise that life is nothing to get serious about. A glance at the brothers Carter tells a lot. There is some confusion about why Billy Carter seems in many respects the quintessential good ole boy, while Brother Jimmy couldn't even fit into the more polished subspecies of conscious good ole boys who abound in small-town country clubs. Billy, amiable, full of jokes, his REDNECK POWER T-shirt straining unsuccessfully to cover the paunch, swigs a beer, carefree on a Sunday morning, as Jimmy Carter, introspective, hard driving, teaches Sunday school. Jimmy sometimes speaks wistfully of Billy's good-ole-boy ease.
>
> Lightheartedness permeates the good ole boy's life-style. He goes by nicknames like "Goober" or "Goat." He disdains neckties as a form of snobbery; when he dresses up, it is to wear a decorated T-shirt with newish jeans or, for state occasions, a leisure suit with a colored shirt. If discussions veer beyond football toward substance, he cuts them off with funny stories.
>
> The core of the good ole boy's world is with his buddies, the comfortable, hyperhearty, all-male camaraderie, joshing and drinking and regaling one another with tales of assorted, exaggerated prowess. Women are outsiders; when social events are unavoidably mixed, the good ole boys cluster together at one end of the room, leaving wives at the other. The GOB's magic doesn't work with women; he feels insecure, threatened by them. In fact, he doesn't really like women, except in bed.

What he really loves is his automobile. He overlooks his wife with her hair up in pink rollers, sagging into an upside-down question mark in her tight slacks. But he lavishes attention on his Mercury mistress, Easy Rider shocks, oversize slickers, dual exhaust. He exults in tinkering with that beautiful engine, lying cool beneath the open hood, ready to respond, quick and fiery, to his touch. The automobile is his love and his sport.

Behind his devil-may-care lightheartedness, however, runs a strain of innate wisdom, an instinct about people and an unwavering loyalty that makes him the one friend you would turn to, not just because he's a drinking buddy who'll keep you laughing, but because, well, he's a good ole boy.

This passage defines the term, *good ole boy*. The author first places him in a likely setting and then offers her definition ("it is a frame of mind based on the premise that life is nothing to get serious about") in the second paragraph. The controlling idea is that the attributes of a good ole boy are lightheartedness (paragraph 3), all-male camaraderie (paragraph 4), and a love of automobiles (paragraph 5). The purpose is to inform and perhaps to amuse as well.

A longer informative passage about good manners also uses definition:

Good manners is the art of making those people easy with whom we converse.

Whoever makes the fewest persons uneasy is the best bred in the company.

As the best law is founded upon reason, so are the best manners. And as some lawyers have introduced unreasonable things into common law, so likewise many teachers have introduced absurd things into common good manners.

One principal point of this art is to suit our behaviour to the three several degrees of men; our superiors, our equals, and those below us.

For instance, to press either of the two former to eat or drink is a breach of manners; but a farmer or a tradesman must be thus treated, or else it will be difficult to persuade them that they are welcome.

Pride, ill nature, and want of sense, are the three great sources of ill manners; without some one of these defects, no man will behave himself ill for want of experience; or of what, in the language of fools, is called knowing the world.

I defy any one to assign an incident wherein reason will not direct us what we are to say or do in company, if we are not misled by pride or ill nature.

Therefore I insist that good sense is the principal foundation of good manners; but because the former is a gift which very few among mankind are possessed of, therefore all the civilized nations of the world have agreed upon fixing some rules for common behaviour, best suited to their general customs, or fancies, as a kind of artificial good sense, to supply the defects of reason. Without which the gentlemanly part of dunces would be perpetually at cuffs, as they seldom fail when they happen to be drunk, or engaged in squabbles about women or play. And, God be thanked, there hardly happens a duel in a year, which may not be imputed to one of those three motives. Upon which account, I should be exceedingly sorry to find the legislature make any new laws against the practice of duelling; because the methods are easy and many for a wise man to avoid a quarrel with honour, or engage in it with innocence. And I can discover no political evil in suffering bullies, sharpers, and rakes, to rid the world of each other by a method of their own; where the law hath not been able to find an expedient.

As the common forms of good manners were intended for regulating the conduct of those who have weak understandings; so they have been corrupted by the persons for whose use they were contrived. For these people have fallen into a needless and endless way of multiplying ceremonies, which have been extremely troublesome to those who practise them, and insupportable to everybody else: insomuch that wise men are often more uneasy at the over civility of these refiners, than they could possibly be in the conversations of peasants or mechanics.

The impertinencies of this ceremonial behaviour are nowhere better seen than at those tables where ladies preside, who value themselves upon account of their good breeding; where a man must reckon upon passing an hour without doing any one thing he has a mind to; unless he will be so hardy to break through all the settled decorum of the family. She determines what he loves best, and how much he shall eat; and if the master of the house happens to be of the same disposition, he proceeds in the same tyrannical manner to prescribe in the drinking part: at the same time, you are under the necessity of answering a thousand apologies for your entertainment. And although a good deal of this humour is pretty well worn off among many people of the best fashion, yet too much of it still remains, especially in the country; where an honest gentleman assured me, that having been kept four days, against his will, at a friend's house, with all the circumstances of hiding his boots, locking up the stable, and other contrivances of the like nature, he could not remember, from the moment he came into the house to the moment he left it, any one thing, wherein his inclination was not directly contradicted; as if the whole family had entered into a combination to torment him.

But, besides all this, it would be endless to recount the many foolish and ridiculous accidents I have observed among these unfortunate proselytes to ceremony. I have seen a duchess fairly knocked down, by the precipitancy of an officious coxcomb running to save her the trouble of opening a door. I remember, upon a birthday at court, a great lady was utterly desperate by a dish of sauce let fall by a page directly upon her head-dress and brocade, while she gave a sudden turn to her elbow upon some point of ceremony with the person who sat next her. Monsieur Buys, the Dutch envoy, whose politics and manners were much of a size, brought a son with him, about thirteen years old, to a great table at court. The boy and his father, whatever they put on their plates, they first offered round in order, to every person in the company; so that we could not get a minute's quiet during the whole dinner. At last their two plates happened to encounter, and with so much violence, that, being china, they broke in twenty pieces, and stained half the company with wet sweetmeats and cream.

There is a pedantry in manners, as in all arts and sciences; and sometimes in trades. Pedantry is properly the overrating any kind of knowledge we pretend to. And if that kind of knowledge be a trifle in itself, the pedantry is the greater. For which reason I look upon fiddlers, dancing-masters, heralds, masters of the ceremony, &c. to be greater pedants than Lipsius, or the elder Scaliger. With these kind of pedants, the court, while I knew it, was always plentifully stocked; I mean from the gentleman usher (at least) inclusive, downward to the gentleman porter; who are, generally speaking, the most insignificant race of people that this island can afford, and with the smallest tincture of good manners, which is the only trade they profess. For being wholly illiterate, and conversing chiefly with each other, they reduce the whole system of breeding within the forms and circles of their several offices; and as they are below the notice of ministers, they live and die in court under all revolutions with great obsequiousness to those who are in any degree of favour or credit, and with rudeness or insolence to everybody else. Whence I have long concluded, that good manners are not a plant of the court growth: for if they were, those people who have understandings directly of a level for such acquirements, and who have served such long apprenticeships to nothing else, would certainly have picked them up. For as to the great officers, who attend the prince's person or councils, or preside in his family, they are a transient body, who have no better a title to good manners than their neighbours, nor will probably have recourse to gentlemen ushers for instruction. So that I know little to be learnt at court upon this head, except in the material circumstance of dress; wherein the authority of the maids of honour must indeed be allowed to be almost equal to that of a favourite actress.

I remember a passage my Lord Bolingbroke told me, that going to receive Prince Eugene of Savoy at his landing, in order to conduct him immediately to the Queen, the prince said, he was much concerned that he could not see her Majesty that night; for Monsieur Hoffman (who was then by) had assured his Highness that he could not be admitted into her presence with a tied-up periwig; that his equipage was not arrived; and that he had endeavoured in vain to borrow a long one among all his valets and pages. My lord turned the matter into a jest, and brought the Prince to her Majesty; for which he was highly censured by the whole tribe of gentlemen ushers; among whom Monsieur Hoffman, an old dull resident of the Emperor's, had picked up this material point of ceremony; and which, I believe, was the best lesson he had learned in five-and-twenty years' residence.

I make a difference between good manners and good breeding;

although, in order to vary my expression, I am sometimes forced to confound them. By the first, I only understand the art of remembering and applying certain settled forms of general behaviour. But good breeding is of a much larger extent; for besides an uncommon degree of literature sufficient to qualify a gentleman for reading a play, or a political pamphlet, it takes in a great compass of knowledge; no less than that of dancing, fighting, gaming, making the circle of Italy, riding the great horse, and speaking French; not to mention some other secondary, or subaltern accomplishments, which are more easily acquired. So that the difference between good breeding and good manners lies in this, that the former cannot be attained to by the best understandings, without study and labour; whereas a tolerable degree of reason will instruct us in every part of good manners, without other assistance.

In this longer passage, the author defines good manners in the first sentence and then expands this in the first three paragraphs to arrive at his controlling idea—good manners can be seen as an art based on good sense. To develop this definition, the author discusses the sources of ill manners (paragraph 6), the overemphasis on ceremony (paragraphs 9, 10, and 11), pedantry in manners (paragraph 12), and confusing good manners with good breeding (paragraph 14). These characteristics of bad manners all result from behavior that ignores common sense. The definition of good manners in this essay provides characteristics that are and are not essential to proper social behavior. Because the author's emphasis is on the subject matter, the essay's purpose is informative.

In sum, definition develops an idea by identifying the essential characteristics of something and by demonstrating how these characteristics separate that thing from similar things.

The final passages of this chapter explore classification and definition as organizational forms. Each passage is analyzed by the "Questions for Determining Controlling Idea, Form, Purpose, and Response." Study them to practice discovering idea, form, purpose, and audience.

THE ETHICAL SYSTEMS OF THE ANCIENTS

Immanuel Kant

The ethical systems of the ancients are all based on the question of what constitutes the *summum bonum*—the Supreme Good—and it is in their answers to this question that is to be found the difference between their various systems. We may call this *summum bonum* an idea, that is, the highest conceivable standard by which everything is to be judged and weighed. To form a judgment of anything we must first sketch a pattern by which to judge it. The *summum bonum* is scarcely possible of attainment and is only an ideal—that is, the pattern, the idea, the archetype for all our concepts of the Good.

What constitutes the Supreme Good? The supreme created good is the most perfect world, that is, a world in which all rational beings are happy and are worthy of happiness.

The ancients realized that mere happiness could not be the one highest good. For if all men were to obtain this happiness without distinction of just and unjust, the highest good would not be realized, because though happiness would indeed exist, worthiness of it would not.

In mankind, therefore, we have to look both for happiness and for merit. The combination of the two will be the highest good. Man can hope to be happy only in so far as he makes himself worthy of being happy, for this is the condition of happiness which reason itself proposes.

They further realized that happiness sprang from man's freedom of will, from his intention to make use of everything with which nature so richly endows him. Of the wealthy man we ask to what use he intends to put all those treasures which he has in plenty. Thus the nature and perfectness of the free will, in which dwells the ground of the worthiness to be happy, constitutes ethical perfection. The physical good or well-being, for which health and wealth are requisite, is not by itself the greatest good; the ethical good, right conduct, worthiness of being happy, must be added to the former, and we then have the Supreme Good. Let us imagine a world inhabited by intelligent beings, all of whom behaved well, and so deserved to be happy, but were destitute and lived in the most wretched circumstances. Such beings would have no happiness, and there would, therefore, be no Supreme Good in these conditions. If, on the other hand, all beings were happy but not well-behaved and not worthy of being happy, we should again have no Supreme Good in such circumstances.

The ancients recognized three forms of the ideal of the *summum bonum:*

1. The Cynic ideal of the school of Diogenes.
2. The Epicurean ideal.
3. The Stoic ideal of the school of Zeno.

The Cynic is the ideal of innocence, or rather of simplicity. Diogenes taught that the highest good is to be found in simplicity, in the sober enjoyment of happiness.

The Epicureans set up the ideal of prudence. Epicurus's doctrine was that the highest good was happiness and that well-doing was but a means to happiness.

The ideal of the Stoics was that of wisdom, and is in contrast with the ideal of Epicurus. Zeno taught that the highest good is to be found only in morality, in merit (and thus in well-doing), and that happiness is a consequence of morality. Whoever conducts himself well is happy.

The Cynics argued that the Supreme Good springs from nature and not from art. Diogenes sought it by negative means. He argued that man is by nature satisfied with little; he has no wants by nature and therefore does not feel privation (that is, the lack of means), and so it is in conditions of privation that he finds happiness. There is much in this argument; for the more plentiful nature's gifts and the greater our store of the world's goods the greater are our wants. With growing wealth we acquire fresh wants, and the more we satisfy them the keener becomes our appetite for more. So our hearts are restless for ever. That refined Diogenes, Rousseau, holds that our will is by nature good, but that we ourselves become more and more corrupt; that nature provides us with all necessaries, but that we create wants for ourselves, and he would have children educated on negative lines. Hume disagrees with these views, and argues that the Supreme Good is a thing of art, and not of nature.

Diogenes teaches that we can be happy without abundance, and moral without virtue. His philosophy is the shortest cut to happiness, for, if we are content with life, it is no hardship to do without things, and we can live happily; and it is likewise the shortest cut to morality, because if we have no wants we have no desires, and in that case our actions conform to morality. To be honest involves no sacrifice; so virtue would be merely an idea. Simplicity is thus the shortest cut to morality.

The Epicureans taught that the Supreme Good was a matter of art, and not of nature, and they thus placed themselves in exact opposition to the Cynics. It is true, said Epicurus, that we have by nature no vices, but we nevertheless have an inclination to vice, and innocence and simplicity cannot, therefore, be secured without the assistance of art. Zeno was in agreement with Epicurus in thus regarding virtue as a matter of art. If, for instance, a simple country girl is free of the usual vices, she is so merely because she has no opportunity of going astray; and if a peasant makes do and is quite content with poor fare, he does not do so because it is all the same to him whether his food is simple or sumptuous, but because it is his lot, and if he had an opportunity of living on a higher scale he would take it. Simplicity, therefore, is only a negative thing. For this reason Epicurus and Zeno accepted art, although in different senses.

The Supreme Good consists of the physical good and the moral good—of well-being and well-doing. Inasmuch as all philosophy strives to bring unity into knowledge and to reduce its first principles to a minimum, attempts have been made to combine into one these two principles of well-being and well-doing. Now, it is the end, and not the means, which determines what we call anything. So, according to the notion of Epicurus, happiness was the end and merit only a means, which would make morality a consequence of happiness. Zeno also sought to unite the two principles, and according to his notion it was morality which was the end, virtue and merit were in themselves the Supreme Good, and happiness was merely a consequence of morality.

For their ideal, their pattern, Diogenes took the natural man, and Epicurus the man of the world. Zeno's pattern or *Idea archetypon* is the sage. The sage is happy in himself, he possesses all things, he has within himself the source of cheerfulness and righteousness, he is a king because he is lord of himself and, being his own master, he cannot be mastered. Such perfection could be attained only by strength in overcoming obstacles, and so a sage was regarded as even greater than the gods themselves, because a god has no temptations to withstand and no obstacles to overcome.

We can also conceive a mystical ideal, in which the Supreme Good consists in this: that man sees himself in communion with the highest being. This is the Platonic ideal, a visionary ideal.

The Christian ideal is that of holiness, and its pattern is Christ. Christ is also merely an ideal, a standard of moral perfection which is holy by divine aid. This ideal ought not to be confused with those who call themselves Christians. These only seek to come nearer to their ideal pattern.

Epicurus taught that virtue had a motive, namely happiness; Zeno took away the motive. Epicurus saw value in merit, but none in virtue, while Zeno exalted the intrinsic value of virtue. Epicurus placed the Supreme Good in happiness, Zeno in virtue. Both were at fault.

Happiness, in the case of Epicurus, was synonymous with pleasure, by which he meant a contented disposition and a cheerful heart; but his philosophy was not, as it has wrongly been taken to be, one of sensual pleasure. He taught that we must so act as to be safe from reproaches from ourselves and from others, and a letter has come down to us in which he invites a guest to dinner with the intimation that he has nothing better to offer than a cheerful heart and a meal of polenta, poor fare indeed for an "epicure." His was the pleasure of a sage, and while he denied worth to virtue, he made morality the means to happiness.

Zeno inverted the position. To him happiness had value, but virtue no motive. Motives are springs of the will which are drawn from the senses. If a man is conscious of deserving happiness, that is not sufficient to appease his desires, and if his desires are unsatisfied he is not happy, even though he feels himself worthy. Virtue pleases uniquely but it does not satisfy; if it did, all men would be virtuous. His very virtue intensifies a man's yearning for happiness. The more virtuous and the less happy a man is, the more painful is the feeling that he is not happy, though deserving happiness. Such a man is satisfied with his conduct, but not with his condition.

Epicurus taught that man would be satisfied with himself if he saw to it that his condition was happy; Zeno, that man would be satisfied with his condition if he so conducted himself that he was satisfied with himself.

A man can be satisfied or dissatisfied with himself either pragmatically or ethically, but he very often mistakes the one type of satisfaction or dissatisfaction for the other. He often mistakes for remorse what is, in fact, a fear of the tribunal of prudence. If, for instance, we slight someone in public we may reproach ourselves in the privacy of our home, but these are the reproaches of the Judge of Prudence within us, since we must suppose that we have made an enemy. The reproach for an action through which damage arises is always a reproach of prudence. If we knew that the other did not notice the offence given we should be satisfied. It follows, therefore, that what we feel is a reproof of prudence which we take for a reproof of morality. Epicurus, however, taught that if we so conduct ourselves as to deserve no reproaches, either from ourselves or from others, we are happy.

The ideal of holiness is, philosophically, the most perfect in that it is the ideal of the highest pure and moral perfection; but, as it is humanly unattainable, it bases itself on the belief in divine aid. Not only does the notion of deserving happiness acquire in this ideal its highest moral perfection, but the ideal itself contains the most potent motive, that of happiness beyond this world. Thus the ideal of the Gospels contains the purest morality as well as the strongest motive—that of happiness or blessedness.

The ancients had no conception of any higher moral perfection than such as could emanate from human nature. But as human nature is very imperfect, their ethical principles were imperfect. Thus their system of ethics was not pure; it accommodated virtue to man's weakness, and was, therefore, incomplete. But the ideal of the Gospels is complete in every respect. Here we have the greatest purity and the greatest happiness. It sets out the principles of morality in all their holiness. It commands man to be holy, but as he is imperfect it gives him a prop—namely, divine aid.

1. *Question:*   What is the subject of the work?

   Answer: Ancient ethical systems.

2. *Question:*   What aspect of the subject is discussed in the work?

   Answer: The basis of these systems, the *summum bonum,* or Supreme Good.

3. *Question:*   What does the author want you to understand and remember, in general, about the aspect of the subject discussed in the work?

   Answer: That the Supreme Good is an ideal, pattern, or archetype used to judge all concepts of good and that what constitutes this ideal is what differentiates the ethical systems of the ancients. The author states this controlling idea as his thesis in the first paragraph.

4. *Question:*   How are the specific ideas presented?

   Answer: The specific ideas that support the controlling idea are presented as forms or types of *summum bonum* (Supreme Good). The author mentions these classifications in paragraph 6 after having clarified the early thinkers' concern for happiness as part of the highest good (paragraphs 2 through 5). The Cynic, Epicurean, and Stoic ideals all concern happiness but differ in what determines that happiness. The sober enjoyment of happiness through simplicity (Cynic) is explained in paragraph 7; well-doing as a means to happiness (Epicurean) is explained in paragraph 8; and happiness as a consequence of morality (Stoic) is discussed in paragraph 9. These forms of the ideal of the highest good are contrasted in these paragraphs, and further details about them are given in paragraphs 10, 12, and 14. The author introduces the mystical ideal (paragraph 15) and the Christian ideal (paragraph 16) for further comparison with the first three forms. The author returns to comparing the ideals of Epicurus and Zeno in relation to human nature (paragraphs 17 through 21) in order to make his concluding remarks in paragraph 23. He explains that the ethical principles of the ancients were imperfect because they were based on imperfect human nature. In addition he shows the ideal of the Gospel to be most complete because of its commitment to purity and happiness with the help of divine aid.

5. *Question:* How do they develop the controlling idea?

   Answer: Classifying three forms of the *summum bonum* or Supreme Good enabled the author to develop his thesis by providing evidence to support it. He demonstrates how each of the three ideals compared with the other and that each was flawed and therefore not the archetype he believes the Supreme Good must be if it is to be the model for all concepts of Good.

6. *Question:* Does the work emphasize the author, the subject or the audience?

   Answer: The essay stresses the subject; therefore, the author's purpose is to inform.

7. *Question:* What response does the author want: empathy, learning or belief?

   Answer: He seems to want learning as the response.

Controlling idea: The Supreme Good is an archetype used to judge all concepts of good, and what constitutes this ideal is what differentiates ancient ethical systems.

Form: Classification.
Purpose: To inform.
Reader Response: Learning.

TO NOBLE COMPANIONS

Gail Godwin

The dutiful first answer seems programmed into us by our meager expectations: "A friend is one who will be there in times of trouble." But I believe this is a skin-deep answer to describe skin-deep friends. There is something irresistible about misfortune to human nature, and standbys for setbacks and sicknesses (as long as they are not too lengthy, or contagious) can usually be found. They can be *hired.* What I value is not the "friend" who, looming sympathetically above me when I have been dashed to the ground, appears gigantically generous in the hour of my reversal; more and more I desire friends who will endure my ecstasies with me, who possess wings of their own and who will fly with me. I don't mean this as arrogance (I am too superstitious to indulge long in that trait), and I don't fly all that often. What I mean is that I seek (and occasionally find) friends with whom it is possible to drag out all those beautiful, old, outrageously *aspiring* costumes and rehearse together for the Great Roles; persons whose qualities groom me and train me up for love. It is for these people that I reserve the glowing hours, too good not to share. It is the existence of these people that reminds me that the words "friend" and "free" grew out of each other. (OE *freo,* not in bondage, noble, glad; OE *freon,* to love; OE *freond,* friend.)

When I was in the eighth grade, I had a friend. We were shy and "too serious" about our studies when it was becoming fashionable with our classmates to acquire the social graces. We said little at school, but she would come to my house and we would sit down with pencils and paper, and one of us would say: "Let's start with a train whistle today." We would sit quietly together and write separate poems or stories that grew out of a train whistle. Then we would read them aloud. At the end of that school year, we, too, were transformed into social creatures and the stories and poems stopped.

When I lived for a time in London, I had a friend. He was in despair and I was in despair, but our friendship was based on the small flicker of foresight in each of us that told us we would be sorry later if we did not explore this great city because we had felt bad at the time. We met every Sunday for five weeks and found many marvelous things. We walked until our despairs resolved themselves and then we parted. We gave London to each other.

For almost four years I have had a remarkable friend whose imagination illumines mine. We write long letters in which we often discover our strangest selves. Each of us appears, sometimes prophetically, sometimes comically, in the other's dreams. She and I agree that, at certain times, we seem to be parts of the same mind. In my most sacred and interesting moments, I often think: "Yes, I must tell———." We have never met.

It is such exceptional (in a sense divine) companions I wish to salute. I have seen the glories of the world reflected briefly through our encounters. One bright hour with their kind is worth more to me than a lifetime guarantee of the services of a Job's comforter whose "helpful" lamentations will only clutter the healing silence necessary to those darkest moments in which I would rather be my own best friend.

1. *Question:* What is the subject of the work?
   Answer: The idea of friends.
2. *Question:* What aspect of the subject is discussed in the work?
   Answer: The type of friends the author desires.
3. *Question:* What does the author want you to understand and remember, in general, about the aspect of the subject discussed in the work?

Answer: The friends she values are those with whom she can share happiness and enjoy life, not those who are with her when there is trouble. Her thesis is stated in the first paragraph of the essay.

4. *Question:* How are the specific ideas presented?

Answer: The specific ideas are presented first by citing the etymology of the words *friend* and *free* at the end of the first paragraph. Each of the three following paragraphs offer examples of the term *friend*. The friend in eighth grade, the friend in London, and the pen pal all are examples of the author's nontraditional approach to friendship.

5. *Question:* How does the author develop the controlling idea?

Answer: Because the author chooses to redefine friendship in personal nontraditional terms, the interrelatedness of the words friend and free and the examples of three highly valued friendships show us the extended use of definition to support a controlling idea. The controlling idea passes over the "friend in time of need" in favor of the "exceptional, inspirational friend," a choice most of us are programmed not to make.

6. *Question:* Does the work emphasize the author, the subject, or the audience?

Answer: The work emphasizes the author's feelings about the friends she values; its purpose is expressive.

7. *Question:* What response does the author want: empathy, learning or belief?

Answer: She wants the reader to accept and sympathize with her values regarding friends. The desired response is empathy.

Controlling idea: The author values friends with whom she can share happiness and enjoy life, not the ones who are with her when there is trouble.
Form: Definition.
Purpose: Expressive.
Reader Response: Empathy.

Exercises

1. Read each of the following articles and decide whether classification, definition, or both organize it.

   a. A culture is not simply an accumulation of folkways and mores; it is an *organized system* of behavior. Let us see some of the ways in which it is organized.

   The smallest unit of culture is called a *trait*. This is a somewhat arbitrary definition since what is a single unit to one individual may appear as a combination of units to another. Hoebel's definition is apt at this point: "A reputedly irreducible unit of learned behavior pattern or material product thereof." Traits of the material culture would include such things as the nail, the screwdriver, the pencil, and the handkerchief. Nonmaterial culture traits would include such actions as shaking hands, tipping hats, the practice of driving on the right-hand side of the road, the kiss as a gesture of affection between the sexes, or the salute to the flag. Each culture includes thousands of traits.

Is the dance a trait? No; it is a collection of traits, including the dance steps, some formula for selecting the performers, and a musical or rhythmic accompaniment. Most important of all, the dance has a meaning—as a religious ceremonial, a magical rite, a courtship activity, a festive orgy, or something else. All these elements combine to form a *culture complex,* a cluster of related traits. Another cluster of objects, skills, and attitudes forms the football complex. The saying of grace, the reading of the Bible, and evening prayers may form a family religious complex. Similarly, there is a dating complex which includes many activities and attitudes with which students may have some familiarity.

The complex is intermediate between the trait and the institution. An institution is a series of complexes centering upon an important activity. Thus the family includes the dating complex, the engagement-and-wedding complex, the honeymoon complex, the child-care complex, and several others. Some complexes are parts of institutions; others, revolving around less important activities—such as stamp collecting—are simply independent complexes.

Linton has pointed out that some culture traits are necessary to all members of the society, while other traits are shared by only some members. A trait required of all members of the society he calls a *universal.* Certain values, gestures, and meanings must be shared by all members if there is to be an orderly social life. When a person approaches us with the right hand extended, we must know whether this indicates a friendly greeting or a physical attack. Without a set of understanding shared by all normal members in the society, such confusion would prevail that the ordinary business of social life would never get done. In our culture one must be monogamous if he marries, must clothe certain parts of the body, and drive on the right side of the street; he must condemn free love and infanticide; he must praise free enterprise and motherhood. Punishment—legal or social, or both—awaits the man who does not conform.

b. NATIONAL PREJUDICES

Oliver Goldsmith

As I am one of that sauntering tribe of mortals, who spend the greatest part of their time in taverns, coffeehouses, and other places of public resort, I have thereby an opportunity of observing an infinite variety of characters, which, to a person of a contemplative turn, is a much higher entertainment than a view of all the curiosities of art or nature. In one of these, my late rambles, I accidentally fell into the company of half a dozen gentlemen, who were engaged in a warm dispute about some political affair; the decision of which, as they were equally divided in their sentiments, they thought proper to refer to me, which naturally drew me in for a share of the conversation.

Amongst a multiplicity of other topics, we took occasion to talk of the different characters of the several nations of Europe; when one of the gentlemen, cocking his hat, and assuming such an air of importance as if he had possessed all the merit of the English nation in his own person, declared that the Dutch were a parcel of avaricious wretches; the French a set of flattering sycophants; that the Germans were drunken sots, and beastly gluttons; and the Spaniards proud, haughty, and surly tyrants; but that in bravery, generosity, clemency, and in every other virtue, the English excelled all the rest of the world.

This very learned and judicious remark was received with a general smile of approbation by all the company—all, I mean, but your humble servant; who, endeavoring to keep my gravity as well as I could, and reclining my head upon my arm, continued for some time in a posture of affected thoughtfulness, as if I had been musing on something else, and did not seem to attend to the subject of conversation; hoping by these means to avoid the disagreeable necessity of explaining myself, and thereby depriving the gentleman of his imaginary happiness.

But my pseudo-patriot had no mind to let me escape so easily. Not satisfied that his opinion should pass without contradiction, he was determined to have it ratified by the suffrage of every one in the company; for which purpose addressing himself to me with an air of inexpressible confidence, he asked me if I was not of the same way of thinking. As I am never forward in giving my opinion, especially when I have reason to believe that it will not be agreeable; so, when I am obliged to give it, I always hold it for a maxim to speak my real sentiments. I therefore told him that, for my own part, I should not have ventured to talk in such a peremptory strain, unless I had made the tour of Europe, and examined the manners of these several nations with great care and accuracy: that, perhaps, a more impartial judge would not scruple to affirm that the Dutch were more frugal and industrious, the French more temperate and polite, the Germans more hardy and patient of labour and fatigue, and the Spaniards more staid and sedate, than the English; who, though undoubtedly brave and generous, were at the same time rash, headstrong, and impetuous; too apt to be elated with prosperity, and to despond in adversity.

I could easily perceive that all the company began to regard me with a jealous eye before I had finished my answer, which I had no sooner done, that the patriotic gentleman observed, with a contemptuous sneer, that he was greatly surprised how some people could have the conscience to live in a country which they did not love, and to enjoy the protection of a government, to which in their hearts they were inveterate enemies. Finding that by this modest declaration of my sentiments I had forfeited the good opinion of my companions, and given them occasion to call my political principles in question, and well knowing that it was in vain to argue with men who were so very full of themselves, I threw down my reckoning and retired to my own lodgings, reflecting on the absurd and ridiculous nature of national prejudice and prepossession.

Among all the famous sayings of antiquity, there is none that does greater honour to the author, or affords greater pleasure to the reader (at least if he be a person of a generous and benevolent heart), than that of the philosopher, who, being asked what "countryman he was," replied, that he was, "a citizen of the world."—How few are there to be found in modern times who can say the same, or whose conduct is consistent with such a profession!—We are now become so much Englishmen, Frenchmen, Dutchmen, Spaniards, or Germans, that we are no longer citizens of the world; so much the natives of one particular spot, or members of one petty society, that we no longer consider ourselves as the general inhabitants of the globe, or members of that grand society which comprehends the whole human kind.

Did these prejudices prevail only among the meanest and lowest of the people, perhaps they might be excused, as they have few, if any, opportunities of correcting them by reading, travelling, or conversing with foreigners; but the misfortune is, that they infect the minds, and influence the conduct, even of our gentlemen; of those, I mean, who have every title to this appellation but an exemption from prejudice, which however, in my opinion, ought to be regarded as the characteristical mark of a gentleman; for let a man's birth be ever so high, his station ever so exalted, or his fortune ever so large, yet if he is not free from national and other prejudices, I should make bold to tell him, that he had a low and vulgar mind, and had no just claim to the character of a gentleman. And in fact, you will always find that those are most apt to boast of national merit, who have little or no merit of their own to depend on; than which, to be sure, nothing is more natural: the slender vine twists around the sturdy oak, for no other reason in the world but because it has not strength sufficient to support itself.

Should it be alleged in defence of national prejudice, that it is the natural and necessary growth of love to our country, and that therefore the former cannot be destroyed without hurting the latter, I answer, that this is a gross fallacy and delusion. That it is the growth of love to our country, I will allow; but that it is the natural and necessary growth of it, I absolutely deny. Superstition and enthusiasm too are the growth of religion; but who ever took it in his head to affirm that they are the necessary growth of this noble principle? They are, if you will, the bastard sprouts of this heavenly plant, but not its natural and genuine branches, and may safely enough be lopped off, without doing any harm to the parent stock: nay, perhaps, till once they are lopped off, this goodly tree can never flourish in perfect health and vigour.

Is it not very possible that I may love my own country, without hating the natives of other countries? that I may exert the most heroic bravery, the most undaunted resolution, in defending its laws and liberty, without despising all the rest of the world as cowards and poltroons? Most certainly it is; and if it were not—But why need I suppose what is absolutely impossible?—But if it were not, I must own, I should prefer the title of the ancient philosopher, viz. a citizen of the world, to that of an Englishman, a Frenchman, a European, or to any other appellation whatever.

c. LIBIDINAL TYPES

Sigmund Freud

Observation teaches us that in individual human beings the general features of humanity are embodied in almost infinite variety. If we follow the promptings of a legitimate desire to distinguish particular types in this multiplicity, we must begin by selecting the characteristics to look for and the points of view to bear in mind in making our differentiation. For this purpose physical qualities will be no less useful than mental; it will be most valuable of all if we can make our classification on the basis of a regularly occurring combination of physical and mental characteristics.

It is doubtful whether we are as yet able to discover types of this order, although we shall certainly be able to do so sometime on a basis of which we are still ignorant. If we confine our efforts to defining certain purely psychological types, the libidinal situation will have the first claim to serve as the basis of our classification. It may fairly be demanded that this classification should not merely be deduced from our knowledge or our conjectures about the libido, but that it should be easily verified in actual experience and should help to clarify the mass of our observations and enable us to grasp their meaning. Let it be admitted at once that there is no need to suppose that, even in the psychical sphere, these libidinal types are the only possible ones; if we take other characteristics as our basis of classification we might be able to distinguish a whole series of other psychological types. But there is one rule which must apply to all such types: they must not coincide with specific clinical pictures. On the contrary, they should embrace all the variations which according to our practical standards fall within the category of the normal. In their extreme developments, however, they may well approximate to clinical pictures and so help to bridge the gulf which is assumed to exist between the normal and the pathological.

Now we can distinguish three main libidinal types, according as the subject's libido is mainly allocated to one or another region of the mental apparatus. To name these types is not very easy; following the lines of our depth-psychology, I should be inclined to call them the *erotic,* the *narcissistic* and the *obsessional* type.

The *erotic* type is easily characterized. Erotics are persons whose main interest—the relatively largest amount of their libido—is focused on love. Loving, but above all being loved, is for them the most important thing in life. They are governed by the dread of loss of love, and this makes them peculiarly dependent on those who may withhold their love from them. Even in its pure form this type is a very common one. Variations occur according as it is blended with another type and as the element of aggression in it is strong or weak. From the social and cultural standpoint this type represents the elementary instinctual claims of the id, to which the other psychical agencies have become docile.

The second type is that which I have termed the *obsessional*— a name which may at first seem rather strange; its distinctive characteristic is the supremacy exercised by the super-ego, which is segregated from the ego with great accompanying tension. Persons of this type are governed by anxiety of conscience instead of by the dread of losing love; they exhibit, we might say, an inner instead of an outer dependence; they develop a high degree of self-reliance, from the social standpoint they are the true upholders of civilization, for the most part in a conservative spirit.

The characteristics of the third type, justly called the *narcissistic,* are in the main negatively described. There is no tension between ego and super-ego—indeed, starting from this type one would hardly have arrived at the notion of a super-ego; there is no preponderance of erotic needs; the main interest is focused on self-preservation; the type is independent and not easily overawed. The ego has a considerable amount of aggression available, one manifestation of this being a proneness to activity; where love is in question, loving is preferred to being loved. People of this type impress others as being "personalities"; it is on them that their fellow-men are specially likely to lean; they readily assume the role of leader, give a fresh stimulus to cultural development or break down existing conditions.

These pure types will hardly escape the suspicion of being deduced from the theory of the libido. But we feel that we are on the firm ground of experience when we turn to the mixed types which are to be found so much more frequently than the unmixed. These new types: the *erotic-obsessional,* the *erotic-narcissistic* and the *narcissistic-obsessional* do really seem to provide a good grouping of the individual psychical structures revealed in analysis. If we study these mixed types we find in them pictures of characters with which we have long been familiar. In the *erotic-obsessional* type the preponderance of the instincts is restricted by the influence of the super-ego: dependence on persons who are *contemporary* objects and, at the same time, on the residues of *former* objects—parents, educators and ideal figures—is carried by this type to the furthest point. The *erotic-narcissistic* type is perhaps the most common of all. It combines contrasting characteristics which are thus able to moderate one another; studying this type in comparison with the other two erotic types, we can see how aggressiveness and activity go with a predominance of narcissism. Finally, the *narcissistic-obsessional* type represents the variation most valuable from the cultural standpoint, for it combines independence of external factors and regard for the requirements of conscience with the capacity for energetic action, and it reinforces the ego against the super-ego.

It might be asked in jest why no mention has been made of another mixed type which is theoretically possible: the *erotic-obsessional-narcissistic.* But the answer to this jest is serious: such a type would no longer be a type at all, but the absolute norm, the ideal harmony. We thereupon realize that the phenomenon of different *types* arises just in so far as one or two of the three main modes of expending the libido in the mental economy have been favoured at the cost of the others.

Another question that may be asked is what is the relation of these libidinal types to pathology, whether some of them have a special disposition to pass over into neurosis and, if so, which types lead to which forms of neurosis. The answer is that the hypothesis of these libidinal types throws no fresh light on the genesis of the neuroses. Experience testifies that persons of all these types can live free from neurosis. The pure types marked by the undisputed predominance of a single psychical agency seem to have a better prospect of manifesting themselves as pure character-formations, while we might expect that the mixed types would provide a more fruitful soil for the conditioning factors of neurosis. But I do not think that we should make up our mind on these points until they have been carefully submitted to appropriate tests.

It seems easy to infer that when persons of the erotic type fall ill they will develop hysteria, just as those of the obsessional type will develop obsessional neurosis; but even this conclusion partakes of the uncertainty to which I have just alluded. People of the narcissistic type, who, being otherwise independent, are exposed to frustration from the external world, are peculiarly disposed to psychosis; and their mental composition also contains some of the essential conditioning factors which make for criminality.

We know that we have not as yet exact certainty about the aetiological conditions of neurosis. The precipitating occasions are frustrations and inner conflicts: conflicts between the three great psychical agencies, conflicts arising in the libidinal economy by reason of our bisexual disposition, conflicts between the erotic and the aggressive instinctual components. It is the endeavour of the psychology of the neurosis to discover what imparts a pathogenic character to these processes, which are a part of the normal course of mental life.

2. Use the seven "Questions for Determining Controlling Idea, Form, Purpose, and Response" to analyze the following article. Summarize your findings by indicating the controlling idea, form, purpose, and response.

EXPRESSIVE LANGUAGE

Amiri Baraka

Speech is the effective form of a culture. Any shape or cluster of human history still apparent in the conscious and unconscious habit of groups of people is what I mean by culture. All culture is necessarily profound. The very fact of its longevity, of its being what it is, *culture,* the epic memory of practical tradition, means that it is profound. But the inherent profundity of culture does not necessarily mean that its *uses* (and they are as various as the human condition) will be profound. German culture is profound. Generically. Its uses, however, are specific, as are all uses . . . of ideas, inventions, products of nature. And specificity, as a right and passion of human life, breeds what it breeds as a result of its context.

Context, in this instance, is most dramatically social. And the social, though it must be rooted, as are all evidences of existence, in culture, depends for its impetus for the most part on a multiplicity of influences. Other cultures, for instance. Perhaps, and this is a common occurrence, the reaction or interreaction of one culture on another can produce a social context that will extend or influence any culture in many strange directions.

Social also means *economic,* as any reader of nineteenth-century European philosophy will understand. The economic is part of the social—and in our time much more so than what we have known as the spiritual or metaphysical, because the most valuable canons of power have either been reduced or traduced into stricter economic terms. That is, there has been a shift in the actual meaning of the world since Dante lived. As if Brooks Adams were right. Money does not mean the same thing to me it must mean to a rich man. I cannot, right now, think of one meaning to name. This is not so simple to understand. Even as a simple term of the English language, *money* does not possess the same meanings for the rich man as it does for me, a lower-middle-class American, albeit of laughably "aristocratic" pretensions. What possibly can "money" mean to a poor man? And I am not talking now about those courageous products of our permissive society who walk knowledgeably into "poverty" as they would into a public toilet. I mean, The Poor.

I look in my pocket; I have seventy cents. Possibly I can buy a beer. A quart of ale, specifically. Then I will have twenty cents with which to annoy and seduce my fingers when they wearily search for gainful employment. I have no idea at this moment what that seventy cents will mean to my neighbor around the corner, a poor Puerto Rican man I have seen hopefully watching my plastic garbage can. But I am certain it cannot mean the same thing. Say to David Rockefeller, "I have money," and he will think you mean something entirely different. That is, if you also dress the part. He would not for a moment think, "Seventy cents." But then neither would many New York painters.

Speech, the way one describes the natural proposition of being alive, is much more crucial than even most artists realize. Semantic philosophers are certainly correct in their emphasis on the final dictation of words over their users. But they often neglect to point out that, after all, it is the actual importance, *power,* of the words that remains so finally crucial. Words have users, but as well, users have words. And it is the users that establish the world's realities. Realities being those fantasies that control your immediate span of life. Usually they are not your own fantasies, *id est,* they belong to governments, traditions, etc., which, it must be clear by now, can make for conflict with the singular human life all ways. The fantasy of America might hurt you, but it is what should be meant when one talks of "reality." Not only the things you can touch or see, but the things that make such touching or seeing "normal." Then words, like their users, have a hegemony. Socially—which is final, right now. If you are some kind of artist, you naturally might think this is not so. There is the future. But *immortality* is a kind of drug, I think—one that leads to happiness at the thought of death. Myself, I would rather live forever . . . just to make sure.

The social hegemony, one's position in society, enforces more specifically one's terms (even the vulgar have "pull"). Even to the mode of speech. But also it makes these terms an available explanation of any social hierarchy, so that the words themselves become, even informally, laws. And of course they are usually very quickly stitched together to make formal statutes only fools or the faithfully intrepid would dare to question beyond immediate necessity.

The culture of the powerful is very infectious for the sophisticated, and strongly addictive. To be any kind of "success" one must be fluent in this culture. Know the words of the users, the semantic rituals of power. This is a way into wherever it is you are not now, but wish, very desperately, to get into.

Even speech then signals a fluency in this culture. A knowledge at least. "He's an educated man," is the barest acknowledgment of such fluency . . . in any time. "He's hip," my friends might say. They connote a similar entrance.

And it is certainly the meanings of words that are most important, even if they are no longer consciously acknowledged, but merely, by their use, trip a familiar lever of social accord. To recreate instantly the understood hierarchy of social, and by doing that, cultural, importance. And cultures are thought by most people in the world to do their business merely by being hierarchies. Certainly this is true in the West, in as simple a manifestation as Xenophobia, the naïve bridegroom of antihuman feeling, or in economic terms, Colonialism. For instance, when the first Africans were brought into the New World, it was thought that it was all right for them to be slaves because "they were heathens." It is a perfectly logical assumption.

And it follows, of course, that slavery would have been an even stranger phenomenon had the Africans spoken English when they first got here. It would have complicated things. Very soon after the first generations of Afro-Americans mastered this language, they invented white people called Abolitionists.

Words' meanings, but also the rhythm and syntax that frame and propel their concatenation, seek their culture as the final reference for what they are describing of the world. An A flat played twice on the same saxophone by two different men does not have to sound the same. If these men have different ideas of what they want this note to do, the note will not sound the same. Culture is the form, the overall structure of organized thought (as well as emotion and spiritual pretension). There are many cultures. Many ways of organizing thought, or having thought organized. That is, the form of thought's passage through the world will take on as many diverse shapes as there are diverse groups of travelers. Environment is one organizer of *groups,* at any level of its meaning. People who live in Newark, New Jersey, are organized, for whatever purpose, as Newarkers. It begins that simply. Another manifestation, at a slightly more complex level, can be the fact that blues singers from the Midwest sing through their noses. There is an explanation past the geographical, but that's the idea in tabloid. And singing through the nose does propose that the definition of singing be altered . . . even if ever so slightly. (At this point where someone's definitions must be changed, we are flitting around at the outskirts of the old city of Aesthetics. A solemn ghost town. Though some of the bones of reason can still be gathered there.)

But we still need definitions, even if there already are many. The dullest men are always satisfied that a dictionary lists everything in the world. They don't care that you may find out something *extra,* which one day might even be valuable to them. Of course, by that time it might even be in the dictionary, or at least they'd hope so, if you asked them directly.

But for every item in the world, there are a multiplicity of definitions that fit. And every word we use *could* mean something else. And at the same time. The culture fixes the use, and usage. And in "pluralistic" America, one should always listen very closely when he is being talked to. The speaker might mean something completely different from what we think we're hearing. "Where is your pot?"

I heard an old Negro street singer last week, Reverend Pearly Brown, singing, "God don't never change!" This is a precise thing he is singing. He does not mean "God does not ever change!" He means "God don't never change!" The difference, and I said it was crucial, is in the final human reference . . . the form of passage through the world. A man who is rich and famous who sings, "God don't never change," is confirming his hegemony and good fortune . . . or merely calling the bank. A blind hopeless black American is saying something very different. He is telling you about the extraordinary order of the world. But he is not telling you about his "fate." Fate is a luxury available only to those fortunate citizens with alternatives. The view from the top of the hill is not the same as that from the bottom of the hill. Nor are most viewers at either end of the hill, even certain that, in fact, there is any other place from which to look. Looking down usually eliminates the possibility of understanding what it must be like to look up. Or try to imagine yourself as not existing. It is difficult, but poets and politicians try every other day.

Being told to "speak proper," meaning that you become fluent with the jargon of power, is also a part of not "speaking proper." That is, the culture which desperately understands that it does not "speak proper," or is not fluent with the terms of social strength, also understands somewhere that its desire to gain such fluency is done at a terrifying risk. The bourgeois Negro accepts such risk as profit. But does *close-ter* (in the context of "jes a close-ter, walk withee") mean the same thing as *closer*? Close-ter, in the term of its user is, believe me, exact. It means a quality of existence, of actual physical disposition perhaps . . . in its manifestation as a *tone* and *rhythm* by which people live, most often in response to common modes of thought best enforced by some factor of environmental emotion that is exact and specific. Even the picture it summons is different, and certainly the "Thee" that is used to connect the implied "Me" with, is different. The God of the damned cannot know the God of the damner, that is, cannot know he is God. As no Blues person can really believe emotionally in Pascal's God, or Wittgenstein's question, "Can the concept of God exist in a perfectly logical language?" Answer: "God don't never change."

Communication is only important because it is the broadest root of education. And all cultures communicate exactly what they have, a powerful motley of experience.

chapter 13
Writing: Classification and Definition

As you saw in the last chapter, both classification and definition impose order, but in different ways. Classification begins with a broad subject and breaks it down into smaller categories. Definition, on the other hand, identifies the special qualities that separate one thing from the others.

Classification and definition both work with details, which are the qualities or characteristics of a thing. Classification, though, forms categories by grouping according to similar qualities, and definition establishes the identity of something by indicating the qualities that make that thing dissimilar.

For example, consider clocks as a subject for classification. Classification begins by determining a broad group of things, all of which share an important element. The members of this group also have less important differences that distinguish one member of the large group from the others. In this case, all clocks indicate time, which is the important element they share. This broad group of similar things can be divided into categories by identifying the less important differences among them. For clocks, these differences could be based on the visual symbols found on the faces of different types of clocks: The two most obvious categories for the faces of clocks are (1) a combination of moving hands and numbers and (2) an electronic display of digits. Each of these categories could be broken into still more groupings. For example, clock faces with hands and numbers could be divided between those that have second hands and those that do not or between those that mark the hours with numbers and those that use geometric shapes in place of the numbers. Digital clocks can be divided into those that display the time continuously and those for which a button must be pressed to illuminate the display, or into categories of those that simply indicate time and those that include other features such as the day of the week. All of these classifications depend on establishing a common element for a broad grouping and then applying a criterion that breaks the larger category into smaller subgroups.

Definition, on the other hand, seeks to work with one item to show how it is both similar to and yet different from the other items. For example, if you wanted to define a "cigar," you would try to articulate its important characteristics:

- Made from tobacco.
- Designed to be smoked.
- No paper covering.
- Generally not inhaled.
- Larger than a cigarette.

These characteristics of a cigar show how definition often depends on two broad types of distinguishing features: an item's purpose and its form or shape. A cigar's purpose is to be smoked, and its form is an uncovered, rolled tobacco leaf, usually larger than a cigarette. This definition also demonstrates how the defining process reveals similarities and differences. A cigar is like other things that are smoked, but it has particular physical characteristics that separate it from cigarettes and pipes.

Writing Classification Essays

Classification is most easily applied to physical objects for which both the broad, common category and the criterion of categorization are easily identified. If you were classifying typewriters, the broad category of mechanical printers is self-evident, and other physical criteria, such as size and power—manual or electric—are readily available. Similarly, cars can be classified according to size or performance characteristics or even price, which is another kind of physical quality, if by physical quality we include any measurable feature.

More interesting, though somewhat more difficult, is the classification of nonphysical, nonmeasurable things, such as ideas. Suppose, for example, you wanted to classify the ways in which individuals find evidence of self-worth. Your broad category would be *Measures of Self-worth*. To discover a useful criterion, ask yourself:

Question: How do we determine our self-worth?
Answer: By measuring or comparing ourselves with some standard.
Question: Where does this standard come from?
Answer: Either from inside ourselves or from other people.

The last answer provides a good basis for subdividing the broad group into internal and external. These categories can, in turn, be subdivided through further questioning.

Internal

Question:	What are internal measures of self-worth?
Answer:	These are measures based on our own standards.
Question:	What kind of standards do we set for ourselves?
Answer:	We set certain standards of excellence.

This last response can generate still more categories of internal measures of worth: physical and mental. These, finally, can be further subdivided to provide the details for an essay.

Physical	*Mental*
Health	Imagination
Appearance	Honesty
Dexterity	Judgment
Strength	Discipline

Similarly, the categories of external measures of self-worth also can be generated through questioning.

External

Question:	What are external measures of self-worth?
Answer:	These are measures provided by sources outside ourselves.
Question:	What kinds of measures, such as these, can be identified?
Answer:	These measures might include financial or social position, career success, awards or prizes, and the approval of respected individuals.

These measures of external success can be divided into categories in the following way, using a criterion that will separate the measures according to the kinds of confirmation of self-worth, financial, career, and approval. When these categories are expanded, you have the details for a substantial essay.

Financial	*Career*	*Approval*
Salary	Position	Family and friends
Social position	Responsibility	Peers
Possessions	Influence	Awards or honors

Either the internal or the external measures of self-worth developed in the preceding categories could form the basis for a classification essay. Suppose you choose the internal measures of self-worth as your approach. Your essay would have two large sections, and each would be divided into four parts, as indicated in the following outline.

Controlling Idea: Internal measures of self-worth can be divided into two broad groups, physical and mental, both of which provide self-imposed standards of excellence.

   I. Introduction.
  II. Physical.
      A. Health.
      B. Appearance.
      C. Dexterity.
      D. Strength.
 III. Mental.
      A. Imagination.
      B. Honesty.
      C. Judgment.
      D. Discipline.
 IV. Conclusion.

Let us assume an informative purpose, with an emphasis on the subject matter, and a broadly defined, adult audience. Because you do not have a specific audience, your examples will be general, things to which most people can relate. The resulting essay might be something like the following:

> At the beginning of Herman Melville's *Moby Dick*, the narrator Ishmael contemplates suicide but decides instead to sign up for a whaling voyage. He is depressed because his life seems to have no purpose or meaning. The ocean beckons to him, perhaps because of its mystery or the adventure it promises. Ishmael's problem, though, is a universal one: we all need to feel that we are leading meaningful lives, that we as individuals are worth something. We do not have to be suicidal to understand that life is much more pleasant if we can find ways to measure self-worth.
>
> Self-worth can be determined by external and internal measures. Perhaps the latter are the most important because they are the freest from accidental circumstances. Among internal measures of self-worth, two broad categories can be distinguished: those based on physical attributes, and those reflecting mental characteristics.
>
> We all are physical beings, and whether or not we acknowledge this, we feel better or worse about ourselves according to how we perceive our physical natures. Foremost among the physical qualities in establishing a measure of self-worth is the simple but important matter of health. If we feel well, full of energy, capable of performing our responsibilities, and, just as important, of enjoying our leisure, we then have a generally good sense of ourselves as physical animals. On the other hand, illness reminds us of our mortality and emphasizes all the other limitations that we might find in our bodies. A sense of good health, therefore, is necessary to a general feeling of worthfulness.
>
> Not only are we physical beings who must feel capable of the activities we undertake, either for serious efforts or for amusement, but most of us also are creatures of vanity. We all want to look good, no matter what style we affect. Our appearance makes some kind of statement about us, about our values, and about our confidence in ourselves. Whether we adopt an attitude of studied informality or

attempt to keep pace with every changing style, it is important to us to be able to look the way we want to. Nobody cultivates acne or other disfigurements, and nobody wants to be either grossly over-weight or severely underweight or to wear truly disreputable clothing, no matter what the style. We each may have a different sense of style, but we all share a need to feel comfortable with our physical appearance.

Another kind of physical standard of self-worth is dexterity, that is, our ability to make our bodies do what we want them to do. This dexterity can be applied to a variety of activities, from athletic en-deavors to macramé. The person who prides himself or herself on his or her proficiency on the tennis court or, on the other hand, on his or her skillfully designed and executed wall hanging is signaling a dedication to physical dexterity as a measure of self-worth.

Though most of us are not weight lifters or body builders, we generally like to think that we have the strength necessary to perform our chores. Whether this strength is measured in endurance or the ability to lift a heavy package or turn a twist-open cap, we all would rather be able to accomplish what we want to do without tiring or having to ask for assistance. For example, changing flat tires, an activity that requires a certain amount of strength and endurance, aside from the mechanical know-how, provides both the obvious ad-vantages of being able to extricate oneself from a deserted highway late at night and the independence of being able to handle such a problem.

The other broad grouping of measures of self-worth, once we have satisfied ourselves about our physical being, is our mental ca-pabilities. An attractive, healthy, dexterous, and strong monkey is still a monkey. Humans like to pride themselves on their position above the animals of the world, on the basis of their greater mental ca-pabilities.

Chief among our mental strengths is our imagination. We have the ability to envision things that do not yet exist, and this ability is one of the characteristics that most clearly separates us from less imaginative animals. The artist facing an empty canvas, the writer staring at the blank page, the cook contemplating empty pots and pans, or even the purchaser of an ancient and rusted automobile all share an imagination that will enable the painter to see form and color on the canvas, the writer to anticipate the words that will com-municate his or her thoughts, the cook to taste and smell the finished product, and the purchaser to envision that automobile transformed into a gleaming and purring vehicle. The greater are our abilities to bring imagination into our lives, the richer we can make our expe-riences, and the better we will feel about ourselves.

Although animals may act according to their instincts, they do not behave ethically or morally. People have the potential for ethical and moral behavior, and the keystone of such behavior is a sense of honesty, both with ourselves and in relation to other people. Our perception of ourselves is governed by our commitment to an honest assessment of our actions. If we are honest with ourselves and know that we have done our best in a particular circumstance, we generally feel contented. And although we are sometimes tempted to be deceitful with other people in order to gain a particular goal, we gain that goal usually with the loss of a certain amount of self-respect.

Life is a complicated business and presents innumerable challenges to our judgment. Every day we are faced with choices, major and minor, ranging from whether to try to beat a red light because we are in a hurry, to selecting friends and associates, all of which reflect our ability to make rational and considered judgments. The person who succeeds in beating the red light, that is, in avoiding a possibly serious accident, probably experiences a sense of relief, but not worthiness, because the act was an example of bad judgment: it was a perfectly avoidable flirtation with disaster. Similarly, the individual who accepts the friendship of a person who can offer only complication and distractions is going to feel that he or she has failed to exercise good judgment. Acting rationally is not very easy, but doing so gives us a feeling of control over our lives and therefore a better sense of our worth.

Most tasks demand a measure of discipline if we expect satisfactory results. In this sense, discipline usually provides rather immediate rewards, no matter what activity is its object. The long-distance runner, the creative artist, the serious student, or the ambitious career person all must learn to sacrifice a degree of pleasure to find success in their chosen activity. However, that success is available to the disciplined individual and immediately increases that person's sense of himself or herself.

All of these categories of internally determined measures of self-worth contribute to our finding purpose and meaning in our lives. Ishmael's voyage turned out to be ill fated, but our life journeys, in less dramatic circumstances, are better or worse, depending on how we can measure ourselves against these criteria.

As with the other sample essays in the other chapters, this one closely follows the outline but finds details to make points not originally in the plan. For example, the comparisons to animals in the first two categories of the second section suggested themselves as a method of comparison/contrast development in the paragraphs in which they occurred. Good writing is always a combination of planning and spontaneous additions, as well as the considered deletions of the revising process.

Writing Definition Essays

As we saw in classification, it is easier to deal with physical objects than with ideas. Similarly, in definition, it is simpler to work with objects that have a definite shape, size, or function. Nevertheless, even physical objects can present problems of definition.

For example, at the front of most classrooms is an object something like a desk but not unlike a table. This object is usually supported by four legs and has a flat top. Often, though, it does not have any drawers. This object, of course, is the teacher's desk, found in many educational environments. It is called a desk because of its function: that is, it serves as a place for books and for writing. It also has the form of a table. If it were removed from the classroom and placed in a cafeteria and if people regularly ate their meals from its surface, it would most probably be termed a table, because the function of a table is to provide a surface on which food, plates, and utensils can be placed. The definition, then, even of a physical object can vary. The same object can be defined differently depending on the purpose to which it is put.

Definitions of ideas avoid problems of conflicts between form and function, as ideas certainly do not have a form and probably cannot be considered to have a particular function. However, the lack of physical attributes also makes the definition of an idea a challenging activity. Without a definite physical reference, we are left to deal with abstractions. These abstractions, though, will finally take on their fullest meaning when they are applied to things we can perceive with our senses.

You will not often want to write a definition essay for its own sake. Rather, you will consider definition in a larger context concerning some issue or problem. In such contexts, definition often is a necessary approach to establishing a sound understanding of the issue.

For example, consider the issue of vegetarianism, the decision to eat only certain, carefully defined foods. Vegetarianism can be adopted for purely nutritional reasons: you can decide that your diet will consist of only certain foods because those are the most healthful for you. In this case, your task would be to define healthful foods.

Vegetarianism can also be seen as a moral issue. Seen from this perspective, the moral question would concern what gives you the right to eat other animals. Raising animals to supply people with food assumes that people possess a moral superiority to the animals they consume. Definition can be used to defend this position by distinguishing one species from another.

Begin by establishing the moral basis for deciding whether or not humans can eat animals:

Question: What gives humans the moral right to eat animals?

Answer: We can eat members of a different species.

Question: Why do we have to distinguish species?

Answer: Otherwise, we would have to say that if it is permissible to eat animals, then cannibalism is permissible.

Question: Then how do you define a species?

Answer: A species is a group of living things that are similar to one another.

Question: Which similarities are important?

Answer: Those that all members share and that nonmembers do not possess.

Question: Which similarities are important?

Answer: Members of the same species look like one another.

Question: That seems vague. What else?

Answer: Well, let's try mating. Members of the same species mate with one another.

Question: What if one member doesn't? Is that member not included in the species? For example, if I choose not to have children, am I then not a member of the human species?

Answer: Of course you are, because you have the capability to mate if you want to.

Question: What if I were sterile and could not have offspring?

Answer: You would still be human because if your reproductive organs were functioning properly, you could mate with a member of your species.

Question: Why?

Answer: Because the important quality is biological compatibility; you could mate with a biologically compatible member of the species.

This last response can serve as a definition of species: members of the same species are biologically compatible with one another and therefore can create additional members of that species.

Suppose you wanted to write an essay that supports your right as a human being to eat animals. Your purpose would be persuasive, in that you would try to convince your audience to think as you do on this issue. The body of your essay would be a development of your definition of species, as that definition is the basis for your position. Your controlling idea would include both the moral basis for your argument and the basis for your definition of species: It is morally acceptable to eat members of a different species, and because humans are a species distinct from other animal species, it is acceptable for humans to eat other animals. In such an essay, your introduction would state your moral basis, and then the body of your essay would show how you can define humans as a separate species. In this development section, you would probably mention several other ways to define the human species before emphasizing the one you have identified as the most important:

  I. Introduction
 II. Inadequate definitions
     A. Appearance
     B. Language
III. Adequate definition
     A. Biological compatibility
     B. Irrelevant exceptions
 IV. Conclusion

Notice that the question of language has been added to appearance as an inadequate basis for defining the human species. You could have chosen language as a defining characteristic for humans, but it is just as useful to concede that some other animal species possess a limited level of language ability. By conceding this point, you can concentrate more effectively on your most important characteristic.

An essay written according to this outline might look something like the following:

> Vegetarians argue that it is immoral to eat animals because there is no moral basis for such a behavior. If we can eat animals, they say, what will prevent us from eating one another, because humans are animals as well? To answer this question, we must first declare a premise from which to argue: humans belong to a species separate from other animals, and therefore we can prohibit cannibalism and still eat steak, because the steak comes from an animal belonging to a different species.
>
> Our problem, then, is to define the human species. We could begin by asserting that members of the same species look like one another. Now, this assertion is generally true, for we can say that an elephant looks more like another elephant than it looks like a canary. However, if we examine this assertion more carefully, we will see that it is too vague to serve as a basis for distinguishing one species from another. For example, some dogs look very much like wolves, and yet we know that they are different from each other in important ways. Most of us would not take our pet wolf for a walk or let it sleep on our bed.
>
> We need to find a more persuasive quality of humans that would separate members of that species from other animals. We could try language ability as a basis for making this distinction. Language ability does work better than appearance, but it is not foolproof. Most animals, to be sure, cannot talk, but some scientists do argue that certain animals have a language ability approaching or perhaps exceeding that of a human child. Chimpanzees, for example, have been trained to the point that they respond to oral language on a rather sophisticated level. One such chimpanzee was taken to the dentist and then taught that the person who worked on her teeth was called a *dentist*. When she was next told that she was going to have to visit this dentist, she exhibited genuine signs of fear and anxiety, just as most humans do when faced with the same prospect.
>
> Language ability alone, then, might not be adequate to explain why we can eat chimpanzee meat if we so chose. We need a still clearer basis of definition.
>
> Probably the best basis of such a definition pertains to reproduction. Although this defining quality is not without its problems, it can be made sufficiently persuasive once we have dismissed the irrelevant exceptions.
>
> Let us say that members of the same species can be defined according to their ability to mate with one another. Of course, we must first dismiss some obvious quibbles. Our definition applies to adult members of opposite gender of a certain species, but it also

includes the immature members of both genders who will grow to sexual maturity.

The important quality, then, that defines a species is the adult member's ability to reproduce with another adult member of that species. Any individual who has this capability can be termed a member of the species, and any individual who does not is, by definition, a member of a different species.

Finally, we must deal with an important class of exceptions to this definition. It is the capability that is important, and not the actuality. If you choose not to have children, you are still a member of the human species because you have the biological capability to reproduce if you want to. Further, even if you are, for whatever reason, sterile, your incapability can be seen as a clearly identifiable and individual biological circumstance. If your reproductive organs were functioning properly, you would be able to procreate; therefore, you are an exception that does not reduce the force of the definition.

Because we have established that the human species is clearly different from other animal species, and because we began with the premise that this difference gives us the moral right to eat members of another animal species, we need feel no guilt the next time we sit down to a steak dinner. No matter how much steak we eat, we are in no danger of becoming a steer.

This essay serves a persuasive purpose, and it is developed by carefully defining a term. You should note, however, that other possibilities could have been introduced into the vegetarian argument. You could, for example, begin with a different premise, that it is immoral to cause pain and that eating other animals inevitably will cause pain. Your definition problem then would be to distinguish those living things that have the capability to feel pain. Such a distinction could focus on the sophistication of the nervous system of the being, and you would have to draw a line at some point, perhaps at the mollusk. Perhaps you would say potatoes cannot feel pain, but some other plants seem to exhibit signs of something like pain, by going into shock when they are roughly handled. However you approached this subject, though, your task would be one of careful and precise definition.

Exercises

1. Choose a broad grouping of similar physical objects, and develop a classification system. Identify a criterion that will break down the broad category into useful subgroups.
2. Choose an idea from the following list, and use it as the broad grouping for a classification system:
   a. Love.
   b. Relationships

    c. Fear.

    d. Jealousy.

    e. Leisure activities.

3. Define an object by stating its physical characteristics. Indicate what part of your definition relates to the object's form and what part concerns the object's purpose.

4. Write a short definition of one of the following ideas:

    a. Pain.

    b. Insecurity.

    c. Time.

    d. Loneliness.

    e. Security.

5. Define a purpose and audience for a classification essay on one of the following topics, and then write the essay.

    a. Newspapers.

    b. Advertisements.

    c. Teachers.

    d. Students.

    e. Part-time jobs.

6. Determine an audience and purpose for a definition essay on one of the following topics, and then write the essay.

    a. A good breakfast.

    b. A healthful activity.

    c. An unpleasant chore.

    d. Creative expression.

    e. An optimist or a pessimist.

Questions for Revision

After you have written your essays for either Exercise 5 or 6, check your work for organization, purpose, and audience by asking the following questions:

Controlling Idea   1. Have I clearly identified the general subject about which I am writing?

    2. Have I emphasized certain aspects of this subject matter?

    3. Have I established a controlling idea by stressing those parts of the subject that I want the reader to understand and remember?

Form   4. Does my controlling idea divide a broad group of things into separate categories? If so, have I established a clear criterion with which to divide the items into categories so that the items in each category are similar to one another and also so that the categories are separated from one another in a logical and meaningful way?

    5. Does my controlling idea define a physical object or an idea? If so, have I presented the attributes of that object or idea in such a way as to show how it is similar to other objects or ideas and how its unique attributes separate it from these other similar objects or ideas?

Purpose   **6.** Does my essay emphasize myself, the subject matter, or the audience?

Audience   **7.** What response do I want from my audience?

Revise your work in light of your answers to these questions so that it demonstrates a clear relationship between its controlling idea and its specific details and establishes a good sense of audience and purpose.

chapter 14
Revision

Revision is often seen as the last step of the writing process. This observation, though substantially correct, is an oversimplification. To be sure, the last activity you ordinarily perform in preparing a piece of writing is revision. However, revision routinely begins much earlier in the process. In fact, many writers revise as they write a first draft. This early revision can be as simple as changing a word for a better choice, or it can be as substantial as redirecting the writing.

Properly understood, the writing process begins in idea generation, perhaps modified by early revision, and ends in revision during which a new idea or two might be introduced. During the middle stages of the writing process, when you are shaping and clarifying your ideas, there should be a balance between discovering ideas and revising. In this sense, revision is an ongoing procedure which becomes the final stage of the writing process. (See Figure 1.)

This pictorial representation can suggest the balance between idea generation and revision. It is more or less accurate for different writers, but it is useful in suggesting that the writing process is comprised of overlapping stages. In the first part of the writing process, you ordinarily concentrate on looking for ideas, and a way to focus these ideas for a particular purpose, and to a specified audience. Your first draft is primarily exploratory. As you put words down on the paper, you stimulate further thinking which produces additional ideas. You also get a sense of how well your controlling idea is going to work, and which details belong in which section of your essay.

In the second stage, you have the opportunity to refine your controlling idea, to reorder details, and to firm up your overall structure. You may still think of important new ideas, and you might make major organizational changes. You will be making sure each paragraph works and develops your controlling idea. You will also be smoothing out your style in terms of sentence structure and word choice. In the second stage you both discover new material and revise what you have already written.

By the time you reach the third stage, your attention should be directed almost entirely toward the finer nuances of revision. You should concentrate

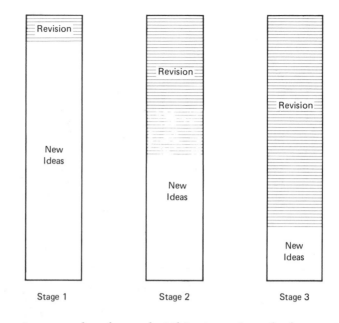

on each sentence, and each word at this stage since the larger structure of your essay will have been established. As part of this final stage, you attend to all the matters of mechanics, such as spelling, punctuation, and points of grammatical usage.

Reading, Writing, and Revision

The three stages mentioned above progress from an emphasis on idea generation to final form of your essay. These stages also reflect another change in your thinking, a movement from inside your mind to a more objective perspective.

When you begin to write, you are self-absorbed. You realize, of course, that what you write will be read by somebody else, and this realization governs your composing from the beginning, from the first idea that occurs to you. But your sense of audience is much less intense when you begin to write because you first have to deal with your own attitudes and beliefs as they relate to your topic. In your first stage, then, you are more concerned about your own thinking than you are about your readers' reactions.

In the middle stages of the writing process though, just as you become more conscious of how your writing is taking shape, you are also beginning to move outside of yourself. You start to view your writing as other persons, your audience, might. You are not only clarifying your ideas for yourself, but you are examining them for their ability to communicate your thoughts to another person.

In your final stage, you should have moved almost entirely outside of your own mind. You now regard what you have written as if it had been written by some other person. You read it as your reader will read it. Your

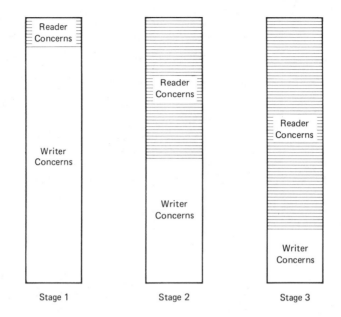

final revisions are made almost entirely from your reader's perspective. You want to be sure your reader will understand your ideas, will react according to your purpose, that is, empathize, learn, or change beliefs. You will want to make sure that you have directed your approach to your audience, assuming neither too much nor too little. That is why you attend to mechanics at this stage: mechanics are more important to your reader than they are to you. Misspellings, for example, might irritate you, but they will much more strongly distract your reader from what you are communicating. (See Figure 2.)

Taking a Paper through Drafts

Let us examine how this process can be illustrated for a particular paper. Three drafts will be provided to represent the three stages as a matter of convenience. Different writers in various circumstances will develop their writing through fewer or more drafts. Below is the first draft of a paper which compares and contrasts two neighborhoods.

> When you move into a neighborhood before you can walk or talk and live there for 20 years, you can hardly imagine a lifestyle different than what you are used to. In Brooklyn, we spoke about different neighborhoods and referred to them as Bay Ridge or East Flatbush, etc. When giving directions we said, "Go two blocks, make a left and the next light make a right." When I moved to Long Island, people referred to neighborhoods as developments. If someone told me they live in the development behind Shop Rite, I'd think they lived in an institution. Also when giving directions, Long Islanders would say, "Go south for 2 miles then east for 6 miles and it's on the left hand side, you can't miss it." I don't like directions like that because I usually "miss" it since I'm not familiar with instructions telling me to go to north, south, east or west.

Another thing are the schools. When I attended the local Catholic School, I depended on the city buses to bring me to and from school since the first grade. I even went home for lunch every day. I never had the opportunity to ride on a yellow school bus and every time I see a group of children waiting on the corner for the bus I wonder if I was a deprived child because I was brought up in Brooklyn. The bus picks them up at 7:00 a.m. and drops them off at 2:30 in the afternoon. They eat lunch in the cafeteria, either by bringing their own or by paying 90¢ for a hot school lunch.

After school I rarely see children outside playing. They are all inside doing their homework or most likely watching T.V. When I came home from school, I never remembered turning on the T.V. I could hardly wait to change my uniform and run outside to join the other kids and start playing until I was called home for supper. I feel sorry for them because their friends aren't allowed out after school.

Before I permanently moved to Long Island, I would visit my family at least twice a month so I was familiar with the neighbors. At that time it was a new development and there were only 4 other families on the block. I was confident that I knew all those people, especially since I've actually been living here for 3 months. To my surprise, the other day I saw a little boy about 4 years old on the lawn next door. When I asked who the new kid was my father said it was Mary's son, he lives there. I couldn't believe I knew that family for 4 years, they live right next door to us, and I never saw him before and what amazed me more was I never knew they even had a son. I don't even know what the people living on the other side of us look like. They moved into the house in April and never go outside except to go to work.

When I lived in Brooklyn, I knew everyone on my block, by name, and half the people within a 15 block radius. Neighbors were extremely nosy, which was good because they were always watching for something suspicious and each wanted to be the first to spot something so they would be the center of attention for a few days.

If I have the opportunity to own my own home on Long Island, I'd hope my neighborhood consisted of relocated Brooklyn families. This way we would all be expecting the same thing and if what we expected didn't happen, we could stick together and make it happen.

This first draft establishes an expressive purpose for the comparison between two neighborhoods because the writer focuses on her perceptions of the differences between the two places. Its controlling idea is not clearly defined but seems to concern her preference for her Brooklyn neighborhood because it offered a stronger sense of community. The sense of audience seems to point to people who would be more familiar with Long Island than Brooklyn, particularly in the references to after school activities. The draft contains a number of mechanical problems which can be attended to in later drafts. For her second draft, the student worked on a clear controlling idea and better sense of audience. Her first draft had enabled her to discover a number of good details which fell into three categories: directions, school, and neighborliness. In the second draft below, she sharpens the organization of these details, and works on her sense of audience, specifically in the fourth paragraph which included some obscure family references.

Although I now live on Long Island, I grew up in Brooklyn, and I'm not sure the change has been all for the better. I have had some adjustment problems after twenty years in an urban setting.

In Brooklyn, for example, we spoke about different neighborhoods and referred to them as Bay Ridge, Bensonhurst, East Flatbush, etc. When giving directions we said, "Go two blocks, make a left and the next light make a right." When I moved to Farmingville, I found out that on Long Island, people refer to their neighborhoods as developments. If someone said they lived in a development behind Shop Rite, and I did not know any better, I thought they lived in an institution. Also when giving directions, Long Islanders would say, "Go south for two miles, then east for six miles, and it's on the left hand side, you won't miss it." I don't like directions like that since I almost always "miss it" because I'm not familiar with instructions telling me to go north, south, east or west.

I have also noticed a difference in school transportation. When I attended the local Catholic School in Brooklyn, I depended on the city buses to bring me to and from school since the first grade. I also went home for lunch every day. On Long Island, though, in the morning I see a group of children waiting on practically every corner for the yellow school bus to come and take them to school. These kids seem to be having a very good time, playing and talking with each other. I used to wonder if I was a deprived child because I was brought up in Brooklyn and never had a chance to ride on the yellow school bus.

The bus picks these suburban kids up at 7 in the morning and drops them off at 2:30 in the afternoon. They eat lunch in the cafeteria, usually a bag lunch, or sometimes a hot lunch purchased for 90¢. But then I remember how nice it was to leave the school for an hour in the middle of the day and eat a lunch served by my mother at my own kitchen table. I don't know which kind of experience is better for a child's development, but I have very warm memories of my own lunch times.

I rarely see these suburban kids outside after school. They seem to vanish into their houses, as if they have had enough of their peers after the day in school. They could be doing their homework, or more likely, they are watching television. When I came home from school, on the other hand, I never turned on the television. I could hardly wait to change from my uniform to street clothes and run outside to join the other kids. I would play with my friends, games like hide'n'seek, or stoop ball, until I was called home for supper. When my younger brothers now come home from school, I feel sorry for them because their friends are not allowed out after school.

People are just not as visible in my new neighborhood. Before we permanently moved to Farmingville, we visited relatives who had moved out from Brooklyn a few years before. We used to visit them regularly, at least twice a month, and so I thought I knew everyone on the block even before we bought our house. After all, our development is still new, and there are fewer than a dozen families on our street. But just the other day, I saw a young boy I had never seen before. I was shocked to discover that he had been living practically next door for four years. I haven't even seen the family who moved in a few doors up the block, and they have been there since April.

When I lived in Brooklyn, I knew everyone on my block by name, and half the people within fifteen block radius as well. My old neighbors were extremely nosy for new information so they could have something to gossip about. There was always someone watching for anything suspicious to happen so he or she would be the center of attention for a few days. Everyone on my old block made it their business to know everything about everyone else. We may have lost some privacy, but we gained closeness as a community.

If I have the opportunity to ever own my own home on Long Island or anywhere else for that matter. I'd hope for relocated Brooklyn families because we would expect the same things from each other—to be friends.

This draft improves upon the first in a number of ways. It is smoother, although some of the mechanical problems remain. More importantly, its controlling idea is more clearly articulated and developed. The writer seems to have discovered that she really preferred her Brooklyn neighborhood much more than she had originally thought. In composing the second draft, she realizes that she misses the kind of people who used to be her neighbors. Perhaps her feelings are conditioned by her early experiences, but since this is an expressive paper she does not have to compare the different environments objectively. For her, as she indicates in the last paragraph, she is most at home with people who grew up in a neighborhood similar to hers in Brooklyn. Her details make these points better in the second draft, as do the transitions she adds at the beginning of the paragraphs. She also simplifies the details about visiting relatives who had moved out before her own family. She understands that her audience does not need to know her family business in detail. What is important is establishing her familiarity with the neighborhood, even before her family bought a house on the same block as the one on which her relatives already lived.

Let's examine these changes from first draft to second in more detail. To do so, we can look for the introduction of new ideas, and for revisions which are motivated by the need to clarify sense of audience and purpose, and by awareness of organization, paragraph structure and sentence fluency.

New ideas: Compare the treatment of bus transportation in the two drafts.

First Draft

Another thing are the schools. When I attended the local Catholic School, I depended on the city buses to bring me to and from school since the first grade. I even went home for lunch every day. I never had the opportunity to ride on a yellow school bus and every time I see a group of children waiting on the corner for the bus I wonder if

I was a deprived child because I was brought up in Brooklyn. The bus picks them up at 7:00 a.m. and drops them off at 2:30 in the afternoon. They eat lunch in the cafeteria, either by bringing their own or paying 90¢ for a hot school lunch.

Second Draft

I have also noticed a difference in school transportation. When I attended the local Catholic School in Brooklyn, I depended on the city buses to bring me to and from school since the first grade. I also went home for lunch every day. On Long Island, though, in the morning I see a group of children waiting on practically every corner for the yellow school bus to come and take them to school. These kids seem to be having a very good time, playing and talking with each other. I used to wonder if I was a deprived child because I was brought up in Brooklyn and never had a chance to ride on the yellow school bus.

The underlined sentence indicates new material, added for the second draft. It further develops the comparison between city buses and suburban school buses. The next paragraph of the revision includes information from the first draft, about lunch time, and then adds new ideas which continue the comparison between the writer's city experiences versus the suburban children's.

The bus picks these suburban kids up at 7 in the morning and drops them off at 2:20 in the afternoon. They eat lunch in the cafeteria, usually a bag lunch, or sometimes a hot lunch purchased for 90¢. But then I remember how nice it was to leave the school for an hour in the middle of the day and eat a lunch served by my mother at my own kitchen table. I don't know which kind of experience is better for a child's development, but I have very warm memories of my own lunch times.

The next paragraph expands upon the draft version which ended with the sentence, "I feel sorry for them because their friends aren't allowed out after school."

Second Draft

I would play with my friends, games like hide'n'seek, or stoop ball, until I was called home for supper. When my younger brothers now come home from school, I feel sorry for them because their friends are not allowed out after school.

Here the second draft provides specific details about after-school activities to make her comparison more vivid.

Audience and purpose: The second draft begins with a different sentence, and breaks the first draft's long introductory paragraph into two:

First Draft

> When you move into a neighborhood before you can walk or talk and live there for 20 years, you can hardly imagine a lifestyle different than what you are used to. In Brooklyn, we spoke about different neighborhoods and referred to them as Bay Ridge. . . .

Second Draft

> Although I now live on Long Island, I grew up in Brooklyn, and I'm not sure the change has been all for the better. I have had some adjusting problems after twenty years in an urban setting.
>
> In Brooklyn, for example, we spoke about different neighborhoods and referred to them as Bay Ridge. . . .

The writer, in the second draft, shows greater awareness of her expressive purpose and begins with a focus on herself rather than the awkward, impersonal "you." She also adds a statement of personal emphasis concerning her adjustment problems which underscores the expressive purpose of her essay. She is not going to compare these neighborhoods objectively; rather, she will compare them in terms which are personally meaningful. By stating this emphasis in the first paragraph, she alerts her audience to her intention that her readers share her feelings.

The first draft's paragraph describing the writer's familiarity with her suburban neighborhood was confusing because it assumed that her audience would need to know about her personal circumstances. The second draft is clearer because it deletes unnecessary personal information and stresses what the reader must know to understand her feelings.

First Draft

> Before I permanently moved to Long Island, I would visit my family at least twice a month so I was familiar with the neighbors. At that time it was a new development and there were only 4 other families on the block. I was confident that I knew all those people, especially since I've actually been living there for 3 months. To my surprise, the other day I saw a little boy about 4 years old on the lawn next door. When I asked who the new kid was, my father said it was Mary's son, he lives there. I couldn't believe I knew that family for 4 years, they live right next door to us, and I never saw him before and what amazed me more was I never knew they even had a son. I don't even know what the people living on the other side of us look like. They moved into the house in April and never go outside except to go to work . . .

Second Draft

> People are just not as visible in my new neighborhood. Before we permanently moved to Farmingville, we visited relatives who had moved out from Brooklyn a few years before. We used to visit them

> regularly, at least twice a month, and so I thought I knew everyone on the block even before we bought our house. After all, our development is still new, and there are fewer than a dozen families on our street. But just the other day, I saw a young boy I had never seen before. I was shocked to discover that he had been living practically next door for four years. I haven't even seen the family who moved in a few doors up the block, and they have been there since April.

This second draft both expands and compresses the information contained in the original. The additional ideas clarify the writer's familiarity with the neighborhood while the deletions eliminate extraneous material. The result is a clearer presentation which more accurately gauges the audience's needs and concerns. The second draft also clarifies the "nosiness" of the writer's neighbors in Brooklyn. This revision shows an awareness of her audience's probable confusion since nosiness is usually perceived as a negative quality.

First Draft

> When I lived in Brooklyn, I knew everyone on my block, by name, and half the people within a 15 block radius. Neighbors were extremely nosy, which was good because they were always watching for something suspicious and each wanted to be the first to spot something so they would be the center of attention for a few days.

Second Draft

> When I lived in Brooklyn, I knew everyone on my block by name, and half the people within a fifteen block radius as well. My old neighbors were extremely nosy for new information so they could have something to gossip about. There was always someone watching for anything suspicious to happen so he or she would be the center of attention for a few days. Everyone on my old block made it their business to know everything about everyone else. <u>We may have lost some privacy, but we gained closeness as a community.</u>

Organization, paragraphing, sentence fluency: We have already noted the new introduction in the second draft. Besides clarifying purpose, the new first paragraph defines the writer's controlling idea: ". . . I'm not sure the change has been all for the better. I have had some adjustment problems after twenty years in an urban setting." The second draft paragraph also adds a transitional phrase which combines it with the controlling idea statement in the introduction: "In Brooklyn, *for example,* we spoke about. . . ."

We have examined the paragraph about school transportation, but note the two different first sentences.

First Draft

> Another thing are the schools.

Second Draft

> I have also noticed a difference in school transportation.

The sentence in the second draft much more accurately introduces the subject matter for that paragraph because the writer focuses upon school transportation, and not the schools generally. Moreover, the transitional word *also* connects this paragraph with the preceding one.

Notice, as well, sentences which are smoothed in the second draft.

First Draft

> They eat lunch in the cafeteria, either by bringing their own or paying 90¢ for a hot school lunch.

Second Draft

> They eat lunch in the cafeteria, usually a bag lunch, or sometimes a hot lunch purchased for 90¢.

The next paragraph again provides a better transition in the first sentence.

First Draft

> After school I rarely see children outside playing.

Second Draft

> I rarely see <u>these suburban kids</u> outside after school.

The phrase <u>these suburban kids</u> more clearly ties this paragraph to the one before it which described the in-school lunch hour of suburban children. Sentences, too, have been polished.

First Draft

> They are all inside doing their homework or most likely watching T.V. When I came home from school, I never remembered turning on the T.V.

Second Draft

> They seem to vanish into their houses, as if they have had enough of their peers after the day in school. They could be doing their homework, or more likely, they are watching television.

We have commented on the revision of the next paragraph, but note how the new introductory sentence ties it to the preceding one.

First Draft

Before I permanently moved to Long Island, I would visit my family at least twice a month so I was familiar with the neighbors.

Second Draft

People are just not as visible in my new neighborhood.

This sentence prepares the reader for the details later in the paragraph which describe the writer's surprise at discovering a child she had never seen before.

This second draft is far from perfect, but it is more clearly focused and smoother. The third draft concentrates on further polishing and eliminating the mechanical errors which persisted through the first two.

Although I now live on Long Island, I grew up in Brooklyn. Because I lived the first twenty years of my life in an urban setting, I have encountered some adjustment problems in suburbia. I am not sure the change has been all for the better for me.

In Brooklyn, for example, we referred to different neighborhoods, such as Bay Ridge, East Flatbush, or Bensonhurst. We gave directions in blocks, "Go two blocks, make a left, and at the next right, make a right." When I moved to Farmingville, I found out that Long Islanders live in "developments," not neighborhoods. The first time a new friend said she lived in a development behind Shop Rite, I thought she lived in an institution. I also had to get used to directions phrased in miles and points of the compass, "Go south for two miles, and then east for six miles, and it's on the left hand side. You won't miss it." I don't like directions like that because I almost always "miss it."

I have also noticed a difference in school transportation. I depended on city buses to take me to the local Catholic school in Brooklyn. I also could take the same bus home for lunch every day. On Long Island, though, every morning I see groups of children waiting at nearly every corner for the yellow school bus to take them to school. Because these kids seem to have such a good time, playing and talking with each other, I wonder if growing up in Brooklyn made me a deprived child who never had the chance to ride the yellow school bus. However, suburban kids do not have the freedom I had as a child.

The bus picks these kids up at the same time every day, at seven in the morning, and then it drops them off at 2:30 in the afternoon. They carry their bag lunches, or buy a hot lunch, which they eat in the cafeteria. But I remember how nice it was to leave school for an hour in the middle of the day to eat a lunch served by my mother at my own kitchen table. I don't know which kind of experience is better for a child's development, but I have very warm memories of my own lunch times when my mother and I would have a chance to be alone with each other.

I rarely see suburban kids outside after school. They seem to vanish into their houses, as if they have had enough of their peers during the time spent in school. Perhaps they stay inside to do their homework, or more probably, they watch television. When I came home from school, on the other hand, I never turned on the television because I could hardly wait to change from my uniform into street clothes so that I could join the other kids outside. I would play with my friends, games like hide'n'seek, or stoop ball, until I was called home for supper. My younger brothers come home from their suburban school and have no one to play with because their friends are not allowed outside in the afternoons.

People are just not as visible in my new neighborhood. Before we bought a house in Farmingville, we visited relatives who had moved out from Brooklyn a few years before. Because of this experience, and because our development is still new, including no more than a dozen families, I thought I knew everyone on the block. But just the other day, I saw a young boy I had never seen before. I was shocked to discover that he had been living practically next door for four years. I haven't seen the family who moved in a few doors up the block, and they have been there since April.

When I lived in Brooklyn, I knew the names of everyone on my block, and half the people within a fifteen block radius as well. My old neighbors were nosy, always watching for anything suspicious, or novel, so they would have something to gossip about. The person who first revealed that the Smith's had bought a new refrigerator would be the center of attention for a few days. My old neighbors made it their business to know everything about everyone else. We may have lost some privacy, but we gained closeness as a community, and because of that feeling, people were always willing to help each other.

If I have the opportunity to own my own home on Long Island, or anywhere else for that matter, I'd hope to find a neighborhood of relocated Brooklyn families. We would expect the same things from each other—to be friends.

This third draft is cleaner and tighter than the earlier two. Most of the changes are on the sentence level, seeking to make each efficient and precise. An occasional new idea, or amplification of a previously stated thought, also helps improve this revision.

In the first paragraph, the third draft improves emphasis and clarity by recasting a couple of sentences.

Second Draft

Although I now live on Long Island, I grew up in Brooklyn, and I'm not sure the change has been all for the better. I have had some adjustment problems after twenty years in an urban setting.

Third Draft

> Although I now live on Long Island, I grew up in Brooklyn. Because I lived the first twenty years of my life in an urban setting, I have encountered some adjustment problems in suburbia. I am not sure the change has been all for the better for me.

The third draft focuses on the controlling idea, that the changes have not been "all for the better" more precisely than does the wording in the second draft. Using the connective word "because" adds to the clarity in the third draft version.

In the second paragraph, the writer has tightened her style and eliminated wordy constructions. For example, "we spoke about different neighborhoods and referred to them as . . ." becomes "we referred to different neighborhoods, such as . . ." She adds one more neighborhood—Bensonhurst—to her list because she has decided to be a little more formal, and formal usage demands three specifics before adding "etc." An "etc." after only a couple of names sometimes suggests that the writer could not provide more specifics, or was too lazy to think of them. The revision gives three, a representative sampling, and dispenses with the "etc."

Other sentences in this paragraph are similarly tightened.

Second Draft

> When giving directions we said, "Go two blocks, make a left and the next light make a right."

Third Draft

> We gave directions in blocks, "Go two blocks, make a left, and at the next right, make a right."

This version is less wordy, and it also attends to mechanics by placing commas where they are needed.

Second Draft

> When I moved to Farmingville, I found out that on Long Island, people refer to their neighborhoods as developments. If someone said they lived in a development behind Shop Rite, and I did not know any better, I thought they lived in an institution.

Third Draft

> When I moved to Farmingville, I found out that Long Islanders live in "developments," not neighborhoods. The first time a new friend said she lived in a development behind Shop Rite, I thought she lived in an institution.

This revision accomplishes several things. It eliminates a problem of agreement in the earlier version ". . . someone said *they* . . ." by rephrasing the sentence. It is more concise and at the same time more vivid because it exchanges the impersonal "someone" for "a new friend." It also places quotation marks around the word "development" to indicate that she is calling attention to the word itself.

The end of this paragraph is both more efficient and effective.

Second Draft

Also when giving directions, Long Islanders would say, "Go south for two miles, then east for six miles, and it's on the left hand side, you won't miss it." I don't like directions like that since I almost always "miss it" because I'm not familiar with instructions telling me to go north, south, east or west.

Third Draft

I also had to get used to directions phrased in miles and points of the compass, "Go south for two miles, and then east for six miles, and it's on the left hand side. You won't miss it." I don't like directions like that because I almost always "miss it."

The revised version uses fewer words to say the same thing, and it ends more emphatically.

In the next paragraph, the writer again smooths the sentences, but she also chooses to add one which provides an important amplification of an idea which leads into the next paragraph.

Second Draft

I have also noticed a difference in school transportation. When I attended the local Catholic school in Brooklyn, I depended on the city buses to bring me to and from school since the first grade. I also went home for lunch every day. On Long Island, though, in the morning I see a group of children waiting on practically every corner for the yellow school bus to come and take them to school. These kids seem to be having a good time, playing and talking with each other. I used to wonder if I was a deprived child because I was brought up in Brooklyn and never had a chance to ride on the yellow school bus.

Third Draft

I have also noticed a difference in school transportation. I depended on city buses to take me to the local Catholic school in Brooklyn. I also could take the same bus home for lunch every day. On Long Island, though, every morning I see groups of children waiting at nearly every corner for the yellow school bus to take them to school. Because these kids seem to have such a good time, playing and talking with each other, I wonder if growing up in Brooklyn made me a deprived child who never had the chance to ride the yellow school bus. However, suburban kids do not have the freedom I had as a child.

The sentences in this version are more subtle and flowing, and they therefore express the ideas better. The added sentence identifies a point of comparison which will be picked up in the next paragraph. One point of usage is also corrected in that the word "school" is not capitalized since the name of a particular school is not mentioned.

The first sentence of the next paragraph refers to the regimentation of suburban children by adding a phrase, "The bus picks these kids up at the same time every day. . . ." The last sentence amplifies the idea of lunch at home with her mother, ". . . but I have very warm memories of my own lunch times when my mother and I would have a chance to be alone with each other."

The main revision in the next paragraph occurs in the last sentence which is less awkward than the verison in the preceding draft.

Second Draft

When my younger brothers now come home from school, I feel sorry for them because their friends are not allowed out after school.

Third Draft

My younger brothers come home from their suburban school and have no one to play with because their friends are not allowed outside in the afternoon.

The next paragraph had been troublesome to the writer from the first draft. It probably needs more work, but this version is better than the earlier ones.

Second Draft

People are just not as visible in my new neighborhood. Before we permanently moved to Farmingville, we visited relatives who had moved out from Brooklyn a few years before. We used to visit them regularly, at least twice a month, and so I thought I knew everyone on the block even before we bought our house. After all, our development is still new, and there are fewer than a dozen families on our street. But just the other day, I saw a young boy I had never seen before. I was shocked to discover that he had been living practically next door for four years. I haven't even seen the family who moved in a few doors up the block, and they have been there since April.

Third Draft

People are just not as visible in my new neighborhood. Before we bought a house in Farmingville, we visited relatives who had moved out from Brooklyn a few years before. Because of this experience, and because our development is still new, including no more than a dozen families, I thought I knew everyone on the block. But just the other day, I saw a young boy I had never seen before. I was shocked to discover that he had been living practically next door for four years. I haven't seen the family who moved in a few doors up the block, and they have been there since April.

This version is tighter, and it makes the point that Long Islanders are not visible since the young boy had been "invisible" up until the writer happened to see him. Nonetheless, it probably still has too much background information which the audience does not really need to know to understand the writer's point. Were she to write another draft of this paragraph, she could just as well cut most of the first half of the paragraph and concentrate more on her feelings when she discovered this "new" neighbor.

In the next to the last paragraph, the writer expands the idea of community in her Brooklyn neighborhood by further defining what she means by "nosy."

Second Draft

My old neighbors were extremely nosy for new information so they could have something to gossip about. There was always someone watching for anything suspicious to happen so he or she would be the center of attention for a few days. Everyone on my old block made it their business to know everything about everyone else.

Third Draft

My old neighbors were nosy, always watching for anything suspicious, or novel, so they would have something to gossip about. The person who first revealed that the Smith's had bought a new refrigerator would be the center of attention for a few days. My old neighbors made it their business to know everything about everyone else. We may have lost some privacy, but we gained closeness as a community, and because of that feeling, people were always willing to help each other.

This revision more clearly explains how neighborly nosiness also leads to neighborly concern, a quality the writer values. Also, her rewriting eliminates another mechanical problem, "everyone on my old block made it *their* business." This pronoun/antecedent agreement problem disappears in the revised version when "everyone" is replaced by "my old neighbors."

The last paragraph remains largely the same with the exception of the last sentence which is shortened for emphasis.

Second Draft

I'd hope for relocated Brooklyn families because we would expect the same things from each other—to be friends.

Third Draft

We would expect the same things from each other—to be friends.

Revision, as demonstrated in the three drafts of this paper, involves a variety of concerns. In the first stage of this process, you will be discovering ideas and defining your audience and purpose. In the second stage, you should pay more attention to overall organization, continue to introduce new ideas, and work on fluency. In later drafts, you continue to refine your style, amplify and emphasize important ideas, and eliminate all mechanical problems. In the process, you move from a focus on yourself as a writer who must discover what you want to say to the reader of your own work, checking it to make sure that you are, in fact, communicating well with your audience.